RELIGIOUS APPEALS IN POWER POLITICS

RELIGION AND CONFLICT

A series edited by Ron E. Hassner

A list of titles is available at cornellpress.cornell.edu

# RELIGIOUS APPEALS IN POWER POLITICS

PETER S. HENNE

CORNELL UNIVERSITY PRESS
*Ithaca and London*

Copyright © 2023 by Cornell University

All rights reserved. Except for brief quotations in a review, this book, or parts thereof, must not be reproduced in any form without permission in writing from the publisher. For information, address Cornell University Press, Sage House, 512 East State Street, Ithaca, New York 14850. Visit our website at cornellpress.cornell.edu.

First published 2023 by Cornell University Press

Library of Congress Cataloging-in-Publication Data

Names: Henne, Peter, author.
Title: Religious appeals in power politics /
 Peter S. Henne.
Description: Ithaca [New York] : Cornell University
 Press, 2023. | Series: Religion and conflict | Includes
 bibliographical references and index.
Identifiers: LCCN 2023014751 (print) | LCCN 2023014752
 (ebook) | ISBN 9781501770500 (hardcover) | ISBN
 9781501772139 (paperback) | ISBN 9781501770517
 (epub) | ISBN 9781501770524 (pdf)
Subjects: LCSH: Religion and international relations. |
 Power (Social sciences)—Religious aspects. | Religion
 and politics—Saudi Arabia. | Religion and politics—
 United States. | Religion and politics—Russia.
Classification: LCC BL65.I55 H48 2023 (print) |
 LCC BL65.I55 (ebook) | DDC 201/.727—dc23/
 eng20230623
LC record available at https://lccn.loc.gov/2023014751
LC ebook record available at https://lccn.loc.gov
 /2023014752

# CONTENTS

*Preface and Acknowledgments*    vii

    Introduction: A Holy Hand Grenade?      1

1. Why, How, and When Religious Appeals
   Matter in Power Politics      14

2. Religious Appeals in a Middle East
   Rivalry: Saudi Arabia and the
   "Islamic Pact"      35

3. US Religious Engagement in the
   Global War on Terrorism      61

4. Russia: Undermining Western
   Opposition to the *Russky Mir*      87

5. Expanding the Analysis      110

    Conclusion: How We Can Better
   Study and Leverage Religion in
   International Relations      124

*Notes*    145

*Bibliography*    179

*Index*    201

# Preface and Acknowledgments

This was not the book I meant to write. My early research—which turned into my first book—and my initial articles examined the ways religion proved to be a problem for state security. The book discussed Muslim states' hesitation to work with the United States on counterterrorism due to the politically powerful Islamic opposition to such policies, which grew from decades-long intertwining of religion and state. My articles discussed the ways religion's potency increases conflict and the negative impacts when states tie themselves to religion.

As I presented this work at conferences, workshops, and job talks, I encountered a frequent question: What about the ways in which religion *helps* states? If religion is so significant, should states not turn to it, rather than to conventional military threats or economic inducements, when developing foreign policy? This question was intriguing and came up often enough that I thought I should explore it. Many foundational works on religion and international relations (which I draw from in this book) raise this possibility. Most, however, discuss only isolated examples or emphasize state use of religion outside of conventional international security issues. Many works in comparative politics demonstrate the manner in which states harness the power of religious belief and organizations for their own benefit. But these focus on domestic politics. A systematic study of religion as a tool in power politics was missing.

So I began the book. I found a great deal of evidence for these states using religion in power politics. Evidence that this was an effective tool, however, was swamped by evidence that policymakers' use of religion in power politics actually made their jobs harder. It made other states nervous and created room for critics of the policies to push back or redefine them.

I worried I had set out to take down overly rationalist and materialist security studies but, in the process, accidentally joined them. Then I realized what I had found. It was not evidence of religion's insignificance; it was evidence of religion's *incredible* significance. Religion is so powerful, and resonates so deeply with global publics, that the very mention of it in power political interactions causes problems for everyone involved.

viii    **PREFACE AND ACKNOWLEDGMENTS**

This book is both an affirmation of religion's importance and a warning against its poorly thought-out use in power politics. It is a critique of contemporary security studies and policy discussions on security issues. But it is also a critique of contemporary research on religion and international relations, which is too focused on highlighting the transformative impacts of religious beliefs. It may not be a great strategy to alienate both sides in a debate, but I hope that, at the least, this book can reinvigorate a dialogue that has gone dormant.

I presented paper versions of chapters at the International Studies Association and American Political Science Association annual meetings, as well as the International Security section's annual conference. I benefited greatly from the feedback from discussants, participants, and audience members.

The ideas in this book also developed alongside two other projects. I participated in the Geopolitics of Religious Soft Power project, a joint effort between the Berkley Center for Religion, Peace and World Affairs and the Brookings Institution and supported by the Carnegie Corporation of New York. Additionally, I received a project launch grant from Notre Dame's Global Religion Research Initiative. This supported a separate project I am working on—using social network analysis to analyze international religion—but the ideas in the two overlap. I also received generous support from the University of Vermont's College of Arts and Sciences to conduct research on this book.

I would first like to thank my wife, Caroline, for her support throughout the writing of this book and my academic career. I also want to thank my daughters, Joanna and Beatrice, for inspiring me to work on this even though I would rather have been playing with them. Mahinder Kingra and Ron Hasser at Cornell University Press—as well as their reviewers and board—were very helpful throughout this process, greatly improving the manuscript with their feedback. I'd also like to thank Ron for organizing this book series, and the publisher for recognizing the importance of this topic. In addition to the formal support I mentioned above, numerous other people have provided input into this book or the paper spin-offs I have presented: Jonathan Agensky, Mary Beth Altier, Victor Asal, Gregorio Bettiza, Bill Braniff, David Buckley, Sean Flynn, Jonathan Fox, Stacie Goddard, Susie Hayward, William Inboden, Jason Klocek, Petr Kratochvil, Peter Mandaville, Tara McFeely, Jeremy Menchik, Daniel Nexon, John Owen, Ahmet Erdi Ozturk, Dave Rubin, Larry Rubin, Nukhet Sandal, George Soroka, Mohammad Tabaar, Monica Duffy Toft, and Melissa Willard-Foster. I would also like to thank Steve Rock, my undergraduate mentor at Vassar College, for hiring me as a research assistant while writing his book on religion and

## PREFACE AND ACKNOWLEDGMENTS

foreign policy—which I reference—inspiring me to pursue both an academic career and this specific topic. Finally, I would like to thank the research assistants at the University of Vermont who have worked on this project: Morgan Brown, Dylan Goetz, Rachel Halpern, Keile Kropf, Karolyn Moore, Evan Smith, Alex von Stange, and Abigail Strauss.

RELIGIOUS APPEALS IN POWER POLITICS

# Introduction

## A Holy Hand Grenade?

In *Monty Python and the Holy Grail*, King Arthur and his knights meet a foe against which their martial prowess fails.[1] Instead of reaching for their swords, they turn instead to the "holy hand grenade of Antioch." After receiving instructions in its use from their cleric, King Arthur launches the holy hand grenade, defeating the enemy.

Many leaders and scholars believe religion will function similarly to this holy hand grenade in international power politics. States appeal to religious values or shared religiosity to build friendly coalitions or break apart rival ones. At the same time, observers of twenty-first century international relations argue that religion is replacing earlier belief systems and shaking the international system; states would thus be wise, they argue, to incorporate these religious appeals into their foreign policy tool kits.

Many others, however, find such a possibility as farcical as the Monty Python sketch. Those responsible for security policy, especially in the United States, tend to downplay and underfund religious initiatives. At the same time, security studies scholars still base their works on rationalist and materialist assumptions that leave little room for religious influences. Both policy and scholarly discussions of international security tend to view religion as a social force or an element of international cultural interactions but see its relevance to areas such as international coalition building as limited.

2    **INTRODUCTION**

As I explain in this book, the truth is somewhere in between. Many states appeal to religion to justify their policies when engaging in international power politics. That is, they justify attempts to build international coalitions by pointing to religion, or they criticize and attempt to break apart rivals through similar religious references. This takes a variety of forms, including the rhetoric accompanying foreign policies, the specific targets of these rhetorical appeals, and the nature and definition of coalition-building initiatives. The religious elements of power politics range from formal religious arguments—referencing texts and tradition—to general appeals to the importance of faith.

These religious appeals have an unpredictable impact on power politics. They are not "cheap talk" or a window dressing for state interests. They reflect the significance of religion in a state's domestic politics as well as the nature of the international crisis. Additionally, under certain conditions, the religious appeals do succeed in strengthening international coalitions or undermining opposing coalitions. That is, they matter. But too often they matter like the aforementioned holy hand grenade tossed into a crowded room.[2] States scramble to figure out what a religious appeal means, tensions rise, and—if the wielder is not careful—the religious appeals can be turned back against them. This answer may not be satisfying to either side in the above debate, but it allows us to make sense of this issue and the broader implications of religion's growing role in the international system.

## Religion and Power Politics

In this book, I use Riesebrodt's approach to *religion* as "a system of practices, related to superhuman powers, that seeks to ward off misfortune, provide blessing and obtain salvation."[3] While personal religious beliefs and religious texts are important, when we discuss the impact of religion on politics—domestic or international—the way these beliefs and doctrines are put into practice is often more significant. Moreover, I focus not on the religion itself but *religious appeals*: references to religious standards and symbols by states in official pronouncements or debates they use to justify policies or critique rivals. My emphasis will thus be on the fact that a state appeals to religion more than the content of the religious argument itself.

I follow Goddard and Nexon to define power politics as "politics based on the use of power to influence the actions and decisions of actors."[4] Specifically, they argue power politics involves attempts to organize or undermine international collective action. I discuss this in terms of building or breaking apart international coalitions intended to advance a state's interest in an international crisis. They discuss a variety of "instruments of power" states can use to do this, including conventional military and economic instruments as well as cultural and symbolic instruments of power. I argue religious appeals are one example of a cultural-symbolic instrument of power states can use to organize international action.

## Why Do States Keep Turning to Religious Appeals? And When Do They Matter?

This book addresses both an empirical and a theoretical puzzle. Empirically, why do we keep seeing states use—or advocate for—religious appeals when attempting to form or break apart international coalitions during crises? Does this represent cheap talk, a principled religious stand, or something else? On the theoretical side, we have found evidence that religion is a useful political tool domestically, influences conflict, and can be a tool for states outside high-stakes security areas. Can religion serve as a tool in something like power politics?

The first part of the puzzle involves explaining the numerous cases of policymakers advocating for or actually using religious appeals in order to integrate or fragment international coalitions. Former US secretary of state Madeleine Albright focused her 2006 memoir on the crucial but underappreciated role of religion in foreign policy. The veteran diplomat agreed with realists that "the main purpose of foreign policy is to persuade other countries to do what we want" but argued "at a time when religious passions are embroiling the globe, that cannot be done without taking religious tenets and motivations fully into account."[5] As she explained later in the book, "the challenge for policy-makers is to harness the unifying potential of faith, while containing its capacity to divide."[6] Unlike many who consign religion to the fringes of international relations or "feel good" stories of cultural exchanges, Albright argued that religion is an essential element of states' foreign policy that leaders must take into account.

US elites across the political spectrum shared this sentiment, often with concrete policies enacted in response. Shortly after the 9/11 terrorist attacks, President George W. Bush met with Jordan's King Abdullah, whom he was hoping to secure as an ally in the global war on terrorism. Bush told Abdullah "our war is against evil, not against Islam," and noted the "thousands of Muslims who proudly call themselves Americans."[7] Senator Joseph Lieberman echoed this, writing on the "theological iron curtain" and called on the United States to engage with and promote the "extensive traditions of tolerant and moderate Islam" to defeat al-Qaeda.[8] During the Cold War, President Eisenhower turned

4    INTRODUCTION

to famous evangelical preacher Billy Graham as "America's pastor," a role that included a foreign policy element when Graham led a series of revivals in West Germany that mixed piety with anti-communist messages.[9]

This occurred during the Obama and Trump administrations as well. In a 2015 column in the Jesuit magazine *America*, John Kerry—then President Obama's secretary of state—wrote that one of the biggest challenges "in global diplomacy today is the need to fully understand and engage the great impact that a wide range of religious traditions have on foreign affairs": he also noted religion's importance in areas ranging from economic development to counterterrorism.[10] Under his direction, the State Department established the Office of Religion and Global Affairs, which increased religious awareness within the State Department and helped build international coalitions related to religious concerns. Likewise, a few years later, Mike Pence—vice president during the Trump administration—pointed to the need to defeat the Islamic State terrorist group and the spread of religious repression: Pence claimed "protecting religious freedom is a foreign-policy priority of the Trump administration."[11] This partially took the form of international coalitions among states and activists to promote international religious freedom.

This is not just a US phenomenon. In a December 2015 op-ed, Yousef al Otaiba—the United Arab Emirates' (UAE) ambassador to the United States—argued that the UAE has "a new vision for the region" that promoted an "ideology of optimism, openness and opportunity."[12] The UAE was trying to limit the threat it faced from the Arab Spring and undermine Qatar's growing prominence and clearly hoped to gain the upper hand through appeals to Islam. In the 1990s, Iraqi leader Saddam Hussein began comparing himself to Saladin, the famous medieval Muslim warrior who fought the Crusaders.[13] Hussein even had a state newspaper call on Arabs to "learn the lesson of Saladin's liberation of Jerusalem" and battle the United States and Israel in support of Iraq.[14] Outside of Muslim countries, China has been sponsoring Confucius Institutes around the world, using religion to expand its appeal despite the government's official atheism. And, under Putin, Russia has been appealing to conservative Christian values to enhance its influence in the world.

What do we make of this? It is difficult to argue that something so common and widespread is irrelevant. Policymakers would not spend so much time on these religious appeals if they thought they did not matter. Yet, we lack hard evidence that these religious appeals are a key element of states' security policies, rather than "cheap talk" that reflects little real effort or resources. We also lack evidence that religious appeals have an impact on international coalition building or fracturing. Religious appeals do seem to resonate with target leaders and audiences, but they rarely have a transformative impact on international issues. Those who believe religion is important need to better understand what impact these appeals have, if any. Skeptics of religion's importance need to explain their frequency.

This also presents a puzzle for the academic study of religion and international relations where research has demonstrated religion's huge impact on the world. Early studies pushed back against the secular biases of international relations and social sciences.[15] Modernization has not erased religion from society, even in the supposedly secularized West.[16] Moreover, this is not just a sociological or domestic political phenomenon. Many states' foreign policies are influenced by religion, either through domestic political pressure from powerful interest groups or the beliefs and perceptions of leaders.[17]

This research cannot explain whether religious appeals matter in international power politics. If religious appeals reflect deep social values, why do states sometimes act contrary to them or formulate many foreign policies that are not religious in nature? Moreover, even the most die-hard realist would admit that states sometimes act based on values like religion. What really matters is whether they stick with these values in high-stakes security situations—such as gaining allies during an international crisis—and whether policies based on these values have any impact.

Other work has found that religion can influence states' foreign policy. Numerous studies have demonstrated the way that religious organizations have worked together to resolve conflicts and advance faith-based policies in international forums.[18] Others have demonstrated that religious beliefs can inspire states to adopt substantive policies in areas such as humanitarianism.[19] Still other work, such as my own, has found that religion increases the severity of conflicts.[20]

This research, however, is also unable to explain the nature and impact of religious appeals in power politics. Much of the work on religion's impact on international relations focuses on areas outside of conventional security issues. Indeed, some of it has framed the research as a way to "move beyond power politics" and broaden definitions of what matters in international relations.[21] This is admirable, and necessary, but can do little to explain states' religious appeals in security areas, or to address broader issues in security studies that I raise in the next section. At the same time, most research on religion and conflict focuses on terrorism and civil wars, which—while important—does not tell us much about the impact of religion on power politics. Religion could very well influence nonstate groups, while conventional statecraft and material concerns override religion in interstate crises. Finally, some of the research that has found religion affects interstate conflict identifies its impact *on* states, rather than as a tool *of* states. That is, it looks at whether policymakers are

6    INTRODUCTION

influenced by religious beliefs or whether states face domestic religious opposition to policies. This again is important but tells us little about whether
states can use religion as a tool in power politics.

That is not to say there is no relevant research, but it has not yet been syn-
thesized to produce a generalizable theory. As I will discuss in the next chapter, some studies in international relations have found cases of states using
religion as a tool in conflicts. Comparative politics has demonstrated the way
states can use religion to try and control domestic dissent. And broader work
in international relations has looked at the way rhetoric and symbols are a useful tool for states to gain an edge in international tensions. In this book, I
draw on each of these areas to produce my theory on religious appeals in
power politics.

## When and Why Religious Appeals Matter in Power Politics

In this book, I explain when and why religious appeals matter in power politics. First, religious appeals are one among many foreign policy tools that states
rely on when forming or breaking apart international coalitions. As Goddard
argued, states' attempts to legitimize their policies are both strategic and "rule-
oriented."[22] This includes religious appeals. That is, they arise from the values and beliefs that constrain and enable domestic and international political
behavior. But they do not represent a principled stand by states on behalf of
their religious beliefs. They also do not represent a triumph of religious motivations over material interests. States can use religious appeals to advance
material interests and deploy them alongside conventional foreign policy tools
like military threats and economic inducements.

Religious appeals matter because of the importance of religion in the world.
Religion remains a significant—and possibly growing—part of many societies'
identities and values. Appeals to such significant values will resonate with
people, affecting their behavior and granting influence to those deploying the
appeals. The religious appeal may even persuade a leader of the rightness and
utility of the policies an international coalition is meant to advance. It may
also gain the attention and support of domestic publics, placing pressure on
their states to join the coalition.

Yet, religion is a complex force; this can lead to several unintended effects.
First, religious rhetoric and symbols often mean different things to different
people. As a result, the targets of religious appeals can adopt the religious arguments for their own purposes, even turning them back against the state deploy-

ing them. Additionally, religion raises the stakes of political debates, making it harder to reach a compromise or back down from aggressive stances. This can increase the tensions surrounding an international crisis, possibly provoking a reaction from rivals of the nascent coalition. Finally, religious arguments sit uncomfortably alongside conventional secular statecraft. As a result, many policymakers struggle to understand the nature and impact of religious appeals, increasing uncertainty in crises and possibly resulting in wasted resources.

States are likely to use religious appeals in power politics under two conditions. The first involves the moral authority of religion in a country, or the extent to which religious actors and arguments attain a prominent place in political struggles.[23] States with a high moral authority of religion are likely to see religious appeals as an important and useful tool to advance their goals. Second, when states face an ideologically charged international crisis, it is not only their security but identity and values that are under threat. As a result, they are more likely to incorporate ideological appeals into international struggles. When both conditions are present, a state is likely to use religious appeals when forming international coalitions.

Religious appeals have an impact on power politics according to their wielder's credibility and the material incentives surrounding their use. Religious appeals must be credible in the eyes of their targets to have an impact; this is a function of both the credibility of the state deploying the religious appeal and the religious arguments' cultural fit with their targets. Additionally, states that have material incentives to cooperate with the international coalition are more likely to respond positively to the religious appeal; states facing material costs from joining will be hesitant to do so. Religious appeals are likely to have their biggest impact when both material incentives and credibility are present, while they will have little influence under opposite conditions. Even intermediate combinations matter, however. When a state's religious appeals are credible but the targets face material disincentives to cooperate, the unintended effects of religion cause a general increase in international tensions and hostility. Finally, when a state is less than credible on religious issues, but targets face material incentives to go along with its efforts, we are likely to see convenient international coalitions form, with uncertainty about how best to apply religious policies and the potential for the religious legitimation to be redirected by its targets.

I test this theory with a qualitative research design. I demonstrate the conditions under which states turn to religious appeals, the nature of these appeals, and their impact on power politics through a series of case studies. I use a combination of typical and diverse case selection to highlight the presence of religious appeals in varying international contexts, as well as within-case

8   INTRODUCTION

variation to demonstrate the impact of different values in the conditions I theorize to matter. Finally, I use a mixture of archival, interview, and media data to demonstrate the validity of my theory and the limits of alternatives.

## Why This Matters: Between Triumphalism and Ignorance

By addressing the gap in our understanding of why states turn to religious appeals in power politics and whether and when this matters, this book can help overcome a frustrating dichotomy in scholarly and policy discussions of religion and international relations. Rather than having to decide between religious appeals transforming or being irrelevant in international security, we can generate nuanced analyses of their various effects. This can revitalize the study of religion and international relations, while also expanding work on rhetoric and values in international relations. Finally, it can contribute to policymakers' efforts to incorporate religion into foreign policy or counter other states' use of it.

Current debates involve a broad gap between what I call religion triumphalists and religion skeptics. Religion triumphalists see religion as a broadly transformative—and often beneficial—force in international relations. This is apparent among those have argued that supporting religious freedom will enhance US security.[24] We can also find it in some scholarly arguments that religion is transforming international relations, possibly for the better.[25] Religion skeptics, by contrast, see religion as having minimal effects. More often, they fail to even consider religion's potential impact; numerous scholar and policy studies that pretend as if religion does not matter. By providing an explanation for states' use of religious appeals that recognizes both their importance and their strategic and unpredictable nature gives a middle course between these extremes.

This is valuable for several reasons. First, this can improve our ability to understand crucial international security issues. We can analyze Russia's appeals to traditional values just as we would its use of hacking or threats to shut off gas supplies; it is one among many power political tools the state deploys. Using this book as a guide, we can produce fine-grained analyses of these religious appeals and their impacts. Likewise, we need to understand whether Islamic appeals by states like Saudi Arabia and the UAE are effective in gaining support from other Muslim states and enhancing their power. This book can help us point to the conditions under which their efforts are likely to succeed. From the US perspective, are appeals to "moderate Islam" and religious engagement initiatives effective in countering terrorism? This book can provide a framework for how to best form international coalitions through these efforts and connect counterterrorism studies to broader security debates.

Second, this book can revitalize the research program on religion and international relations. The research program on religion and international relations has demonstrated religion's importance and found significant religious impacts on unconventional security issues ranging from peace building to terrorism. The program has had less success forcing "conventional" security discussions to include religion. Several scholars responded to 9/11 by pointing to international relations' blind spot on religion.[26] Major names in international relations embraced the significance of religion, producing edited volumes with prominent publishers.[27] Yet, religion never became a mainstream topic in international relations, while the above efforts never produced the sort of sustained engagement seen in research into areas like the democratic peace or humanitarian interventions. Providing detailed evidence that states not only use religious appeals as a tool in power politics, but that these religious appeals have a noticeable impact, will make it harder for mainstream security studies to ignore religion. Likewise, the novel approach I take in this book can provide guidelines to move research on religion and international relations forward.

Additionally, this book can complement the research on rhetoric, values, and symbols in international relations from which I develop my theory. This broad research program tends to ignore religion: but applying it to the study of religion and international relations can demonstrate the need to better incorporate religion into it and expand the impact of its theories. Moreover, it can suggest new avenues of research, by pointing to the significant unintended effects from values and rhetoric these studies often ignore.

Finally, the book contributes to policy discussions. Calls and efforts to incorporate religion into the foreign policy of the United States and other states, as well as the work of organizations like the United Nations, continue. There has been some progress in this area. Think tanks and foundations like the Council on Foreign Relations, the Chicago Council on Global Affairs, the Pew Research Center, the Center for American Progress, and the Mellon Foundation run programs on religion or reports on religion. New initiatives and outlets have emerged to discuss and advocate for religion's role in foreign policy. These include journals such as the *Review of Faith and International Affairs* and *Providence: A Journal of Christianity and American Foreign Policy*. They also include think thanks and advocacy groups, such as the Institute for Global Engagement, the Religious Freedom Initiative, the International Center for Religion and Diplomacy, the Cambridge Institute for Religion and Global Affairs, and Georgetown University's Berkley Center for Religion, Peace and

10    **INTRODUCTION**

World Affairs. Indeed, I have been involved in several of these efforts, writing reports for the Center for American Progress and the Berkley Center, and working with the Pew Research Center.[28]

The problem, however, is integrating this work with broader policy discussions on security studies. These initiatives and arguments struggle to gain purchase, especially in high-stakes security areas as conventional military and economic discussions push religious discussions aside. Religious discussions often end up confined to "soft" areas of foreign policy. Alternately, they "preach to the choir"; projects on religion and conflict only include experts who already accept its importance, while those on conventional security issues completely ignore religion's presence. Ideally the two groups would engage in dialogue.

Several observers have lamented this situation. Jean Bethke Elshtain argued religion is often "seen in simplistic alternatives," as "either a source of sanctimonious aspirations . . . that are politely ignored in 'real' statecraft" or as "the source of all the terrorist extremism."[29] Thomas Farr has argued the State Department tends to downplay religious factors when approaching international issues, limiting the effectiveness of their analyses.[30] International relations scholar Ron Hassner has made a similar point about the military, calling for religious literacy to be a part of military planning.[31] By demonstrating how religious appeals can serve as a potent tool in power politics—if used carefully—this book can make it easier for advocates of religion in foreign policy to make their case. I provide specific suggestions for formulating policies based on my findings in the conclusion.

## What about Soft Power?

Readers may wonder why this book does not focus on soft power. As Nye famously defined it, soft power is the ability to "get others to want what you want" and can be as important as "hard power," which is based on military and economic resources.[32] Nye pointed to a vibrant culture as well as public education campaigns as ways states can build up soft power, increasing the attractiveness of their foreign policies. One could argue that the religious appeals I discuss in this book are a form of soft power, as states appeal to shared culture and values to enhance support for their international coalitions.

As I expand on in the conclusion, I think there are a few limitations to focusing this book on soft power. First, soft power can be a rather vague term, referring to any use by states of culture or symbols in foreign policy.[33] Properly defined, soft power is a passive resource that enhances states' other capabilities.[34] By contrast, religious appeals are an active tool states draw on in international crises. Defining religious appeals as soft power would thus confuse the issue. Religious appeals do relate to soft power, however, even if they do not completely overlap. As Mandaville and Hamid discussed, religion can serve as a form of soft power; Mandaville expanded this in an edited volume to which I contributed.[35] Religious appeals are distinct, however, as the mobilization of this soft power in the form of states' credibility on religious issues. This has implications for the policy prescriptions I derive from my work.

## Outline of the Book

This book makes its case through a theoretical chapter, several case studies, and a conclusion. The theoretical chapter presents the foundations for my argument. I specify what I mean by religion, religious appeals, and power politics. Following that, I survey research on both legitimation and rhetoric in international relations, and religion and politics to provide the foundations for my argument. I then present my theory on why religious legitimation matters, the conditions under which states are likely to use it, and the conditions under which it is likely to have an impact. I also discuss the qualitative research design of the book.

I turn next to the case studies. The first is Saudi Arabia's efforts to form an Islamic Pact as part of its 1960s rivalry with Egypt. I discuss the high moral authority of religion in Saudi politics and the ideologically charged nature of the rivalry with Egypt. I provide evidence that Saudi Arabia deployed religious appeals as a serious and strategic tool in its power politics. I then discuss the conditions affecting the appeals' impact; Saudi Arabia's credibility on Islamic issues and the material disincentives of target states to join its Islamic Pact. This limited the ability of Saudi Arabia to form a durable coalition, but it did disrupt regional relations, unsettling Egypt and worrying the United States.

The second case is the United States' use of religious engagement to build international coalitions as part of its global war on terrorism. Like Saudi Arabia, religion has a high moral authority in the United States, playing an important part in American politics even if it is officially secular. The global war on terrorism—the US response to the 9/11 terrorist attacks—was likewise an ideologically charged crisis, in which al-Qaeda attempted to mobilize Muslims against US dominance, and the United States appealed to common values—including shared "moderate" religiosity—to create a countervailing coalition. I demonstrate that these led the United States to adopt religious appeals as part of its effort to mobilize states and societies against al-Qaeda. I then discuss the

## 12   INTRODUCTION

conditions affecting this strategy's impact; the United States' credibility on "moderate Islam" and engagement with Muslims was often limited, but Muslim states and social groups faced material incentives to work with the United States. Convenient coalitions thus formed; some deeper connections emerged, but many of the interactions were stymied by the United States losing control of the religious narrative and its general unfamiliarity with the religious policies it proposed.

The third case is Russia's use of religious appeals in its attempts to undermine Western opposition to its dominance of the *Russky Mir* or "Russian world." Russia has attempted to maintain control of former Soviet states it sees as its historical sphere of influence, even as Western alliances expanded into this region. Despite the official atheism of the Soviet Union, the Orthodox Church has regained a prominent place in Russian politics. This, combined with the ideological nature of its struggle against the West, led Russia to deploy religious appeals to undermine Western influence. Russia has framed itself as a defender of traditional values, which has resonated among conservative groups in Western Europe and the United States. This led some of them to call for closer ties with Russia and oppose harsh Western reactions to Russian aggression. Yet, Western states have material interests in opposing Russian influence. As a result, tensions have increased between the two sides, with the former hardening its stance against the latter.

The final substantive chapter is a series of shorter case studies that provide more information on the importance of varying levels of the theorized conditions. Saudi–Iranian tensions over Bahrain's independence demonstrate religious states do not draw on religious appeals in nonideological crises. Likewise, European countering violent extremism efforts demonstrate states do not turn to religious appeals when they have a low moral authority of religion, even in ideological crises. Saddam Hussein's failed use of religious appeals to combat Operation Desert Storm and Thailand and Cambodia's competing use of religious appeals to gain support in their border dispute, demonstrate what happens in cases of low credibility and low material incentives. By contrast, the Vatican's intervention in the Syrian civil war and Iran's postrevolutionary Middle East mobilization demonstrates the success of religious appeals in cases of high credibility and material incentives. Finally, the backlash China has faced over its use of Confucius Institutes to gain support for its Belt and Road Initiative provides further insight into cases of low credibility and high material incentives.

In the concluding chapter I discuss the book's implications. I argue there is indisputable evidence that religious appeals can be an important part of power politics. Yet, conditions often combine in an unstable manner, producing the unexpected effects of religious legitimation I discussed above. I then extend the analysis by applying my theory to more recent cases. The concluding chapter also discusses the broader scholarly and policy implications of the book. Mainstream international relations must start accepting religion's importance in power politics, but scholars of religion and international relations must shift their approach as well. We limit the scope of our studies by emphasizing religious beliefs' hold over states or instances of religion overriding material concerns. Instead, we must focus on international religious politics as a set of interactions and practices that overlap with material factors. The book can also speak to policymakers. Considering the minimal cost of issuing religious appeals and their clear effects, it appears to be a cost-effective tool in power politics. But it is also unpredictable and must be approached with care; I provide specific guidelines in that chapter.

# CHAPTER 1

# Why, How, and When Religious Appeals Matter in Power Politics

States use religious appeals as a tool to support or undermine international collective mobilization alongside other foreign policy tools. Religious appeals matter because they emphasize a significant aspect of many leaders' and societies' identities. They also mobilize publics and shift the nature of political discourse. States are most likely to use religious appeals when they have a high domestic moral authority of religion and when they face an ideologically charged international crisis. The religious appeals' impact depends on the credibility of the appeals and the material incentives facing the target.

This chapter proceeds in four sections. First, I define what I mean by religious appeals and power politics. Second, I survey relevant research in international relations. I then present my theory, before discussing the book's research design and empirical expectations.

## What I Am Explaining

In this book I draw on Goddard's work to focus on states' legitimation of their policies, or the rhetoric states use to justify their policies.[1] As Goddard argues, legitimation matters by "giving meaning to behavior" and influencing how other states respond to a state's policies.[2] This relies on two assumptions: that

14

rules and values matter in guiding state behavior but also that—as Goddard puts it—"actors are less socialized and more strategic than in many constructivist accounts."[3] That is, while rules and values matter in international relations, they do not drive state behavior; instead, states draw on them strategically and purposefully.[4]

I expand on Goddard's definition in two ways. First, she analyzes legitimation strategies that accompany a state's rising power in the international system. I focus on state behavior in international crises, rather than broader power transitions. Second, and accordingly, I am approaching this as a tool in crises rather than longer-term legitimation strategies. I therefore focus specifically on religious appeals, or the *invocation of religion in order to justify policies or critique a rival.* That is, I examine the use of religious rhetoric to justify or legitimate a state's policies. This relates to the discussion by Sandal and Fox—and Fox and Sandler in a separate work—of religious legitimacy as a potential tool for states.[5] I use the term *appeals* to tie it closer to the work on rhetoric and international relations that I discuss below.

I speak of this in terms of a *wielder* and a *target.* The wielder is the state using the religious appeals, while the target is the state toward which the appeals are directed. This could involve the claim that a state's policies are in line with religious beliefs. It could also be an appeal to a shared religious identity to convince another state to align itself with the state launching the appeal. It may also be an appeal to religion generally, rather than a specific religion, with the wielder addressing common elements of faith across religions.

States can use religious appeals in many contexts: in this book I focus primarily on international power politics. According to Goddard and Nexon's definition, this is the "politics based on the use of power to influence the actions and decisions of actors that claim, or exercise, authority over a political community": international power politics involves international collective mobilization "oriented toward expanding influence at the expense of rivals."[6] State policies in power politics involve efforts to integrate collective mobilization or to fragment opposing collective mobilization. States do this by drawing on various "instruments of power," which include traditional economic and military instruments as well as cultural and symbolic instruments like religious rhetoric.

I elaborate on Goddard and Nexon's power politics framework as well. First, I discuss this specifically in terms of international coalitions. Second, their framework is a mechanism-based one that attempts to highlight the processes through which states use instruments of power rather than the conditions under which this occurs or is likely to be successful. I argue that we can emphasize the context-dependent nature of religious appeals but still theorize

16    **CHAPTER 1**

about when they are likely to have an impact: I discuss this further in the research design section later in the chapter. Additionally, I expand the definition of impact to include mixed or unpredictable effects.

# Strengths and Weaknesses of Existing Research

This book draws from international relations research that argues, in Goddard and Kreb's words, "public talk"—specifically legitimation—is a crucial aspect of power politics.[7] While few studies have dealt explicitly with the impact of religious appeals on power politics, numerous works can provide resources to address this topic. Many studies emerging out of constructivism have analyzed the impact of rhetoric and legitimacy broadly defined, specifying when states use it, why it matters, and the conditions under which it matters. Likewise, studies on religion and international relations have looked at the ways religious arguments influence politics. While there are some limitations in both sets of works, they provide a foundation through which we can theorize religious appeals in power politics.

## General Works on Legitimacy and International Relations

Many have argued the way that states justify their behavior grants influence in international relations. Goddard argued states use "legitimation strategies" to mobilize domestic and international publics in support of the state's policies, and to undermine opponents' attempts to mobilize support.[8] Busby claimed that moral movements influence states through public shaming and praise and strategic framing that pushes states to act.[9] Pouliot argued that security communities arise not through the internalization of a shared identity, but through a series of interactions that create habits of cooperation.[10] Others pointed to the use of values by transnational movements and states to coerce behavioral changes.[11] Still others argued rhetoric can clarify the meaning of events, granting influence as a result.[12] Even realists like Walt argued legitimacy can be an important resource.[13]

Some of this work looks at when rhetoric and legitimacy are likely to come up in international relations, and when they have an effect. Studies have found states are likely to draw on claims of legitimacy when they face threats to their security—requiring ideological defenses—or there are recognizable symbols available for use in political debates.[14] In terms of their effectiveness, many point to whether or not they are credible with their audiences, which is partly a function of whether the state is acting in line with the values they espouse.[15] Others point to the material incentives involved.[16]

## Religion and Politics

The study of religion and politics can provide similar insights. Grzymala-Busse argued religious communities—specifically Christian churches—can gain moral authority over politics, granting them influence over leaders and policies by mobilizing mass support or justifying state action.[17] Others have similarly found that religious claims and appeals can be effective in domestic political debates.[18] Hassner argued religious actors can use their rhetoric to gain political influence and drive political struggles.[19] Others have found religious ideas served a powerful role in Iranian and Turkish politics.[20] Similar studies have looked at the ability of religious actors to mobilize support for humanitarian norms and to influence states through appeals to religious beliefs.[21] Some have looked at the ways states use religious foreign policy to gain domestic and international support.[22] Still others discussed the role of networks in spreading religious beliefs and upending state power.[23]

As with general work on legitimation in international relations, some of this looked at the conditions under which states are likely to turn to religion and when this has an effect. Some of the research on when states turn to religion has to do with the prominence of religion in a state's society and institutions.[24] Others found it has to do with the opportunities provided by the international context.[25] In terms of religion's impact, most emphasize the credibility of the actors making the religious arguments. This is a function of the credibility of the religious arguments and the credibility of the actors themselves.[26] Some have also looked at the material interests involved, specifically the political power of religious groups and political elites.[27]

Several studies noted mixed and unpredictable effects of religious appeals, however. That is, many found that while the injection of religion into politics had a significant impact, it was not always a positive one. Many noted that they raise divisions in political debates.[28] They also expose actors to charges of hypocrisy.[29] Others have found that the use of religion in foreign policy can create both domestic and international crises, as they create new political debates that may be hard to control and predict.[30]

The above work has demonstrated that rhetoric and legitimacy—religious and otherwise—grant influence in international relations. Research could be improved in a few areas, however. First, general work in the area of rhetoric and legitimacy tends to focus on its positive impacts, such as reducing conflict or fostering cooperation. It also focuses on cases in which it clearly drove

18    CHAPTER 1

international events. This overlooks the possibility noted by work on religion and politics that such ideological or cultural appeals could have negative or unintended consequences. Second, research on religion and international relations tends to resist clear specification of the conditions under which religion is likely to function as a tool for states, instead emphasizing the process through which this occurs. While this still yields useful understanding of international relations, the broader work on legitimacy in international relations provides a model to have a more explicit argument about when religious appeals will matter without taking away from the richness of the analysis. Finally, the study of religion and international relations has tended to focus on issues outside of core security concerns or, when it does study core security concerns, it emphasizes the role of religion in nonstate actors' violence. Broader works in international relations have not avoided this area, suggesting the study of religion and international relations could push itself further.

# Religious Appeals and Power Politics

In this section I synthesize existing works on religion and politics and legitimation in international relations to develop a theory on why and when religious appeals affect power politics. Drawing on the research discussed in the previous section, I argue that religious appeals have an impact due to the significant influence religion has over many societies, even though they are strategic tools used by states. These appeals can persuade political actors to join or leave a coalition and can mobilize international publics. However, states do not always draw on them. Religious appeals arise when a state has a high moral authority of religion and it is facing an ideologically charged international environment. Likewise, religious appeals do not always affect power politics, and their effect is not always the one the wielder intended. Their effect depends on a combination of their credibility and the material incentives facing their targets.

## The Nature and Impacts of Religious Appeals

My starting point is an assumption about the significance of religion in the world. Religion remains a potent and complex force that drives and transforms political debates. Regimes recognize this when they turn to religious appeals as a strategic tool in power politics. When states deploy religious appeals, they can produce both expected and unexpected effects. The expected effects work on two levels: persuading leaders of the wielder's good intentions and resonating with domestic audiences. The unintended effects, however, arise from the complexity of religion. Religious appeals intensify tensions, can be turned back on their wielder, and confuse policymakers formulating and responding to them.

First, despite the rise of secular belief systems and modernization, religion remains an important—and possibly growing—force. Many societies define themselves along religious terms, while their religious beliefs influence their perception of political issues.[31] Religious institutions wield significant moral authority throughout the world.[32] Religious arguments also form the basis for mass support for leaders and policies.[33] Finally, the transnational nature of religion leads to greater identification with causes and peoples abroad.[34]

Religion is also complex and unpredictable. Religious beliefs can be manipulated by elites, leading to unforeseen consequences of religious arguments in political debates.[35] Leaders may gain political support by appealing to religious values, but they can also open themselves up to charges of hypocrisy by publics who expect them to act in line with religious values.[36] The mobilization of religious values in conflicts can lead to both peace and violence.[37] And the transnationalization of political debates through the global scope of religion can disrupt the normal functioning of states and societies.[38]

In line with the work on legitimacy and international relations covered in the previous section, appealing to such an important element of the world will resonate with regimes and societies. When the targets of religious appeals share the same religious beliefs as the wielder of religious appeals, they may be more amenable to the wielder's arguments as they are in line with their own practices and values. Even when they are not of the same religion, they may recognize the general form of the religious appeals and appreciate the wielder's desire to increase the significance of religion.

That being said, religious appeals are a strategic tool. When a state issues a religious appeal, it is not the result of deep-seated principles overriding material concerns. Likewise, it does not indicate that a state is attempting to form an international coalition in order to spread its religious beliefs. Instead, states issue religious appeals alongside other foreign policy tools they can use to organize coalitions, such as economic inducements or military threats. Under certain conditions—which I discuss below—regimes recognize the potential power of religious appeals and deploy them in power politics alongside more conventional foreign policy instruments.

The use of religious appeals can translate into specific impacts on power politics. Some effects are expected. Religious appeals can persuade a targeted regime of the proposed international coalition's value, increasing the likelihood they will join. That is, the target recognizes the shared values contained within the appeals, and this makes them more amenable to the proposed action. A state's leader may be unwilling to join an international coalition to isolate an aggressive state due to fears of threats to its security or from domestic opposition. If, however, the coalition's organizer argued the coalition was in line with shared religious values, it may make it easier for the leader to accept the coalition, or at least give them cover when justifying it to their people. This is a common mechanism that was proposed in the studies covered in the previous section of both general rhetoric in international relations and in religion and politics.

The second effect is that religious appeals mobilize domestic publics either for the wielder's initiative or against its rivals. Even if leaders remain unconvinced by the religious appeals behind calls to join international collective action or to abandon allies, domestic publics could be receptive. This is because domestic publics do not have the imperative of regime security driving their actions and may be more amenable to acting based on their values. They may thus agree with the wielder's religious appeals and pressure their leaders to act accordingly. Religious arguments have been shown to be particularly effective in mobilizing such domestic support.[39] For example, a leader may be wary of an international coalition that would necessitate costly commitments such as sanctions or military action. If the coalition's organizer framed it in terms of popular religious arguments, the leader's populace could enthusiastically embrace the coalition, calling on their leader to join it.

Not all effects of religious appeals are expected, however. This is a blind spot of general works on legitimation in international relations, as they tend to study cases of rhetoric increasing cooperation and reducing conflict. Studies on religion and international relations, by contrast, have looked into the ways that the use of religion in politics can cause negative outcomes. Specifically, the complexity of religion I noted above raises potential problems for states that attempt to wield it in the form of religious appeals.

First, religious appeals can easily slip out of the wielder's control and be redirected back to them. Religious discourse is complex, with multiple possible interpretations of any international issue or state policy. And, of course, religion is not just religious texts, but the practices and daily rituals of its members. As a result, religious sentiment is often shaped by states at the same time that a state's religious argument may end up having a different or uncertain meaning when it reaches its target audience. Political struggles may then erupt over clarifying and claiming the religious meaning of the statement. In practice, much of the use of religious rhetoric by states has led to unexpected or ambiguous messaging that often backfires on the political elites using the religious arguments. Discussions about what, for example, Islam says about

# HOW RELIGIOUS APPEALS MATTER IN POWER POLITICS    21

something like terrorism are not as simple as consulting a guidebook. Instead, there are often centuries of theology and religious texts to consult and debate. Likewise, Catholics worldwide have debated the legacy of Pope John Paul II, simultaneously claiming him as a progressive and a traditionalist force.

In the context of power politics, this means religious appeals may end up serving purposes contrary to intentions of the state wielding them. A rival may adopt the religious arguments but claim that the wielder is acting contrary to religious beliefs while the rival is advancing them. Alternately, a target may claim to agree with the religious appeal and join the coalition but then use religious language to frame policies as religiously inspired that are out of line with the international coalition's interests. In both cases the wielder of the religious appeal will have a harder time managing the international coalition as a result.

Second, religion can "raise the stakes" of a political dispute, making it harder for each side to come to an agreement and increasing their sense of threat. When religion becomes a part of domestic or international conflicts, it justifies dramatic action by those involved due to their belief they are satisfying divine commands or performing for a divine audience.[40] Religious conflicts are harder to resolve, as religious issues are more likely to be indivisible, or potential resolution is more likely to threaten combatants' identities.[41] This occurs even with nonviolent domestic conflicts, as religious arguments increase mistrust and make it harder for opposing sides to find common ground. This is arguably the case for international tensions as well. An international disagreement over competing claims to regional authority is difficult to resolve, but material interests can be divided and reconciled. If the disagreement expands to involve competing beliefs or competing religious–secular ideologies, it is harder for the regimes involved to back down without undermining the basis for their continued power. They will be sensitive to any religious appeals as part of the crisis, potentially expanding and prolonging it.

Some of this has to do with anxiety over religious appeals' domestic resonance. Most governments around the world recognize their societies are highly religious. For example, pre-Justice and Development Party (AKP) Turkey's official secularism required repeated and intense involvement of the military in domestic politics in order to hold off religious challenges to secularism; communist China has similarly exerted significant resources toward controlling and repressing religious communities in that country. After the Islamic Revolution in Iran, neighboring states feared its revolutionary Shia appeals would resonate with their publics, laying the foundation for ongoing tensions between these countries. And states like Cuba have tried to cut off their domestic Christian populations from international religious organizations, to avoid destabilizing outside influence. Thus, even if the religious legitimation fails to produce

## 22   CHAPTER 1

or fragment international coalitions, it can still deeply unsettle international relations.

Finally, religion sits uncomfortably alongside conventional international practices: unfamiliarity with it can lead to ineffective initiatives and wasted resources. The contemporary international system is primarily composed of secular norms, like sovereignty and liberal claims. Conventional international politics involves appeals to material interests and, if values are invoked, they tend to be secular ones like democracy or human rights. As Waltz argued, realpolitik, defined "ever since Macchiavelli" through "interest . . . necessity and *raison d'état*," is the primary method "by which foreign policy is conducted" in international politics.[42] Those who have pushed back on this and argued that norms matter tend to emphasize secular beliefs.[43] This can be seen in the difficult attempts of religious actors to engage with the United Nations.[44] Thus, religious language and symbols stick out from regular interactions.

As a result of this novelty, states are uncertain how to process or respond to religious appeals. Their foreign ministry or defense staff are trained to deal with military doctrine, economic shocks, or diplomatic procedures; they are less prepared for appeals to religious doctrine or identity. For example, many noted the way religiously inspired events like the Islamic Revolution in Iran or the 9/11 attacks caught both policymakers and scholars off guard.[45] Similarly, some have expressed concern at the lack of religious literacy among policymakers.[46] Because of this novelty of religion, states will be unsure how to interpret religious appeals and how to respond to them. Similarly, even those wielding the appeals will not have extensive experience or competence in their use and may be unable to properly formulate them or evaluate their effectiveness. This can inject a dangerous degree of unpredictability into international crises, exacerbating already tense situations (see table 1.1).

## When States Draw on Religious Appeals

Thus, religious appeals can have distinct effects on target states. States do not always use religious appeals in power politics, however. This is a strategic tool, one among many, rather than a constant reflection of a state's values. States will turn to religious appeals when international issues meet two conditions: the state involved has a high moral authority of religion and the issue is ideologically charged.

The first condition under which we are likely to see religious appeals in international power politics involves the moral authority of religion in a state's domestic politics. Religion has an effect on politics because of what Gryzmala-Busse

## HOW RELIGIOUS APPEALS MATTER IN POWER POLITICS

*Table 1.1* The expected and unexpected effects of religious appeals

| EXPECTED | UNEXPECTED |
| --- | --- |
| Mobilize domestic publics | Redirected back on wielder |
| Persuade leaders | Increase tensions in crises |
| | Create uncertainty over policy initiatives |

calls its moral authority. However, as she notes, this moral authority varies across countries. She argues it comes from the political tactics of religious organizations: in order to remain politically successful, churches have to maintain the appearance of being above the political fray.[47] Some discuss it as the result of historical legacies, such as leaders' political survival strategies.[48] Others argue it arises from political institutions and their connections to religion, with religion more salient in political debates when there are close ties between religion and state.[49]

For countries with high moral authority for religion, religion plays an important part in its political debates and institutions. In these states, political figures are wary of offending religious sensibilities for fear of attracting public ire.[50] High moral authority means political debates tend to revolve around religious issues.[51] Likewise, leaders have a harder time ignoring public pressure due to the need to justify their policies through religion.[52] A high moral authority of religion in domestic politics also increases international attention in political debates, as there is greater identification with religious kin and issues abroad, and greater transnational connections through religious networks.[53]

This aspect of domestic moral authority for religion is well documented in the comparative politics literature, but I would argue it extends to states' foreign policies. When religion is highly salient in domestic politics, it becomes a commonly accepted element of policies and arguments that states are expected to follow in their international affairs as well. States' foreign policies will thus be partly inspired by religious concerns, and religious justifications and arguments will be part of their international affairs. This can affect international crisis behavior as well as states' attitudes toward international law.[54]

The second condition under which we are likely to see religious appeals in international power politics is the extent to which ideology or identity matters in an international issue. International issues involve not just territory and resources but ideological and identity challenges. Some international issues merely involve states contesting material resources based on rational self-interest. However, this is not constant across the international system, and specific issues

## 24    CHAPTER 1

will vary according to their ideological or identity-based content.[55] Religion—specifically Islamist politics—became a major part of opposition to the US global war on terrorism, while political Islam has served more broadly as a competing ideological framework to liberalism.[56] And Protestant–Catholic struggles transformed European international relations in the early modern era.[57]

When an issue is suffused with ideological and identity challenges, states may feel a greater threat to their legitimacy and act accordingly. Transnational ideological polarization risks undermining regimes' foundations for rule.[58] For example, several episodes in Middle East history demonstrate the role of religious divides in heightening Middle Eastern states' threat perceptions.[59] Accordingly, in such situations ideology and identity will be tools states rely on. States have intervened in others' politics in order to spread their ideology and take advantage of the transnational ideological polarization.[60] They also engage in conflicts and long-running rivalries in order to head off threats to their identity.[61] Likewise, when religious issues are more salient in a conflict, we are more likely to see religious practices become a part of the battlefield.[62]

States are most likely to draw on religious appeals in power politics when these two conditions are present. For states with a high domestic moral authority of religion, appeals to religion will be a prominent and commonly accepted part of their politics. This will primarily occur in the domestic realm: the regime will use religion to justify their policies and existence. However, when such states face international issues in which ideological and identity issues are salient, they will also use these religious appeals in international power politics. If the international issues involve religion, states will use religious appeals to contest the nature of the religious issues at stake, arguing they are more worthy of support than those of their rivals. If the crisis involves nonreligious ideologies or identities, the state uses religious appeals to critique states relying on other beliefs (see table 1.2).

Religion will be a less prominent element of power politics in other possible combinations. When a state with high domestic moral authority of religion confronts an international issue in which ideology and identity are not salient, the state's religious appeals will be confined to domestic politics and we will see appeals to material benefits or secular values. When a state with low domestic moral authority of religion confronts an ideological or identity-based international issue, it will attempt to push back on the ideological nature of the issue with its own secular or materialistic claims. And when a state with low domestic moral authority of religion engages in an issue in which ideology and identity are not salient, we will see "standard" international relations.

## HOW RELIGIOUS APPEALS MATTER IN POWER POLITICS

*Table 1.2* When states use religious appeals in power politics

| | MORAL AUTHORITY OF RELIGION | |
|---|---|---|
| IDEOLOGICAL CRISIS | HIGH | LOW |
| Yes | Religious appeals in power politics | Nonreligious ideological appeals in power politics |
| No | Religious appeals confined to domestic politics | No religious appeals |

## When Religious Appeals Matter

In contrast to some who expect religion to transform international relations, I argue that religious appeals do not always have an impact on power politics, let alone one beneficial to international society or intended by the wielder. Specifically, the effect of the religious appeals depends on the credibility of the wielder and the material incentives of the target.

The credibility of the wielder has a major impact on religious appeals' impact. Some of this has to do with the wielder itself. That is, does the wielder act in line with religious principles? Or is its behavior clearly discordant with the religious rhetoric it is advancing? States are more likely to successfully justify their policies when they act in line with established belief systems. Likewise, states that have a history of supporting the moral causes that they claim drive their policies are more likely to gain influence. This extends to religion. Religious organizations that are more widely respected and more able to frame their actions as benefiting the common good have more political influence in domestic politics.[63] For example, the Vatican has been able to draw on its credibility as a mixture of official statehood and religious organization and religious leaders leverage the respect they have acquired to build peace.[64]

Credibility also relates to the cultural fit between the appeals and the target audience. That is, does the target audience recognize the values the wielder is appealing to, or are they foreign or contrived? Some of this has to do with the religious arguments in the appeals. Are they based on recognizable doctrine and texts, or are they an extreme interpretation of the faith? Much of it, however, has to do with the cultural practices and values based on the religion, which are not always directly arising from religious texts. That is, how does the target society interpret and act out their religious beliefs in their daily lives? If the religious appeals resonate with these cultural expressions, they can have an impact.

In addition to credibility, another condition is the material incentives the targets face. Specifically, would they face material costs by going along with

26    **CHAPTER 1**

the religious appeals? Alternately, would they gain material benefits from co-operating with the wielding state? Social movements have had more of an impact on state behavior when the states have a material incentive to adopt their moral policies.[65] In the international realm, rising states are more likely to adopt values-based rhetoric to reassure powerful states and prevent them from blocking their rise when unsettled situations leave states more concerned about the potential for conflict.[66] This holds for religious appeals as well. As works on religion–state connections and politics have found, religious beliefs or issues do not drive behavior on their own: we see dramatic effects when states have an incentive to act in line with religious pressure.[67]

Drawing on Busby's work, I argue that religious appeals' effects come from the combination of these two conditions. When the appeals resonate and a state faces material incentives to cooperate, we are likely to see a significant effect on international collective action. The religious appeals will promote the collective mobilization the target is organizing, or will undermine the collective mobilization by its rival. By contrast, when the appeals do not resonate and a state faces material disincentives, we will see little effect. The state will fail to either organize collective action through its religious legitimation or stop a rival's efforts.

I break with Busby, however, by arguing that the intermediate effects—which he saw as insignificant—still indicate religious appeals matter in international relations. It is in these cases that the unexpected effects of religious appeals are most likely to be noticed. When the religious appeals resonate and a state faces material disincentives to go along with their wielder, we will see a general increase in tensions even if the collective action does not come together. States know they will face material costs for going along with the collective action the wielder is attempting to mobilize, in terms of threats to their security by more powerful states or a loss of economic opportunities. These tend to be more immediate than the imperatives of religious arguments: policymakers thus prioritize them. However, the significance of religion in international relations remains. Regimes will be wary of religious appeals' impacts on their domestic publics and the general destabilizing effect of religion on international issues. They will try to counter these impacts by aggressively countering the wielder state, either with competing appeals or military and economic actions. This increases the overall tensions in the crisis.

When religious appeals are only partially credible, but states face material incentives to cooperate, we will see convenient collective action form. States may not take seriously the wielder of the religious appeals, or not believe in the substance of the religious appeals. Yet, they realize they can benefit by going along with the wielder's initiatives. As a result, the religious appeals can

# HOW RELIGIOUS APPEALS MATTER IN POWER POLITICS

*Table 1.3*  When religious appeals affect power politics

| | MATERIAL INCENTIVES TO JOIN COALITION | |
|---|---|---|
| CREDIBILITY OF WIELDER | YES | NO |
| *High* | Religious appeals contribute to international coalition building | Religious appeals increase tensions in a crisis |
| *Low* | Religious appeals create shallow coalition, wielder loses control | No effect of religious appeals |

help justify the international collective action and present a pleasing face for policies that may otherwise be difficult to formulate, but the collective action will not persist once the material incentives change. Moreover, as the religious appeals' formulation and impact is shallow, leaders will be unsure how to deploy and respond to it; resulting policies may be ineffective or counterproductive. Finally, because religious appeals' impact is not based on leaders and societies internalizing the religious arguments, the complex nature of religion can take over. Targets of the religious appeals may misunderstand and misapply the appeals, and they may even twist the meaning of the initial rhetoric for their own purposes (see table 1.3).

## Summary, Clarifications, and Alternative Explanations

Thus, I argue that religious appeals can have a major impact on power politics. When states with a high domestic moral authority of religion face an ideologically charged international dispute, they may draw on religious appeals as one among many tools to promote or undermine collective action. This can mobilize domestic publics and persuade target leaders. These effects depend on the combination of the credibility of the appeals and the material incentives facing the target, with even intermediate effects having an impact.

Some clarifications are needed to my argument. One concern may be that I am treating religion the same as any other belief system. Have not scholars been arguing that religion matters because it is distinct and dramatic? One reason I am not basing my argument on this claim is that I worry many early works on religion and international relations overemphasized religion's transformative nature. Religion does matter in international relations, but its "return" has not fundamentally changed how the international system works. Scholars of religion and international relations risk leaving their theories easily disproven if they make such grand claims.

Alternately, one could object I am claiming too much about the uniqueness and power of religion. I assume many things about the importance of religion

28    CHAPTER 1

in today's world and the impact it has on states. If these are not true, then my theory falls apart. These are assumptions, but I include evidence in each of the case studies about religion's impact on the states and social groups involved. A related concern is that, if I am arguing states strategically use religious appeals, does that suggest religion has no independent effect on international relations? I would argue against that. Many studies on legitimacy and international relations note that states strategically use ideals and values but that does not mean these ideas are insignificant. Additionally, I address this claim as the instrumentalist counterargument later in the chapter.

One could also argue that the material incentives are "doing most of the work." That is, apparent cooperation with a state using religious appeals is due to its material power, not the religious appeals themselves. As we will see, there are unique impacts on power politics from religious appeals even as material incentives vary. An explanation of power politics without attention to the role of religious appeals would be incomplete. Granted, a skeptic could still claim these intermediate effects do not count as "real impacts." This a broader point about the narrowness of the debate on ideas in international relations, which I will address in the book's conclusion.

Additionally, there may be issues with levels of analysis. When I discuss wielders and targets of religious appeals, I sometimes focus on leaders, sometimes on regimes, and other times on domestic audiences. This is because the theory cuts across traditional levels of analysis, in line with the complexity of religion itself. Confining the analysis to one level of analysis may undermine some of its explanatory power. In the case studies I will use "leader" when I am discussing specific leaders, "regimes" when I am discussing the people in charge of a state, and "state" when I am discussing official actions by a country.

I also want to address alternative arguments. One is what I call the *religion skeptics*. These scholars would reject the significance of religious appeals in power politics. As Goddard and Krebs note, "many realists . . . see public rhetoric as a mere fig leaf covering the naked pursuit of interest."[68] At best, then, religious appeals, would be just another "fig leaf," meant to hide the self-interest motivation of a state. Religious appeals may also be confined to low priority areas of foreign policy.

We can find some examples of these religion skeptics specifically discussing international alignment and coalitions.[69] Many others, however, discuss ideology and culture in general. Conventional realist theories explicitly reject the role of culture and values in alliances.[70] Neoclassical realists would allow for some influence of identity on international alignment, but they tend to argue that states' foreign policies—once formulated—will follow conventional realist contours.[71] More recent rationalist works point to regime type or domestic politics to explain international coalition building.[72] Others point to regimes' calculation of potential partners' reliability, states' learning, and calculating their interest in the alliance, or even literal payments to explain alignment and alliance ties.[73] Despite the great variety of such theories, they tend to see alignment as a process driven by a rational calculation of state interests.

A related counterargument comes from the *instrumentalists*. One could argue that states do draw on religious appeals in power politics, and that these do have an impact on international relations. But leaders are just using religious appeals as a cynical political tool. This is a common rebuttal to evidence of religion's importance in politics but is really an example of "shifting the goalposts" rather than undermining an argument. Unless one is claiming something about the deepest beliefs of policymakers, it does not matter whether they *really* believe in the ideals they point to. All that matters is their impact. Indeed, if leaders draw on ideas and these ideas affect politics, even though the leaders are not being sincere, this will only strengthen claims of ideas' importance. As Goddard and Krebs argued, elites may be strategic, but they are also acting within a "given 'cultural tool-kit' . . . that includes rhetorical resources."[74] I do not see this as a serious counterargument but will address it in each of the cases to deal with potential critics.

Alternately, some are *religion triumphalists*. These scholars would argue that religion is a transformative force in the international system, replacing previous concerns with material gain and maybe even power itself. This counterargument would expect religious appeals to reflect a principled stand by the wielder on behalf of their religious beliefs. The state's goal is to spread its religious values through international coalitions, rather than advance material interests. Additionally, they would expect such appeals to matter despite material disincentives, and to produce dramatic—and beneficial, from the wielder's perspectives—changes in state behavior. There are several examples of this in the literature.[75]

# Research Design

Demonstrating the impacts of religious appeals in power politics involves several difficult methodological challenges. Rather than downplay them, I want to be transparent about the obstacles I faced in this book. First, I expect states to turn to religious appeals along with other power political tools: the use of religious appeals is highly context dependent. As a result, I am unlikely to be able to

30    **CHAPTER 1**

measure religious appeals as a variable that has consistent effects across different countries and issues. Additionally, we are unable to set up a strict comparative case design in which the cases "control for" all possible confounding variables. Finally, the nature and impact of religious appeals tend to be rather indirect, complicating searches for evidence.

These challenges are real, but we should not shy away from important questions just because they are difficult to answer. Instead, I draw on the growing literature on qualitative methodology to present a valid explanation despite the above challenges. I theorize the conditions under which religious appeals are likely to have an impact and use a combination of diverse, typical, and within-case comparison to gain leverage over this topic. Finally, I test my theory by looking for evidence that would be unlikely to exist if I were wrong.

## A Conditional Mechanism Research Design

Before I discuss my specific case selection techniques and methods of analysis, I first want to discuss the general methodological approach I take in this book. The standard methodological approach involves measuring the explanatory variable and dependent variables and demonstrating that changes in the former correspond to the latter.[76] In this approach, the qualitative analysis serves as a stand-in for a large-$n$ quantitative analysis. In my case, I would clarify—possibly even quantify—the various conditions I discussed above as variables and use them to explain the incidence and effects of religious appeals across a variety of cases.

There is an alternative approach, however. Studies can focus on the process leading to an outcome, or the mechanism connecting a cause and effect.[77] This avoids inappropriately imposing a quantitative standard on qualitative work that most quantitative work in political science cannot even satisfy and captures the complexities of social and political issues.[78] Numerous qualitative studies in international relations, as well as works specifically on religion and international relations, have drawn on these approaches. Some do so explicitly, while others implicitly use the language and approach of such methods.[79]

I follow this approach. The conditions I posit as giving rise to religious appeals and influencing their effects are highly context dependent. Any attempt to quantify and measure them consistently across all countries and times would be suspect. As a result, I do not specify what counts as—for example—credibility or material incentives ex ante; I instead base them on the specifics of each case study. Additionally, we cannot specify the weight of religious appeals' impact compared to other power political tools.

## Case Selection

I follow the case selection techniques of similar studies to test my theory on religious appeals and power politics, while expanding on their approach using advances in qualitative methodology. The standard approach involves choosing cases that control for alternative explanations by finding ones that are similar in all ways except the expected input and outputs. Yet, the aspiration to control for all possible counterarguments in order to demonstrate the validity of a theory requires an experimental standard that most observational studies cannot meet.[80]

Indeed, many existing studies on legitimacy and international relations do not attempt to reproduce this experimental standard. Some use cases meant primarily to be confirmatory.[81] They generally follow Seawright's and Gerring's "typical case" selection technique, in which the cases chosen are "well explained by" the theory.[82] Others use a diverse set of cases, in which cases vary along the full range of relevant factors: these can both explain and confirm the theory.[83] Finally, some use a diverse case selection technique that formally specifies how the cases vary.[84] Studies on religion and international relations adopt similar case selection techniques. Many studies focus on one crucial case.[85] Others adopt a diverse selection technique, identifying cases that vary in important ways that help clarify the role of religion.[86] Finally, some adopt more formal case selection techniques.[87]

I follow these existing studies' approaches, while more formally specifying the case selection techniques. I use a combination of diverse and typical case selection techniques, while leveraging within-case comparison to provide greater insight into the conditions leading to religious appeals' use and impact. My theory would expect to find the use of religious appeals in each of these cases; however, they are also strong candidates for my counterarguments, as I will discuss in each chapter. They thus both illustrate my theory and weaken counterarguments. At the same time, finding evidence that religious appeals are an important part of foreign policy—with clear impacts on power politics—across diverse cases strengthens support for my theory. I complement these in-depth case studies with shorter case studies. Some compare episodes within each country case in which states used religious appeals and those in which they did not. Additionally, I broaden the diverse case selection to include more variation on the conditions under which states use religious legitimation and their impact.

The primary cases are Saudi Arabia's 1960s rivalry with Egypt, the United States' efforts to craft counterterrorism coalitions after 9/11, and Russia's twenty-first century struggle with the West over control of former Soviet states.

32    CHAPTER 1

These cases are very different—in terms of religious traditions, position in the international system, regime type, and economic and military power—but demonstrate surprising similarities in terms of the reasons they draw on religious appeals and these religious appeals' impact on international power politics. Additionally, I use a variety of shorter case studies to illustrate broader variety in the conditions I theorize. These include variations in the conditions under which states use religious appeals, and variations in the conditions under which religious appeals have an impact.

## Methods and Data

Finally, I need to clarify the specific methods I am using to assess the presence and impacts of religious appeals. Most similar studies do not explicitly discuss their methods: they tend to delve into the process through which their hypothesized conditions activate the mechanism and how this affects a political or social situation. This technique is often called process tracing.[88] Process tracing can take a variety of forms. I use a specific type that emphasizes the likelihood of finding a piece of evidence. Even if the evidence does not clearly explain how an outcome came to be, if its existence is unlikely if my theory is incorrect, it would strengthen my theory's validity.[89] Likewise, if evidence for alternative explanations is missing—or contrary evidence exists—this invalidates them.[90] If I am able to find evidence that eliminates alternative explanations, and other evidence that supports mine, that will strengthen my theory.

I draw on a diverse set of primary and secondary data in this book. In the Saudi case I combine secondary studies with original archival research on Saudi foreign policy in the 1960s. In the US case I combine secondary studies with interviews with policymakers and experts. And the Russia case draws primarily on a mix of secondary studies and media articles. This variety of data is a strength, rather than weakness, however. Drawing on various types of data is a form of triangulation: it can overcome limits with any specific piece or type of data, and demonstrate that evidence for my theory is present in a variety of forms.[91] Admittedly, this data is imperfect. However, the qualitative methods I am using can allow us to gain some explanatory leverage while clarifying areas of uncertainty. The case selection highlights the existence of the mechanism, while the process tracing gives us confidence about its impacts. This is similar to much quantitative work in international relations, which often relies on imperfect data. Instead of abandoning any hope of gaining insight from such data, quantitative scholars turn to statistical methods that address the data issues and are (ideally) transparent about their limitations. I will take a similar approach in this book.

## Empirical Expectations

Based on the above discussion, I have a set of empirical expectations for my explanation, as well as for alternative explanations. The first involves the conditions I specify. States with high religious moral authority have ties between religion and state, and political debates that revolve around religion. Likewise, ideologically charged international crises are those in which both sides see a threat to their identity or values as well as physical security. Religious appeals are credible when the targets see the wielder as in line with the religious rhetoric, and the rhetoric fits the beliefs of the targets. Finally, targets have material incentives to go along with the religious appeals when they would gain economic or military resources through cooperation: disincentives involve threats to their wealth or security by cooperating. If my theory is correct, regimes should use religious appeals in power politics in the presence of these conditions, and there should be evidence the religious appeals are a reaction to their joint presence.[92]

My theory also specifies the nature of the religious appeals and their impact. I should find evidence that regimes view religious appeals as a strategic tool, not an end in themselves. I should also find evidence that states take religious appeals seriously as an element of their power politics. If we observe expected effects, I should see evidence either of leaders being persuaded to work with the wielder in response to religious appeals, or domestic publics responding positively to the appeals and calling on corresponding actions by their states. If unintended effects are present, I should find evidence of targets' concern about the impact of religious appeals, with corresponding aggressive actions. I should also find evidence of targets referring to the religious appeals in service of their own interests, not those of the wielder. Finally, there should be evidence of religious appeals or responses to these appeals being ineffective or poorly implemented.

I can specify expectations for alternative explanations as well. If the *religion skeptic* argument is accurate, I would find no evidence of religious appeals, or religious appeals that are minor and tangential aspects of power politics. Additionally, these religious appeals would have no noticeable impact on state behavior. As I noted above, the empirical implications of the *instrumentalist* approach are unclear, so I will address them in more depth in each case study. Alternately, if the *religion triumphalist* argument were correct, I would find evidence that religious appeals represent states' attempts to act on and spread their religious values, often in contrast to material concerns. Additionally, their impact would tend toward the more dramatic of those I have theorized, such as persuading leaders to change their behavior.

## Conclusion

In this chapter I theorized the nature and impacts of religious appeals on power politics. Religious appeals are a strategic tool that states draw on as a recognition of religion's importance in their own and others' societies. Religious appeals can produce both expected effects and unexpected, disruptive effects. When states with a high moral authority of religion face an ideologically charged international crisis, they will use religious appeals along with other foreign policy tools to build international coalitions and advance their interests. The impact of these religious appeals depends on the credibility of the wielder and the material incentives facing their target. This contrasts with religion skeptics, who would argue religious appeals have little impact on power politics, or religion triumphalists, who would expect religious appeals to override material concerns and transform international crises. I test this argument through a qualitative research design. The next chapter presents the first of my case studies, Saudi Arabia's attempt to build an "Islamic pact" in the 1960s.

# CHAPTER 2

# Religious Appeals in a Middle East Rivalry
Saudi Arabia and the "Islamic Pact"

In 1967, US officials asked Saudi Arabia to "discontinue its propaganda attacks" on Egypt.[1] Faisal bin Abdulaziz Al Saud—the Saudi king—had been touring regional countries, issuing calls for "Islamic solidarity" and attempting to form an international coalition organized around Islam, the Islamic Pact. These appeals were targeted at Egypt, as Saudi Arabia hoped both to create a coalition of like-minded monarchies and to spread its Islamic ideology as a counter to the popularity of Egypt's secular pan-Arabism. The United States had earlier noted this was "one of the major irritants in Saudi relations with Nasser," and that the "radical Arab governments' sharp reactions" to Faisal's efforts have polarized the region.[2]

Some may argue these religious appeals were a tangential aspect of this "Arab Cold War." The Islamic Pact never formed, and regional power shifts—with Egypt falling and Saudi Arabia becoming the dominant state—occurred due to the Arab loss in the Six-Day War and the rise of oil prices in the 1970s. Others may argue this represents religious values overriding security concerns, with religion serving as a more powerful tool in international relations than conventional statecraft. I argue, instead, that Saudi religious appeals were a strategic tool it drew on in power politics, reflecting the domestic and international context. The religious appeals had substantive impacts on regional politics, although their primary effect was to increase tensions rather than form a durable international coalition.

36    CHAPTER 2

The chapter proceeds in four sections. I first discuss Saudi Arabia's importance to the question of religious appeals in power politics. I then discuss the Saudi use of religious appeals, including the background of the crisis, the conditions leading to the appeals' use, and their impacts. Finally, I assess the overall validity of my theory in this case, and reject counterarguments, before presenting conclusions.

## The Debate over Islam in Saudi Foreign Policy

In this section I demonstrate both religious skeptic and religious triumphalist explanations should be able to explain the Saudi rivalry with Egypt. The ultimate failure of these explanations undermines these counterarguments—that religion is either tangential to material factors or a transformative force—and strengthens my own theory. Saudi Arabia is a country with significant material resources that manages both extra-regional allies—the United States—and regional geopolitical rivals. At the same time, it is a country whose very existence depends on Islam, with Islam manifesting in nearly all of its policies.

Saudi Arabia has had to balance its religious commitments with realpolitik considerations since its creation. The kingdom has been dependent on the United States for security and financial support. It has also had several rivalries with its neighbors throughout its history—including Egypt in the 1960s, Iraq in the 1990s, and Iran since the 1979 Iranian Revolution—forcing it to be cautious and prudent in its application of Islam to foreign policy. Additionally, Saudi Arabia's primary export is oil, which arguably has as much, if not more, influence on its foreign policy than does Islam.

Accordingly, many Saudi observers suggest religion is an insufficient explanation for Saudi foreign policy. Some studies of Saudi foreign policy focus on oil politics, with Islam playing only a minor part.[3] Others go further, arguing that the apparent ideological motivations behind Saudi Arabia are actually an oil-fueled attempt at self-protection.[4] Still others emphasize conventional geopolitics over the role of Islam in Saudi politics.[5] Even analyses that deal more directly with Islam place it secondary to conventional security motivations, accepting that there is a theological dimension to issues like the Saudi–Iranian rivalry but arguing that geopolitical competition is the primary reason for tensions.[6]

Others, however, do emphasize the role of Islam in Saudi foreign policy. Studies on religion and international relations have pointed to Saudi Arabia as an example of religion's continued importance in the world. Some argued Saudi Arabia used its control of Islam's holiest sites to gain support among Muslims.[7] Others pointed to the transnational Islamic movements Saudi Arabia

## RELIGIOUS APPEALS IN A MIDDLE EAST RIVALRY          37

helped form and its use of religious arguments in international organizations.[8] Studies of the Middle East have also pointed to the importance of Islam in Saudi foreign policy, arguing it both affects Saudi threat perception and serves as a tool in attempts to maintain its security.[9]

Thus, both religion skeptic and religion triumphalist explanations are apparent for this case. Religion skeptics would argue that Saudi Arabia was concerned about Egypt's material power, and its threat to Saudi domestic stability. They would claim key aspects of Saudi policy in response had to do with ensuring US support and engaging in a proxy war with Egypt in Yemen. The Islamic Pact, to them, was a low-priority window dressing on these more important issues. Alternately, religion triumphalists could argue that Saudi foreign policy reflected its Islamic principles, and that its attempts to spread this religious ideology resonated broadly in the region. As I show in this chapter, neither of these explanations is accurate.

## Methodological Note

I should first raise some methodological points about this discussion. Due to the historical nature of this case and the lack of publicly available Saudi foreign policy archives, I am unable to present direct evidence of Saudi decision making and its impacts. Instead, I use US archival records—from the Johnson administration—on Saudi foreign policy. This can provide access to the nature of Saudi foreign policy because of the close ties between the United States and Saudi Arabia in this period, and US desire to work with Egypt. Additionally, the records include numerous transcriptions of conversations with Saudi and Egyptian leadership, so it is not completely dependent on US interpretations of Middle East states. Finally, I draw on translated media articles from the Middle East—made available through the Foreign Broadcast Information Service—to provide a broader perspective on the impacts of Saudi efforts. I should also note that the relevant Arabic word, *tahalluf*, can be translated as pact, alliance, or league. The sources alternated between these. I will use Islamic Pact in order to remain consistent.

There are some potential issues with this data. Some of the archival records do rely on US officials' perceptions of Saudi foreign policy and regional reactions to it, which may raise concerns about validity. In order to address this, I provide details on each piece of evidence to clarify its source. I also attempt to combine US officials' perspectives with either regional voices or corresponding secondary literature, such as memoirs and biographies of key figures. The translated regional media should also allay concerns about bias in the sources. However, I discuss caveats to my analysis at the end of the chapter.

38    **CHAPTER 2**

# Saudi Use of Religious Appeals in the 1960s

Saudi religious appeals in its struggle with Egypt were part of these broader tensions. The 1960s Saudi–Egyptian rivalry involved both a high moral authority for religion on the Saudi side and an ideologically charged international crisis. Saudi efforts to create an Islamic Pact involved strategically drawing on its religious traditions in order to build an anti-Nasser coalition.

## Background: Saudi Arabia and the Cold War

The Saudi–Egyptian rivalry occurred in the context of the long-standing US–Saudi alliance and Cold War intrusions into the Middle East. Saudi Arabia and the United States formed an alliance in 1945, after US President Roosevelt met with the Saudi king and founder ibn Saud. This constituted an "oil for security" deal, in which Saudi Arabia would ensure a steady and stable oil supply and the United States would protect Saudi Arabia from threats.[10] These included neighboring states, Soviet expansion, and domestic unrest. Despite periodic tensions, this alliance has persisted through the twenty-first century.

However, Saudi Arabia did more than just provide oil. It was also an important part of the US struggle against the Soviet Union. In the 1950s, Eisenhower hoped Saudi Arabia could rally Muslims against Egyptian—and by extension Soviet—influence in the region.[11] The Saudis also built the Dhahran airfield in 1945, which allowed US air forces access to the Middle East. Saudi anti-communist efforts expanded as time went on, with the Saudis sponsoring anti-communist efforts globally.[12] In the Middle East, Saudi Arabia became a key part of the US "Twin Pillars" policy, alongside Iran; these two US-aligned states were instrumental in limiting the spread of communism through the region.

The Saudi rivalry with Egypt complicated these efforts. Gamal Abdel Nasser Hussein was a socialist who accepted Soviet support starting in 1955. However, Nasser saw himself primarily as an anti-imperialist, and was a founding member of the Non-Aligned Movement. Recognizing this, the United States hoped to draw Nasser away from Egypt and leverage his influence over Arab politics.[13] This, in turn, aggravated Saudi Arabia, which worried the United States would abandon it to what it saw as Egyptian aggression.

## Conditions Predicting Saudi Use of Religious Appeals in Power Politics

The moral authority of Islam in Saudi Arabia is incredibly high. Islam in some ways defines Saudi politics. This is obvious in the makeup of Saudi political institutions. The kingdom of Saudi Arabia is officially Islamic, using the Qur'an as its constitution. The judiciary is made up of Islamic clerics, while an official security force enforces conservative Islamic behavior. The kingdom's rulers also justify their control over the country through Islam.

Additionally, religious and traditional cultural practices are an essential element of its foreign and domestic policies. Saudi elites used Islamic to secure political power, and control domestic politics.[14] As a result, Saudi leaders often deploy religious arguments to maintain their power and justify policies. For example, after the *ikhwan*—an Islamic paramilitary force—revolted against the Saudis early in their history, the Saudis appealed to religion in order to justify stopping the militia.[15] This was also apparent when Saudi Arabia was formulating its response to Saddam Hussein's invasion of Iraq; then crown prince Abdullah Al Saud called for religious leaders to agree to any policy the regime adopted.[16] Religious appeals matter internationally as well. For example, Saudi Arabia felt compelled to support Islamic causes around the world because of the importance of charity in Islam and its desire to maintain its "Islamic credentials."[17] And King Saud bin Abdulaziz Al Saud, Saudi Arabia's second ruler, told the United States he hoped to lead a pan-Islamic movement.[18]

This high moral authority occurred alongside an ideologically charged international crisis in the 1960s' Egypt–Saudi rivalry. Conservative monarchies like Saudi Arabia vied with revolutionary nationalist regimes like Egypt for influence.[19] Nasser dominated regional discourse, appealing to shared Arab values and attempting to advance his pan-Arab ideology at the expense of conservative Western-aligned monarchies.[20] These symbolic claims included Arab nationalism and Palestinian rights, which served as Nasser's tools to unify and gain control over regional politics.[21] Saudi Arabia saw this pan-Arabism as a threat to its survival, and turned to Islam to counter Nasser's appeal.[22] This caused the rivalry to take on an ideological character, as states on each side turned to their competing ideologies to gain an edge over their rivals.[23]

This rivalry included actual fighting through the proxy war in North Yemen.[24] In 1962, elements of the North Yemen army overthrew the country's monarch in order to set up a republic. This coup soon became embroiled in regional politics as Egypt's president, Gamel Abdel Nasser, openly supported the republican cause. The Saudi regime, wary of the coup inspiring domestic unrest and fearful of Nasser's growing influence, supported the royalist forces. The war dragged on through the 1960s, bogging down Egyptian forces and contributing in part to the Arab defeat in the 1967 war with Israel.

40    **CHAPTER 2**

## Saudi Islamic Appeals in 1960s Power Politics

Due to the confluence of a high moral authority for religion and an ideologically charged international struggle, Saudi Arabia turned to religious appeals. Specifically, Saudi Arabia attempted to form an international coalition by appealing to shared Islamic faith. The Saudi regime saw these appeals as a crucial part of its foreign policy, deploying them strategically in interactions with other states.

### THE ISLAMIC PACT AND RELIGIOUS APPEALS

Saudi Arabia attempted to create an Islamic Pact, but this was not merely a coalition of Muslim countries. King Faisal hoped to use Islam as an ideological counterweight to Nasser's influential pan-Arabism. Saudi Arabia used Islam as a means to criticize Egypt through propaganda efforts. Saudi Arabia also called for Islamic solidarity among conservative Muslim states, in an attempt to bind them together in an anti-Nasser alliance. The United States was a target of Saudi religious appeals as well; Saudi Arabia used Islamic arguments to convince the United States it was the most credible US partner in the region. Finally, Saudi Arabia justified its foreign policies by referencing in Islam.

The most straightforward example of Saudi Islamic appeals were Saudi officials justifying some of their foreign policies by referring to Islam. Sometimes this was an attempt to persuade US officials of policies' value. In a May 1964 meeting, Faisal pushed back on US claims that Nasser's actions in Yemen had no connection to Soviet Communism by arguing that Nasser could not be trusted; this was because "Nasser did not believe in God" and thus had "no standards of honesty."[25] Saudi Arabia also justified its Yemen policies through Islam: in a 1966 meeting between US National Security Council adviser Robert Komer and Prince Sultan bin Abdulaziz, Sultan argued that an accord on Yemen with the United Arab Republic was for the good of all Muslims.[26]

Other Saudi Islamic appeals were strategic tools. One was propaganda. Saudi Arabia used religious propaganda to combat both Nasser and communism. In an April 1967 meeting between the US ambassador and Faisal, Faisal raised Saudi "public media" efforts that were meant to "[stress] Islam as [a] defense against godless Communism."[27] While he argued they had not "deliberately attacked Nasser" and that Nasser's anti-Saudi propaganda was more direct, the US ambassador characterized the propaganda as "instruments of attack."[28] Specifically, the ambassador noted that "the banner of Islam and anti-Communism had clearly been waved as direct attacks on [Egypt]."[29] While the archival sources did not discuss the content of the propaganda, US officials did suggest Saudi Arabia "discontinue its propaganda attacks" as part of a move toward reducing tensions between the two.[30] Thus both the United States and Egypt took this seriously.

Saudi Arabia also hoped to promote Islamic solidarity. Under Faisal, Saudi Arabia tried to expand its power by organizing other states along Islamic lines. This took the form of an Islamic Pact, in which conservative Muslim countries would be united (assumedly under Saudi leadership). In June 1966, a US citizen who had been working with the Saudi regime noted—in a call with US national security adviser Walt Rostow—that Faisal "is trying to rally the Arab world to resist Communism and Nasser's radicalism by evoking the spirit of the Muslim faith."[31] As part of this, Faisal traveled to Turkey, Morocco, Guinea, Mali, and Tunisia in late 1966; in a memo, Rostow argued that since Guinea and Mali are "Nasser's territory," Faisal was trying to "build support for himself and his Islamic Pact."[32] Additionally, in December 1965, Faisal made a series of "goodwill" visits to Iran, Kuwait, Sudan, and Jordan, which included "expositions of his conviction of the need for 'Islamic solidarity.'"[33]

Several of Faisal's speeches to Muslim audiences demonstrate this attempt to form an Islamic Pact. In a 1966 speech, Faisal argued "if this appeal [to Muslim solidarity] displeases some circles and some evil powers such as imperialism, communism or Zionism, I am absolutely sure that the Muslims . . . will support their righteous religion, join forces and cooperate with this just cause and with piety."[34] And in Tunis in 1966, he said "I would like to draw the attention of all Arab brothers that they are, more than anyone else, responsible for this call [for Islamic solidarity], because God has chosen His Prophet from among them."[35] This had its roots in his early 1960s efforts. In a speech at a 1962 international Islamic conference, Faisal "invoked Islam as a counter-ideology" to Nasser, declaring "those who disavow Islam and distort its call under the guise of nationalism are actually the most bitter enemies of the Arabs, whose glories are entwined with the glories of Islam."[36]

These appeals were clearly power politics. Faisal claimed his efforts as "aimed at bringing the Islamic peoples together and upholding the principles of the religion," and denied it was overtly focused on Nasser.[37] Yet, US officials assessed that Faisal did seem to "consider his Islamic policy as a means of countering the Arab socialist movement and of checking Nasser's strength," in a 1966 briefing for Faisal's US visit.[38] In a separate analysis, US officials noted Faisal viewed these calls for Islamic solidarity as "a weapon in his diplomatic arsenal helping to strengthen his defenses against [Egypt]" and "[stake] his claim to a measure of leadership in the Islamic world."[39]

Saudi Arabia also tried to use religious appeals to persuade the United States of its value as an ally, and of the need for continued US support for Saudi

## 42    CHAPTER 2

security. This primarily revolved around the US rivalry with the Soviet Union. Faisal presented Saudi Arabia as a bulwark against communist influence in the Middle East by appealing to Islam. In a 1966 meeting King Faisal "forcefully and at length argued [for the need] for action [to] stop the Communist penetration" of the Middle East, calling for forceful US action and explicitly contrasting it with US inaction in Vietnam in 1954.[40] Faisal also noted that his goal—"whether on the Arab or the Islamic level"—was to "cooperate with others" in the region to "stem [the] Communist tide."[41] Similarly, in a 1966 meeting with the US secretary of state, Prince Sultan argued "the threat of Communism in the Near East was the biggest danger" but that "Islam was the strongest shield against Communism."[42] He added that Saudi Arabia "endeavored to work against Communism on the basis of their religion," and that Nasser's efforts in Yemen were part of "the long-range Communist blueprint."[43] In another meeting with US officials, Sultan argued that their "religion was a good shield against Communism," but it is "bound to crack" if exposed to pressure.[44] Thus, Saudi Arabia used its Islamic credentials and appeals in an attempt to bind the United States to Saudi Arabia and ensure its support.

## Saudi Religious Appeals as a Foreign Policy Tool

These religious appeals by Saudi Arabia were both a strategic tool and a substantive element of its foreign policy. Saudi Arabia did not define its foreign policy by Islam, and instead used conventional diplomatic language when discussing its concerns and ambitions. Yet, it did view the appeals, and the issues in which it deployed them, as an important tool in the pursuit of its interests.

First, the Saudi–Egyptian rivalry, and its proxy war in Yemen, was not a religious conflict. This is important to emphasize as I am not arguing that religion drives states' foreign policy; instead it serves as one among many tools for states to advance their interests. Saudi motivations included conventional realpolitik considerations. Likewise, Saudi Arabia had specific, tangible goals, rather than vague religious aspirations.

At several points, Saudi Arabia used conventional foreign policy language to explain and justify its interventions in Yemen. In an April 1967 meeting with US embassy officials about Saudi policy in Yemen, Faisal did not mention Islam in his defense of the Saudi intervention. Instead, he emphasized things like the need to defend against Egyptian aggression and a desire to be responsive to Yemeni royalist requests for aid.[45] In a separate meeting that month on mediation between the Saudis and Egypt, US Ambassador Hermann Eilts noted that Saudi priorities included stopping Egyptian bombing of Yemen.[46] In another cable, US officials noted that Faisal defended his continued intervention in

Yemen by pointing to Saudi Arabia fulfilling earlier agreements on disengagement while Egypt did not, and the failure of the United States to do anything about Egyptian duplicity.[47] He also noted Nasser's desire to stall by pretending to negotiate until he was in a better position.[48] This is all conventional statecraft we would expect to hear in any international crisis. If Saudi Arabia's attempt to counter Egyptian influence was instead motivated by Islam, Saudi leaders would rely on Islamic justifications to defend their positions.

There are other examples of such conventional realpolitik. In a meeting with US officials, Faisal emphasized the most important issues in Yemen as ensuring the "Yemeni people have the right to decide their future," and Yemeni royalists' right to "defend themselves."[49] Additionally, after the United States claimed continued Saudi support for royalists could lead to a wider war, Faisal declared he did want a "peaceful settlement" but that he believed Nasser was trying to "gain time and to get renewed US aid," rather than genuinely negotiating, although he did also raise the broader threat of communism.[50] In another 1967 meeting, Faisal emphasized the requests for aid from Yemeni royalists as the justification for Saudi intervention.[51] And, in an earlier cable, the United States raised rumors of a break in diplomatic ties between Egypt and Saudi Arabia due to Saudi anger over Egyptian "harassment" of Saudi nationals.[52] This plethora of nonreligious defenses of Saudi efforts to block Nasser suggests the Saudis did not see it as a religious conflict.

There were also signs Saudi Arabia was willing to negotiate with Nasser; that is, it did not see the struggle as an uncompromising religious mission. In April 1967, King Faisal was—according to top Saudi diplomat Omar Saqqaf— "tired of [the] Yemeni war" and was "interested" but "skeptical" about mediation efforts.[53] Saqqaf also believed that Faisal would be "willing [to] restrain Yemeni Royalists" in exchange for an end to Egyptian bombing of Yemen.[54] And in an April 1967 memo, US officials believed that while Faisal claimed his goal in Yemen was the "removal of any vestige [of Egyptian] influence," in reality he would be satisfied with the removal of Egyptian forces and the leader of Yemeni Republicans, Abdullah al-Salal.[55] Similarly, in March 1964, Faisal met with an unidentified individual who later relayed the meeting to US officials. Faisal reportedly specified his demands for Egypt in Yemen as "claims for property damage and loss of life" from Egyptian bombing of Yemen and "compensation for confiscated Saudi property."[56] If this was a religious conflict for Saudi Arabia, they would have held firm until all opposing forces were destroyed. Instead, Faisal approached it like any conventional international crisis.

Moreover, the religious appeals Saudi Arabia deployed in its tensions with Nasser were a conscious policy it used in certain situations. If this were a case of religion influencing foreign policy, we would see such appeals across issue

44    **CHAPTER 2**

areas. King Faisal intentionally restricted religious propaganda against other Arab states initially, and only turned to it as the tensions with Egypt intensified. A 1965 US memo reported that Saudi Arabia was not allowing any criticism of secular Tunisian president Habib Bourguiba—despite ideological differences—and Faisal had a "distaste for inter-Arab propaganda campaigns."[57] Moreover, Saudi use of religious appeals declined after the 1967 war, again indicating they were a conscious targeted policy, not a ubiquitous feature of Saudi foreign policy. For example, in an October 1967 meeting with US State Department officials in which they discussed inter-Arab relations and tensions with Israel in the wake of the Six-Day War, Faisal did not mention Islam at all.[58]

Thus, Saudi Islamic appeals were not a case of religion motivating Saudi foreign policy. Instead, they were one among several tools Saudi policymakers turned to in international power politics. That does not mean they were inconsequential "cheap talk," however. Saudi Arabia did see its intervention in Yemen—and the broader rivalry with Nasser—as a major foreign policy initiative. This is crucial to demonstrate, as it shows that Saudi Arabia took this issue seriously and religious appeals were not confined to "soft" cultural outreach. Faisal's religious appeals were tied to one of the key themes in his foreign policy, the idea that the divide between religious and atheist states represented a major threat to Saudi security. This is why, according to biographer Alexei Vassiliev, Faisal "devoted so much time and so many resources to promoting the solidarity of Muslim states."[59] Similarly, as tensions with Egypt persisted despite mediation efforts, Faisal began "to actively propagate the idea of rallying round not only Arab but also Muslim forces to counter Egypt's nationalist policy."[60]

This can be seen in a few specific instances. In February 1966, Faisal sent his brother, Prince Sultan, to the United States with a letter requesting US help on Yemen. US State Department officials noted this was "highly unusual," indicating the severity of the threat Faisal believed he faced.[61] In a contemporary meeting with the US ambassador in Saudi Arabia, Faisal discussed what he saw as the "growing Communist threat," which the king believed could spark a conflict similar to that in Vietnam.[62] Faisal claimed Nasser was "providing a protective screen" for Soviet influence in the Middle East.[63] Similarly, in August 1964, Faisal requested a special meeting with the ambassador in order to relay reports that Egyptian aircraft flying from Yemen had crossed the border with Saudi Arabia, and Egyptian forces were heading toward its territory.[64] The king interpreted this as a threat to Saudi security.[65] Saudi religious appeals during Saudi Arabia's tensions with Nasser were thus related to deep-seated concerns about the regime's material and ideological security.

Saudi Arabia faced some costs for its use of religious appeals. This demonstrates that it took these religious appeals seriously as a policy tool and was willing to deploy them even if it faced potential penalties as a result. As I will discuss in detail below, the United States became frustrated with Saudi Arabia at several points due to its continued intervention in Yemen. Moreover, Saudi Arabia knew of these potential costs, and was still willing to proceed. In a December 1963 meeting, Saqqaf asked US officials whether it was still the US position that it "would not defend Saudi Arabia [in the event of] resumption of aid to Royalists."[66] This was a subtle attempt to probe the limits of US patience with Saudi support for the royalists, of which the United States was not a fan.

## The Impact of Saudi Religious Appeals

Saudi Arabia used religious appeals in this crisis through its attempt to build an Islamic Pact to counter Nasser. These religious appeals had a clear impact on regional politics. As Saudi Arabia under King Faisal was credible on religious issues, but targets faced material disincentives to cooperate with the Islamic Pact, it was not the intended effect, however. The Islamic Pact never came together, and Saudi religious appeals primarily increased regional tensions.

### CONDITIONS AFFECTING THE IMPACT OF SAUDI RELIGIOUS APPEALS

The impact of Saudi religious appeals related to my theorized conditions. First, Saudi Arabia under King Faisal was a credible speaker on Islamic issues. Faisal was well known as a personally pious man, represented in Saudi media as "the authentic Muslim king."[67] He called for the pragmatic implementation of Wahhabi Islam during his reign.[68] Moreover, Faisal's domestic "power base" included the Islamic clerical elite.[69] Many regional Muslims looked to Faisal as a counterweight to secular leaders like Nasser. For example, many Islamists fled crackdowns in Arab nationalist states by relocating to Saudi Arabia. And Muslims outside the region saw him as their champion, as seen in Pakistan renaming a city after him.[70]

Faisal also gained a reputation as an effective and relatively reformist leader. His brother Saud, who preceded him on the throne, was famously inept in both domestic and foreign affairs. Saud was a poor steward of the country's oil wealth, spending it on frivolous and ineffective projects.[71] Faisal changed that, improving the governance of the kingdom. He also implemented important reforms, leading to respect even from the Grateful Dead, who dedicated their 1975 album, *Blues for Allah*, to him after his assassination.[72]

While Saudi Arabia was credible on the religious appeals it used, its targets faced material disincentives to joining the Islamic Pact. At this point, Egypt

46    CHAPTER 2

was the dominant material power in the region. According to the Correlates of War National Material Capabilities data, Egypt had three times the resources of Saudi Arabia, in terms of both military capabilities and overall material capabilities.[73] Moreover, Egypt had demonstrated its military prowess and willingness to fight through its victory in the Suez crisis and intervention in Yemen. Going against Egyptian wishes thus threatened states' security.

States also faced domestic material disincentives to working with Saudi Arabia due to Egypt's influence over popular movements. Several conservative regimes had fallen to Arab nationalist revolutions, and the remaining states feared domestic unrest. Nasser stoked these fears by appealing directly to Arab publics, leading states to worry about upsetting him and facing domestic protests as a result.[74] Even external powers like the United States hoped to court Nasser due to his influence in the region, and thus had a disincentive to work too closely with Saudi Arabia against Nasser.[75]

Saudi Arabia could provide some material incentives to potential coalition members, but these did not outweigh the threat from Egypt. Saudi Arabia's close ties with Western states could theoretically extend to its allies. And it did work with regional states to provide economic support. States' primary concern remained Egypt, however. For example, Jordan was a conservative monarchy that hoped to stay on good terms with the United States, but its fear of Egypt undermining its regime led it to keep some distance from Saudi and US plans and to participate in Egyptian initiatives.[76]

## The Impact of Islamic Appeals

As expected, Saudi religious appeals had an impact on this crisis. Both regional states and the United States adjusted their behavior in response to the religious appeals. Some conservative states responded positively to the appeals, although there was a limit to the extent to which they would join the Islamic Pact. Arab nationalists, in turn, vociferously opposed Saudi efforts, and saw them as a threat. The United States likewise worried about their destabilizing effect and was not convinced to help Saudi Arabia in this initiative.

### Regional Rival Concerns about the Islamic Pact

Saudi Arabia's regional rivals were worried about its appeals. A briefing memo for Faisal's 1966 US visit noted that his Islamic Pact was "portrayed in Cairo as a move to align the reactionary powers against the progressives."[77] In response to the Islamic Pact, Nasser "accused Faisal of being a 'traitor to the Arab cause,' and declared that Islamic solidarity was 'an American-British conspiracy.'"[78] And a CIA analysis from that year notes that Nasser had "come to view Faisal's new campaign for Islamic solidarity as a Western-inspired tactic to rally opposition against him and Egypt's brand of socialism."[79] This suggests that Nasser was worried about the ideological nature of the alliance: this was not just a case of balancing. Another US assessment noted that Egyptian worries about Faisal's "anti-Nasser Islamic Pact" were heightening the former's "distrust" of the latter.[80] Similar reports came out of the Soviet Union. A May 1967 Soviet report noted a youth conference in Egypt included a denunciation of the "Islamic pact" as part of broader "American imperialism."[81]

Expressions of concern also came directly from Egyptian officials. In February 1966, Egyptian vice president Anwar Sadat met with President Johnson and top US officials. During this meeting, he sought US assurances that the United States was not involved with Faisal's Islamic Pact.[82] This suggests that Egypt was worried about Faisal's efforts, and it was deemed serious enough to raise with the United States. A March 1967 Egyptian state media pronouncement criticized UK involvement in the Middle East, noting that Britain was the "ally and supporter" of conservative governments in the region and that the "remnants" of conservative forces include the "debris of the projected Islamic pact."[83] An August 1966 Egypt state media broadcast discussed Faysal's trip meant to "promote the Islamic alliance" as a "continuation of and a substitute for CENTO [Central Treaty Organization]."[84]

There are numerous reports of similar concerns in Egyptian media. In a 1966 statement, Mohammed Haykal—the editor of Nasser-aligned Egyptian paper *al-Ahram*—argued that Saudi Arabia had been supporting the Muslim Brotherhood and "engaged in a series of suspicious trips" as part of an "open imperialist master plot." He argued that Saudi Arabia's declaration of an Islamic Pact was a "revival of the Baghdad Pact and Eisenhower doctrine."[85] Another editorial that year argued King Faysal's visit to Washington, DC, was about "enlisting more support" for his projects including his "Islamic Pact," which it argued was another example of "Arab reaction attempting to turn its allies against forces of liberation."[86] Other editorials attacked the Islamic Pact as an abandonment of "the liberation of Palestine," and an "imperialist bridge" across the Persian Gulf.[87] In a September 1966 editorial in *al-Jumhurnya*, the author discussed Faysal's tour of countries he hoped to recruit into the Islamic Pact and his "call to use Islam as a political means to fight liberation in the Arab world"; the editorial argued the "man in the street in the Arab and Islamic world knows that this project is but a continuation of the old, desperate attempt to revive the Baghdad Pact."[88] An April 1967 Cairo Voice of the Arabs broadcast argued that the United States was behind the "so-called Islamic Pact by assembling a cluster of agent reactionary rulers."[89] A June 1966 *al-Ahram* editorial discussed the "Islamic pact plot" that had been "exposed,"

48    CHAPTER 2

and expressed concern that it was directed as "progressive liberated trends in the area" and that Faysal hoped to gain US support for his project. The editorial also noted that it was "not a coincidence" that "Jordan has assumed a contemptuous attitude towards the Palestinian liberation front."[90]

These reactions went beyond rhetoric. US officials believed that Nasser's fear of the prospective Islamic Pact was affecting his judgment in foreign policy, leading to erratic decisions. A 1966 memo notes that Faisal's calls for "Islamic solidarity" was "one of the major irritants in his relations with Nasser," and that the "radical Arab governments' sharp reactions" to Faisal's efforts had polarized the region.[91] In June 1966, the US ambassador to Egypt noted that Nasser was "over-reacting to fancied US support for [the] Islamic 'Pact.'"[92] Similarly, in 1966, Central Intelligence Agency (CIA) analysts argued that, as a result of Nasser's concerns about the Islamic Pact, he was discussing forming an openly anti-Saudi coalition and "considering terminating the détente" with Saudi Arabia.[93] Palestinian writer Said Aburish corroborates this in his biography of Nasser, arguing these Islamic appeals had a particular "potency" and that the combination of Saudi efforts alongside US and Israeli antagonism led to the sense that "the odds were stacked against him."[94] Likewise, in a February 1966 interview with Iraqi media, Nasser reported that his conversations with Iraqi authorities over the Unified Political Command—meant to be the first stage in a political union between the countries—revolved partly around attempts to counter the Islamic Pact.[95]

Other radical Arab states also reacted negatively. Iraq expressed concern about Saudi efforts, noting to a US diplomat in 1964 that the Saudi–Egyptian tensions may lead to a "renewed alignment of the monarchies" against Nasser and his allies, including Iraq.[96] Similarly, Syria "condemned" Saudi Arabia as a "'reactionary' pursuing strictly personal ends, whose appeal for Islamic unity was directed against Arab Nationalists."[97] Syria even called for an "emergency conference in Damascus of the revolutionary Arab states": this irked Egypt, which saw itself as the convener of such gatherings, demonstrating the importance of the situation to Syria.[98] A June 1966 Syrian state media pronouncement expressed concern about Faisal meeting with the shah of Iran, noting they were "not satisfied protecting the bases of their masters" and were instead "coordinating their efforts with the reactionaries of the Middle East" through the "Islamic Pact" to "strike every progressive liberation movement in the region."[99] In September 1966, a Syrian military office spoke to Egyptian media about Faisal's "desperate attempts to establish an Islamic alliance," and argued it was part of a "broader war on the Arab people."[100] A January 1966 "Voice of the Arabian Peninsula" broadcast out of Damascus discussed concerns about US and British arms supplies to conservative states, linking "this armament with the Islamic alliance which the imperialist powers advocate through that country."[101]

Syria attempted to actively counter Saudi efforts. In April 1967, the Syrian chief of state gave a speech in which he connected the Islamic alliance to a long line of "imperialism" in the region; he combined this with a call to action, stating the "Arab revolutionary forces are confident of final victory over imperialism" and "traitorous reactionary regimes."[102] Hafez Asad—then defense minister—in May 1966 attacked the Islamic alliance and called on the Syrian people to treat the "enemies of the revolution and people" as "Zionists" and "attack them where they are and uproot them."[103] Around the same time, a Syrian state media report pointed to the Islamic alliance, and argued that the "aggressive imperialist forces will learn how the Arab people can burn the air in defense of their unity."[104]

Arab nationalist and anti-imperialist organizations were also critical of the Islamic Pact. In October 1966, an opposition group in Iran argued efforts to "rig up an Islamic alliance" were part of a conspiracy by "colonialists and their stooges" but that "such so-called holy alliances will not bear the fruits that the imperialists desire."[105] A June 1966 statement by the Iraqi Communist Party argued the Islamic alliance was part of a broader plan to send arms to Saudi Arabia and Jordan as part of a planned attack on Syria and Egypt.[106] In May 1966, the chairman of the Palestine Liberation Organization, when asked about the "Islamic pact," said the "Palestinian people have nothing to do with any pacts" and that they "march with a single pact only—the pact of the Arab nation."[107] A statement by the General Federation of Trade Unions out of Damascus in June 1966 argued the "call for the establishment of an Islamic alliance has been revealed" as part of "shabby imperialist ambitions."[108] A July 1966 editorial in a Syrian Ba'ath Party newspaper noted the "Islamic alliance" was part of a "reactionary-imperialist-Zionist" plot in the region to preserve divisions among Arab states.[109] A January 1967 statement from a Third World solidarity conference held in Damascus attacked Saudi Arabia for its role in the war in Yemen, and argued the Islamic alliance was an attempt to support the "political line hostile to democracy and the people."[110]

These organizations also called for states to take action to prevent the formation of the Islamic Pact. A statement by the "Free Bahrainis" based in Damascus in March 1966 discussed the "dreadful imperialist conspiracy against the freedom, safety, progress and future of the Arab people." They argued "Arab reaction, instigated by imperialism," tried to create a "reactionary imperialist pact . . . the Islamic pact" and that this necessitated a "popular Arab reply."[111] After a May 1966 meeting of Arab communists, the activists called for the "unification of efforts of all national and progressive forces in the face of

50    **CHAPTER 2**

the Islamic alliance."[112] In September 1966, the Arab Lawyers Federation called on Egypt to work with other Arab states to combat the Islamic alliance.[113]

### Conservative State Support for the Islamic Pact

There was also some indication that conservative states and prominent Muslims were attracted to the Islamic Pact. Faisal's hosts reportedly "favorably received" him during his trips to Muslim countries in which he attempted to gain support for the Islamic Pact.[114] A US memo prepared in preparation for Faisal's 1966 US visit noted that Saudi Arabia had received "some expression of sympathy" from Jordan and Iran on its Islamic Pact.[115] Specifically, a CIA assessment noted the shah responded positively to the Islamic Pact, as it would help to counter the threat posed by radical Arab states.[116] Additionally, Faisal bonded with Kamel Mrouh, a Lebanese Shia who ran the *al-Hayat* newspaper, over his Islamic outreach effort.[117] Through *al-Hayat*, Mrouh "heralded the ideas of Muslim solidarity and served as Faisal's mouthpiece in the Arab world."[118] According to Mrouh's son, he helped reconcile Faisal with the shah of Iran, a useful strategic partner.[119]

There is evidence that Iran shared Saudi priorities. The shah of Iran was wary of Nasserism, and hoped to work with Faisal to combat Egypt's influence. In a 1964 meeting with the US ambassador, the shah raised his "preoccupations with Nasser and concern for the security of the Persian Gulf."[120] Additionally, Abbas Aram, the Iranian foreign minister, argued in a meeting with a top State Department official that Iran is a "well-wisher of the Arabs" but the "problem is Nasser," who Aram believed was a Soviet tool to control the Gulf.[121] The shah also spoke of Faisal "with respect" in 1968, even as the two were experiencing tensions over borders.[122] The United States believed Iran was considering helping Saudi Arabia support royalist forces in southern Yemen after the British withdrew.[123]

Iran also seemed to directly support the Islamic Pact. Syria criticized Iran for speaking in favor of the Islamic alliance during a June 1966 visit to Morocco.[124] A "Voice of Iraq" broadcast similarly criticized Iran for working with Saudi Arabia on the Islamic Pact to oppose the "aspirations of our people."[125] During a December 1965 visit of Faisal to Iran, Faisal spoke of the importance of "adherence to Islamic principles" to strengthen ties between the two countries.[126] A joint press release from that visit appealed to their common Islamic beliefs, and their desire to "call a conference of Islamic chiefs of state" to "pave the way for an identity of views and protection of their interests."[127] In May 1966, an Iranian newspaper wrote an angry editorial in response to a threatening speech by Nasser against Saudi Arabia, noting Saudi Arabia's defense of the "Almighty's holy sanctuary."[128]

Other states seemed drawn to the Islamic Pact. Syria criticized Kuwait for "deporting all progressive Arabs," noting "imperialism" is keeping "Kuwait from the march of the liberated Arab countries" partly through "binding it to the Islamic alliance."[129] After Faisal's trips in support of an Islamic alliance, the leader of the Sudanese Ummah Party expressed support for an Islamic summit led by King Faisal.[130] During a 1966 meeting between Faisal and the king of Morocco in Morocco, Hassan II said he "welcomed the call for the rapprochement of Islamic peoples" and supported the idea of an "Islamic call."[131]

### Limits to Reception of the Islamic Pact

Yet, there was a limit to which conservative Arab states would sign on to the Islamic Pact, and the United States never supported it. While the United States thought Saudi Islamic appeals were having an impact on the region, they were not effective in binding the United States to the Saudi cause. Notably, US officials did not believe Faisal's claims that the war in Yemen was against communism. In a 1966 memo to President Johnson, Rostow noted that they could continue discussing with Faisal the "Communist penetration in the Middle East" and hoped to "bring him to a more realistic view of what Communism is."[132] This wry aside by Rostow indicates he, and others in the administration, believed Faisal was overplaying connections between Egypt's Yemen intervention and the Soviet Union. In a separate memo from that year, US officials claimed that Saudi Arabia had a "grossly exaggerated impression of the extent of Communist bloc presence" in the region.[133]

Some US reactions to Saudi Islamic appeals veered toward the dismissive. US officials pretended to care about Faisal's appeals to the communist threat to keep him happy. This was apparent in a 1966 memo from Komer to Johnson about Prince Sultan's US visit, in which he asked permission to say a few "non-things" to the Saudi prince, including that Johnson had "ordered a prompt and careful re-examination of the risk of Communist takeover in Yemen."[134] And, in an earlier memo to the president, Komer noted that the State Department wanted Johnson to send a "Presidential message" to Faisal as "assurance," adding that "it's almost become a matter of giving Faysal [sic] a top-level pat on the head every six months."[135]

Additionally, the United States did not take Saudi Arabia's side on Yemen. US officials believed Saudi Arabia was just as disruptive as Egypt. A 1966 memo noted that Faisal's "hesitation to allow" a regime transition from the royal family "prolongs the disruption in Yemen."[136] It also argued that if Faisal was "truly intent on opposing the Communist position in Yemen," he would support an alternative to the oppressive royalists.[137] Additionally, a summary of US security commitments to Saudi Arabia from that year noted the United

52    **CHAPTER 2**

States had "stressed to the Saudis that US protection of their integrity must not serve as a shield behind which they could continue to stimulate hostilities in Yemen."[138] This indicated a US desire to avoid giving Saudi Arabia a "blank check" in the conflict. A memo from Rostow to Johnson in advance of Faisal's 1966 visit called on Johnson to "downplay" the importance of the visit and avoid giving Faisal greater prestige in the Middle East that he could use to antagonize Nasser.[139]

US efforts to keep Saudi Arabia happy were mostly due to economic and strategic concerns. For example, the United States worried about Saudi Arabia turning to France or the UK instead of the United States for its arms purchases. In November 1963, the State Department informed the US embassy in Saudi Arabia that a British arms salesman was piquing the interest of Saudi Arabia: they worried this would complicate the Saudi reliance on US arms and training.[140] And, in April 1965, Rostow wrote a memo to McGeorge Bundy, former national security adviser, in which he said a recent message to Faisal should "Keep Faisal calmed down" and "help sell up to $200 million worth of hardware in competition with UK and France."[141] At the same time, the United States recognized that Saudi Arabia was an important player in the region, which it needed on its side. In 1968, Secretary of State Rusk sent a memo to President Johnson urging he meet with Crown Prince Khalid while he was on a medical trip to the United States. In it, Rusk said the US "stake in Saudi Arabia is high," and the ties between the two countries were one of the only ways the United States could "preserve [its] troubled relationship with the Arab area."[142] Additionally, in a memo requesting the president meet with Prince Sultan, Komer referred to Saudi Arabia as an important "client" the United States needed to satisfy.[143]

At the same time, the United States believed that Saudi efforts were destabilizing. In a 1967 memo on the potential for mediation between Egypt and Saudi Arabia, US officials suggested Saudi Arabia "discontinue its propaganda attacks" and "soft-pedal contacts with [the] Moslem Brotherhood [sic]" in Egypt.[144] A contemporaneous memo, giving directions to the US embassy in Egypt from the State Department, made similar points.[145] This suggests the United States saw Saudi religious appeals as an obstacle to resolving tensions with Egypt, providing indirect evidence of their effectiveness. Additionally, the United States grew frustrated with Faisal's efforts to form an Islamic Pact and sympathized with Nasser's concerns over this initiative. A 1966 briefing paper noted that, while Nasser's "delay" in removing troops from Yemen was part of the problem, Faisal's efforts to build an Islamic Pact were also contributing to ongoing tensions.[146]

Moreover, besides the above examples, the impact of Saudi religious appeals on potential allies was muted. The memo that discussed interest in Jordan and Iran also noted that Saudi appeals received only "polite interest" elsewhere.[147] And in neither Jordan nor Iran did Saudi religious appeals draw them into a durable Islamic alliance or cement Saudi leadership over the states. This is apparent in a few specific exchanges with these two states.

First, much of Jordan's deference to Saudi Arabia had to do with its desire for Saudi funding. Jordan noted its reliance on Saudi aid in several meetings with US officials. In February 1967, Jordanian prime minister Wasfi Tell told the US ambassador of recent efforts to obtain funding from Saudi Arabia for military and economic development projects.[148] Similarly, in early 1968, Jordanian chief of staff General Amer Khammash visited Saudi Arabia where he received "little encouragement" of additional Saudi funding, which he relayed to US embassy staff.[149] Likewise, at several points, Jordan expressed frustration with insufficient funding from Saudi Arabia. In November 1966, King Hussein met with the US ambassador to request help in gaining funding from Saudi Arabia: during the meeting, General Khammash argued their urgent need meant "there was simply no time for the long drawn out negotiations that were inevitable" when dealing with Saudi Arabia.[150] At another point, Prime Minister Tell—in response to a US question over Saudi funding—said "Saudi mental processes were so slow that quote [*sic*] even when they agree in principle—and in all sincerity—it takes months for them to act."[151] Additionally, in January 1967, Hussein told US embassy officials that he hoped for Saudi funds, but "the low level of Saudi comprehension and interest in his problems did not encourage" him.[152] Thus, Jordan appeared drawn to Saudi Arabia not because of the power of Saudi religious appeals, but because it needed Saudi money.

Moreover, at times, Jordan explicitly rejected Saudi leadership. Jordan was not happy with having to accept Saudi troops on its territory in the run-up to the 1967 war. According to a December 1966 memo, King Hussein reportedly was irritated at Saudi and Iraqi troops being placed in Jordanian territory, and hoped to increase the strength of Jordan's military to obviate this need.[153] Similarly, at one point Jordan proposed a joint East Arab military command that did not include Saudi leadership.[154] Likewise, a US intelligence study on Jordan from December 1966 made no mention of Saudi influence over the kingdom.[155] Thus, Saudi religious appeals did not translate into Jordan accepting Saudi dominance in the region. Jordan also tried to mediate between Egypt and Saudi Arabia on Yemen, as in a June 1965 message from King Hussein.[156] Jordan state media released a strong reaction to an Arab nationalist writer who claimed Western military support for Jordan was part of a "reactionary" plot, reiterating Jordanian support for Arab causes, thus distancing itself from Saudi Arabia.[157]

54    CHAPTER 2

The Islamic Pact seemed conspicuously absent from Jordanian communications. In a February 1966 communiqué released after a meeting between the two monarchs that discussed their support for the Arab League and Palestine, as well as general attempts to develop "close ties" among Islamic states and "fight atheism and deviance," nothing was said about the Islamic Pact.[158] An April 1966 announcement following a Jordanian delegation to Saudi Arabia similarly did not mention the pact.[159] When asked by the *Christian Science Monitor* about attempts to increase Islamic solidarity, Hussein gave an evasive answer, pointing to the importance of "[exerting] every effort to solve problems" among states in the "Islamic world": he noted that "Islam is our roots" but that states must be "built on the best things we can gain from our modern experiments."[160]

Iran, similarly, did not accept Saudi leadership. In a May 1965 memo, Iran's foreign policy priorities centered on Afghanistan, Pakistan, and Iraq, indicating little attention to Saudi interests.[161] At other points, Iran hoped to manage Middle East affairs by working with Turkey and Pakistan, not Saudi Arabia. For example, in mid-1967, the shah met with the leaders of the two countries to discuss plans for resolving the Arab-Israeli conflict.[162] Similarly, a background paper for the shah's 1967 US visit highlighted the "close ties" Iran had with Pakistan and Turkey.[163] Additionally, Iranian officials at several points noted to US officials that Iran, not Saudi Arabia, should be the leading power in the region. In a 1964 meeting between US officials and Iranian foreign minister Abbas Aram, Aram attempted to convince the United States to place more pressure on Nasser. In order to demonstrate Iranian credibility, he said the "other Arab countries" are "afraid of Nasser" but Iran "was not afraid."[164] Similarly, a May 1968 US memo noted an "Iranian assumption that Iran has the mission of controlling the Gulf."[165] And in a June 1968 meeting with the secretary of state, the shah even compared Saudi Arabia unfavorably to Iran, arguing that Iran was "progressive" while Saudi Arabia was "paternalistic" and backwards.[166]

Iran was also jealous of US support for Saudi Arabia, believing the United States supported the Saudis over Iran. A May 1966 CIA report claimed the shah had reacted angrily to a top US official's recent visit to Egypt. When he heard US officials had warned Nasser against taking action against Saudi Arabia, he reportedly "slammed [his papers] down on the desk and said 'if only the United States would support us as it does Faysal [*sic*].'"[167] He added that it was "unfortunate" that the United States had not reacted similarly against apparent Egyptian threats against Khuzestan.[168] Similarly, in November 1969, Iranian ambassador Hushang Ansary met with the US secretary of state to pass on comments from the shah. The shah was concerned about what he termed "undue support" for Saudi Arabia, which he believed would "create problems of prestige" for Iran in the region.[169] The secretary believed the shah hoped the

"US will pick Iran as its 'chosen instrument'" in the Middle East.[170] Thus, Saudi religious appeals were not effective in convincing Iran to follow the Saudi lead in the region.

Additionally, both Jordan and Iran had their own reasons for cooperating with Saudi Arabia, unrelated to Saudi Islamic appeals. Jordan was a target of Nasser's criticism due to its monarchical government and US ties. In a December 1966 speech, King Hussein furiously pushed back on—to use the US embassy paraphrase—the "attack" of "Arab brothers and their officials" on Jordan: he added that "some Arab factions are trying to destroy Jordan."[171] While he did not specifically mention Nasser, this was clearly directed at Egypt. Similarly, Iran was worried about Nasser's ideological appeal, but was also concerned that Nasser harbored territorial ambitions for Iran's majority-Arab Khuzestan province.[172]

# Analysis

The above discussion demonstrates Saudi Arabia used religious appeals as a tool in its attempt to form an international coalition and break apart a rival coalition. The moral authority of religion in Saudi politics combined with the ideological crisis it faced in the rivalry with Egypt led it to draw on religious appeals. These appeals were strategic and part of its security policy. Additionally, evidence indicates their impact was primarily to heighten regional tensions due to the combination of Saudi credibility and material disincentives to participate in its international coalition. The evidence also allows us to reject counterarguments, with a few caveats I can address.

This was a clear case of the use of religious appeals in power politics. Saudi Arabia hoped to form an international coalition to counter Egypt's influence in the 1960s. This would take the form of an Islamic Pact. One of the ways Saudi Arabia tried to create this coalition was by appealing to shared Islamic faith and criticizing the secular ideology of its rivals. Saudi Arabia used these religious appeals to integrate its coalition—convincing states like Iran or Kuwait to align with Saudi Arabia—and fragment the Egypt coalition by targeting borderline states like Jordan.

Moreover, the evidence demonstrates the conditions under which states use religious appeals and their nature. Some of the reports clearly state that Saudi Arabia turned to these religious appeals due to the ideological threat Egypt posed. Likewise, there is some evidence of Faisal and other Saudi policymakers arguing their country's Islamic values could hold off communist expansion, indicating the religious appeals were connected to the domestic moral

56    **CHAPTER 2**

authority of religion. Additionally, the evidence that Saudi Arabia treated the religious appeals as both strategic and part of a high-stakes security issue indicates the nature of religious appeals in power politics.

The findings also demonstrate the impact of religious appeals. There is evidence that target states responded positively to Saudi appeals, with some positive social response as well. There was much more evidence that Arab nationalist states and social organizations saw Saudi Islamic appeals as a threat. US observers also worried about Saudi religious appeals, recognizing their potential to destabilize the region. Numerous actors acknowledged the significance of religious appeals in regional politics.

Of course, the Islamic Pact did not come together, but this still supports my theory. Given the mixed material incentives, I expected the religious appeals to primarily increase regional tensions. This is what we saw. Arab nationalists reacted hostilely to Saudi efforts, calling for more aggressive actions against Saudi Arabia and its allies. Nasser was concerned about the Islamic Pact, which reportedly affected his foreign policy decision making. Thus, Saudi efforts to form an Islamic Pact made an already tense situation even more tense. This would be likewise unlikely if my theory were wrong.

Granted, the evidence did not clearly state why Arab nationalists responded so hostilely. Similarly, the reports did not definitely state the nature of these impacts was due to Faisal's credibility and mixed material incentives of targets. I can address these concerns, however. First, while evidence was limited, it is likely that Arab nationalist response to Saudi religious appeals had to do with their potential ideological threat. Many of the critiques of Saudi Arabia pointed to fears of neocolonial control over the region rather than the power of political Islam. Yet, many did reference Saudi Arabia's ideological threat, rather than the potential for material domination. If Arab nationalists were not concerned about the ideological challenge of Saudi religious appeals, it is not clear why they would spend so much time critiquing the Islamic Pact instead of its general ties to the United States.

Second, regional audiences—even hostile ones—seemed to accept Faisal's credibility when responding to Saudi religious appeals even as they noted material disincentives to working with Saudi Arabia. There were a few indications that the positive impact of Saudi religious appeals had to do with Faisal's credibility. The relationship between Faisal and Mrouh appeared based on the latter's respect for the former's piety. Likewise, the shah of Iran defended Saudi Arabia against attacks due to its Islamic nature. Moreover, even Faisal's rivals did not attack his credibility on Islamic issues; instead, they focused on his dedication to Arab causes and ties to the United States. In terms of the material incentives, Jordan expressed frustration at receiving insufficient aid from Saudi Arabia and attempted to mediate tensions with Egypt. Iran was similarly wary of granting Saudi Arabia too much authority. This suggests that even potential Saudi allies had material disincentives to joining Saudi Arabia's international coalition. We thus have a situation in which regional audiences saw Saudi religious appeals as credible calls to action but were either hostile to such action or wary of taking part in it.

We can also say a few things about how Saudi religious appeals had an impact. There was some evidence that Saudi appeals helped to persuade other states of the desirability of its initiative, even if they did not ultimately sign on. There was more evidence both of domestic mobilization and fear of such mobilization in response to the religious appeals. Some studies note Egypt's concern with Saudi Arabia had to do with Saudi support for Egyptian Islamists and the threat they posed to Nasser.[173] Thus, the disruptive impact of Saudi religious appeals seems to have related to fears of these appeals resonating with and stirring up domestic political groups.

I can also reject alternative explanations. First, the religion skeptic counterargument fails. This argument would require evidence that the religious appeals were only for low priority issues, and that regional states did not take the Islamic Pact seriously. That was clearly absent. Saudi Arabia used the religious appeals as a crucial part of a high-stakes security issue. Moreover, both rivals and allies responded to these religious appeals. This explanation is invalid.

A related counterargument is the "instrumentalist" critique. Skeptics could argue the religious appeals were just cynical tactics by Saudi Arabia, especially given their strategic nature. However, this critique is poorly defined and primarily involves shifting the goalposts. It is unclear what exactly such a claim means, since we can never *really* know what someone is thinking, especially a historical figure. Finding evidence of religious appeals' use and impact should be enough to demonstrate they matter.

But the instrumental critique is common enough that I should respond to it. All those who met or studied Faisal agree he was a deeply pious man. This influenced his politics as well as his personal life. It even affected Saudi international relations, as Faisal refused to establish diplomatic contacts with the Soviet Union due to its atheist ideology. And, as I discussed, Islam played an important role throughout Saudi politics, with Saudi leaders expected to justify and frame their policies through Islam. It is possible Saudi policymakers only used religious appeals because they knew the appeals would be popular domestically. But all available evidence suggests Faisal and many other Saudi elites truly saw Islam as an important element of their politics. Beyond that,

58    **CHAPTER 2**

the dominant ideology in the 1960s was secular pan-Arabism: if Saudi Arabia was just trying to appeal to popular sentiments it would have mimicked Nasserism rather than trying to push Islam.

The religion triumphalist counterargument is also insufficient. It would require evidence showing Saudi Arabia saw its religious appeals as a way to act on its Islamic values, and that they were a transformative foreign policy tool. Such evidence was also absent. Islam did not define Saudi foreign policy in a manner we would expect if religion truly overrode material constraints in international relations. Religious appeals were one among several tools Saudi Arabia drew on. Their impact was not due to other Middle East states hearing the appeals and consulting their own religious beliefs for guidance. Moreover, the fact that the Islamic Pact failed to come together would undermine arguments for religion's transformative impact.

An additional counterargument specific to Saudi Arabia is its role as an oil producer. Saudi status in the world depends on this, granting wealth—which it can translate into international influence—and security guarantees from the United States. Those who study Gulf politics may be frustrated oil played such a small part in this chapter. It did factor into the mixed material incentives target states of Saudi Arabian appeals faced. And Saudi oil wealth gave it the resources to support Islamist groups in the region. However, Saudi wealth increased dramatically in the 1970s as oil prices went up, giving the Saudis more resources to try and dominate regional politics.[174] Moreover, even if Saudi oil gave it resources and sway over states, it would be hard to claim this filtered down to positive reactions among domestic audiences. Arab nationalists clearly tied concerns about Saudi Arabia to its religious appeals, not its provision of oil wealth. Such an argument is thus incomplete.

There are some caveats to all this. Some has to do with the evidence. Most of my evidence is secondhand. As I noted at the beginning of this chapter, this is unavoidable, but I was transparent with the source of the evidence and present corroborating statements by Middle East leaders when possible. Additionally, I triangulated this with secondary sources: the archival evidence expands upon, and does not contradict, the existing literature. Another caveat would be that the impact of the religious appeals was not concrete enough. That is, we saw neither the formation of an official alliance nor the outbreak of hostilities as a result of Saudi appeals. Instead, this was merely increased diplomatic friction. In terms of Middle East politics, though, an observer should recognize that a state action that leads to concerns by outside powers and angry denunciations by rival states and organizations is having a substantive impact. This is important on its own, as it can make it more difficult to conduct routine diplomacy or respond to crises that break out. Additionally, such friction is not evenly distributed, and certain states may benefit more from increasing tensions. This arguably occurred with Saudi Arabia. In the run up to the Six-Day War, Egypt faced increasing challenges both from conservative states like Saudi Arabia and radical Arab nationalists.[175] These pressures ultimately ended Egyptian dominance of the region, enabling Saudi Arabia's rise. The need to recognize the process of power politics as important on its own is broader than just this chapter, however, and I will address it in the conclusion.

## Conclusion

Saudi Arabia drew on religious appeals as part of its 1960s rivalry with Egypt, which took the form of efforts to form an Islamic Pact and advance its Islamic ideology to undermine Egypt's secular pan-Arabism. The high moral authority of religion in Saudi domestic politics meant its leaders recognized the importance and power of religious appeals and turned to them as one among several policy tools in power politics. Additionally, the ideological struggles in the rivalry with Nasser in the 1960s led the Saudis to anticipate the religious appeals would resonate in Middle East politics. As a result, Saudi Arabia used religious appeals as part of its power political attempts to form a coalition and counter Egypt's appeal: this was a serious and strategic aspect of Saudi Arabia's foreign policy.

These religious appeals affected regional politics greatly. Saudi Arabia under its then-ruler King Faisal was a credible speaker on religious issues, although regional states faced significant material disincentives to work with Saudi Arabia. This inhibited the formation of the Islamic Pact, but Saudi efforts still had an impact on the region by unsettling relations and increasing tensions. Targets of Saudi Arabia's religious appeals—conservative regional states like Jordan and Morocco—responded favorably but did not wholeheartedly sign on to Saudi Arabia's plans. Saudi rivals, by contrast, saw Saudi efforts as a challenge and threat to their security, and responded by trying to mobilize action in response. The United States, meanwhile, generally supported Saudi Arabia but worried its client state was creating problems through its infusion of Islam into regional tensions.

Thus, contrary to religion skeptics, Saudi religious appeals in this case mattered. Arguing against this involves dismissing the voluminous evidence of regional leaders referencing Saudi efforts to create the Islamic Pact when explaining their policies. That being said, the religious appeals did not matter in the way Saudi Arabia intended. Saudi religious appeals failed at their primary purpose: forming an anti-Nasser alliance that would undermine his power. And

Saudi religious appeals did not convince the United States to support the Saudi position on Yemen. What Saudi religious appeals did accomplish, however, was to unsettle regional politics and ratchet up tensions. This certainly counts as an impact.

Some readers, especially those who champion religion's role in international relations, may come away unsatisfied with this chapter. While my findings undermine traditional analyses of power politics that ignore religion, they do not provide the dramatic evidence for the transformative impact of religion on international relations that many are looking for. Instead, the chapter suggests those interested in demonstrating religion's importance in international relations will need to change their focus: I return to this in the book's conclusion.

# CHAPTER 3

# US Religious Engagement in the Global War on Terrorism

After the shocking terrorist attacks of 9/11, the United States ramped up its military might to defeat al-Qaeda. But US policymakers realized they needed to do more than just capture and kill terrorists. They needed to form a coalition with Muslim states and societies, encouraging them to support counterterrorism operations and reject al-Qaeda's message. The United States appealed to religion as part of this effort. Specifically, the United States attempted to promote more "moderate" expressions of Islam in order to combat al-Qaeda (and later the Islamic State of Iraq and Syria [ISIS]) extremism and encouraged Muslim communities to engage with each other and the US government.

While many of the specifics of this case are different from Saudi Arabia's attempt to form an Islamic Pact—in terms of time period, the nature of the countries, and the specifics of the programs—it is a similar example of a state wielding religious appeals in order to mobilize an international coalition. As with Saudi Arabia, it arose due to the high moral authority of religion in US politics and the ideologically charged nature of the international crisis the United States faced. US policymakers took these religious appeals seriously as a potential foreign policy tool, even if they never invested sufficient resources in them. The United States, however, was less than credible on Islamic issues, even as Muslim states and societies faced material incentives to work with US policymakers. Many Muslim states thus joined in US efforts, while Muslim social

62    **CHAPTER 3**

organizations tried to work with the United States even as they were wary of US intentions. This led to a situation in which some authoritarian Muslim states co-opted US religious narratives, and both US policymakers and Muslim groups were unsure how best to formulate religious engagement efforts or determine whether they were working.

In this chapter, I will first discuss the debate over the role of religion in US foreign policy more broadly. I will then present my analysis. First, I will discuss the high moral authority of religion in US politics and the ideological struggle it faced in the global war on terrorism, leading it to turn to religious appeals. I will then discuss the credibility and material incentives involved and present the evidence for US religious appeals' complicated impact. Finally, I will analyze this evidence's implications for my theory and alternatives and provide conclusions.

## Debating the Role of Religion in US Foreign Policy

Like Saudi Arabia, the United States is a typical case for both my argument and counterarguments. It has been the dominant state in the international system since World War II, whether measured via economic or military might. The United States spent the Cold War fending off a challenge from the Soviet Union and has endeavored to maintain its primacy in the face of peer competitors and asymmetric threats since the Cold War ended. It thus should be a perfect case for religion skeptic counterarguments. At the same time, the United States' struggles have always been ideological, drawing on its potent civil religion. The United States has relied on moral—often religious—arguments to justify its foreign policies since it was formed; it therefore also seems a good case for religion triumphalists. There is thus a debate, sometimes implicit, over the extent to which religion drives and serves as a tool of US foreign policy that can inform a study of US religious engagement in the global war on terrorism.

Most studies of US foreign policy note the importance of the United States' moral self-image in its place in the world. Studies note the United States' emphasis on spreading its liberal values, which has had a significant influence on US foreign policy.[1] Yet, many argue power and interests ultimately drive the United States' role in the world. Some claim the United States' idealistic rhetoric masks its interest-driven foreign policy.[2] Others point to the limits of the United States' ability to influence the world through appeals to values.[3]

Yet, religion is often ignored in these discussions of US foreign policy. Many studies that acknowledge the role of US culture in explaining its foreign policy downplay or overlook the religious elements of US culture.[4] This oversight of the role of religion is especially glaring in studies on the US global war on terrorism and other counterterrorism initiatives, which often do not discuss the religious aspects of the struggle between the United States and al-Qaeda.[5]

There have been attempts, however, to make clear religion's importance as both an influence and a tool. Scholars have surveyed the influence of religion on US foreign policy, both during the Cold War and after its end.[6] Others have argued that religion can serve as a tool to bring people together.[7] Some of this has looked specifically at the United States' religious outreach in the global war on terrorism. Several works claim religion could be a beneficial tool in US counterterrorism efforts.[8] Others, however, have expressed concern about these efforts.[9]

Just as with Saudi Arabia, then, one could make both a religion skeptic and a religion triumphalist argument about US efforts in the global war on terrorism. Religion skeptics would accept the important role religion plays in US politics and the appeals US leaders make to it when formulating foreign policy. Yet, they would argue that high-stakes security situations like the war on terrorism require leaders to put aside ideals and focus on core national interests. They would claim appeals to religion in the global war on terrorism were only window dressing, not taken seriously by either their speakers or their audience. Religion triumphalists, in turn, would argue that US religious appeals are the expression of deep-seated US principles and serve as a powerful tool in organizing international efforts against terrorism, even if some question their ethical desirability. I argue neither approach captures the significance and complex impacts of US religious appeals in this case.

## Methodological Note

This chapter is based on interviews I conducted with former policymakers and counterterrorism and counterextremism practitioners in Washington, DC, and over the phone, in the fall of 2019. The interviews were semi-structured; I asked each the same basic questions but allowed the respondents to provide whatever information they saw as relevant. Some of the interviews were anonymous in order to allow respondents to feel comfortable discussing sensitive issues. As all respondents were currently or previously working in the area of this analysis, the interviews can provide firsthand information on the nature and effectiveness of US religious appeals in counterterrorism. There may be some concerns about the reliability of this information, as the respondents all worked in some way on these religious appeals. As readers will notice, however, respondents were candid about the limitations of religious appeals, so

64    CHAPTER 3

there is little evidence that they were presenting skewed information in order to make the case for their preferred policies.

## Background: Al-Qaeda and the Global War on Terrorism

Al-Qaeda emerged in the wake of the Soviet invasion of Afghanistan. Al-Qaeda founders Osama bin Ladin and Abdullah Azzam organized Arab fighters who traveled to the country. After the war ended, bin Ladin expanded his operations to wage a transnational struggle against US influence over Muslim countries. Al-Qaeda set up cells around the world and began formulating its doctrine of the "far enemy"; as Gerges discussed, al-Qaeda was distinct from other Islamist militants in its focus on the United States over Muslim governments.[10] Bin Ladin argued that attacking the United States would force it to withdraw, weakening governments in the Middle East and elsewhere, and allowing them to be overthrown. Al-Qaeda acted on this plan through a series of attacks in the 1990s, such as the coordinated bombings of US embassies in Kenya and Tanzania in 1998.

Despite this growing threat, terrorism was not a priority for the United States. Much of the US national security apparatus had been directed toward the Soviet Union. As a result, progress against the Soviets was seen as paramount to other concerns, blinding the United States to the threat posed by instability in Afghanistan after it helped organize the Arab fighters there. Moreover, with the end of the Cold War, the United States struggled to determine a proper grand strategy and assessment of the new threats it faced. As a result, US policymakers ignored the signs that al-Qaeda was focused on striking the United States.

This led to the 9/11 attacks in which a team of al-Qaeda hijackers crashed planes into the World Trade Center and the Pentagon. An additional plane was forced down by its passengers in Pennsylvania. The United States responded by reorienting its foreign policy toward fighting al-Qaeda, launching the global war on terrorism. George W. Bush ordered an invasion of Afghanistan, followed soon after by an invasion of Iraq. The United States expanded its counterterrorism capabilities, both through new agencies such as the Department of Homeland Security and new priorities for existing organizations. The United States also pressured other countries to crack down on terrorist financing and activities and cooperate with US counterterrorism efforts.

This global war on terrorism had mixed results. Al-Qaeda was disrupted, culminating in the 2011 raid in which US forces killed bin Ladin.[11] Yet, al-Qaeda persisted as a weakened force through several of its franchises. Additionally, ISIS, which was initially an al-Qaeda franchise, became a major terrorist threat. This group seized territory in the Middle East, launched several franchises in different countries, and inspired many people in Western countries to support the group or even travel to Syria and join.

## US Religious Appeals in the Global War on Terrorism: Theory and Evidence

US religious appeals were part of this struggle against terrorism. Religion has always been a major element in US politics, infusing its domestic political debates and influencing foreign policy decisions. Likewise, al-Qaeda's challenge to the United States involved not just a security threat but a perceived critique of US values and an attempt to mobilize Muslims worldwide against US leadership and undermine US Muslim allies. As a result, the United States used a variety of religious appeals as serious but strategic tools in its attempt to form an international coalition against al-Qaeda and other terrorist groups.

### Conditions Influencing US Use of Religious Appeals

Religion has a high moral authority in US politics. Religion, primarily Protestant Christianity, has been an important element of US politics and society since before the country's founding. The "founding myth" of British settlers in New England involved a struggle for religious freedom.[12] Additionally, the first US settlers thought they saw a divine purpose in their move to the United States.[13] Once the United States became independent, its founders hoped to keep religion safe from government interference.[14]

Moreover, even while America is officially secular, its secularism encourages religious expression. In contrast to states like Turkey and France, the US political system enabled and even encouraged public religiosity.[15] As a result, US politics is marked by the promotion of religious expression by government officials.[16] This takes the form of a "civil religion," in which "collective political identity has been expressed as a nation self-consciously 'under God.'"[17]

Religious arguments, accordingly, hold a lot of weight in US political debates. Evangelical Christians, for example, have tended to vote as a bloc; they "provided roughly 40 percent" of the vote for George W. Bush in 2004.[18] Moreover, religious figures and organizations are often prominent in US politics, wielding significant sway over voters and politicians. Religious organizations influence voters by both informing their votes and mobilizing them politically.[19]

## CHAPTER 3

US politicians likewise draw on religious language when discussing their policies and platforms. Politicians often appeal to religious beliefs when making pronouncements.[20] For example, President Eisenhower famously added "one nation under God" to the pledge of allegiance in order to increase US morale in the face of the Soviet threat.[21]

Religion has also been a recurring element in US foreign policy. Early in the United States' history, it struggled to extricate itself from European influence and establish a sphere of influence in the Americas. This had clear realpolitik motivations, but US leaders saw it as a religious charge as well. Manifest Destiny, which justified America's westward expansion, was tied to religious beliefs.[22] Moreover, the idea of "US exceptionalism," which has motivated America's foreign policy for centuries, arose from the United States' sense of religious mission.[23] And President McKinley, who initiated imperial missions outside of North America, conceived of these policies as "part of a divine plan."[24] Likewise, Christian groups in the United States have often called for a foreign policy based on their religious views.[25] This is apparent in George W. Bush's efforts to resolve the civil war in Sudan, which were connected to his evangelical Christian faith and advocacy by evangelicals.[26]

But religion was not just a motivation for US foreign policy; policymakers turned to it as a tool.[27] The Cold War was a geopolitical struggle, but it was also an ideological one, as the United States' democratic capitalism clashed as a values system with the Soviet Union's communism.[28] Thus, US leaders tried to counter the Soviet ideological threat with religion. For example, President Truman appealed to Christianity when trying to establish ties with Western Europe and contain the Soviet threat. Truman often drew on religious language when trying to gain support for the Marshall Plan; "through labor and industry, with the blessing of God," Truman pronounced, "these sorely stricken nations shall again become masters of their own destiny."[29] Truman also appointed an envoy to the Vatican in the hope of recruiting the Catholic Church in the struggle against the Soviets.[30]

The United States also used religious appeals to draw non-Western societies into the struggle with the Soviet Union. Fearing President Gamal Abdel Nasser's influence in the Middle East—which they saw as favoring the Soviets— the Eisenhower administration hoped Saud—then the king of Saudi Arabia— could become an important religious figure and counter to Nasser. Some in the administration referred to him as a potential "Islamic Pope."[31] The United States also worked with conservative Christians in South Korea to expand their influence in the wake of the Korean War.[32] And in South Vietnam, the United States worked with Catholics to ensure pro-US figures were dominant in that country's politics.[33]

This continued after the Cold War. While the ideological struggle with the Soviet Union was over, the United States hoped both to maintain its international primacy and to expand the liberal international order against authoritarian challenges and political instability. One manifestation of this was the official embrace of international religious freedom promotion as part of its foreign policy.[34] The codification of this policy, via the 1998 International Religious Freedom Act, was due to a broad coalition of faith groups that pressed the Clinton administration to take action.[35] This was accompanied by faith-based foreign aid, the promotion of "moderate Islam" under Bush, and President Obama's countering violent extremism policies.[36] Beyond specific policies, post-Cold War presidents "used religious language and allusions to deliberately cut across partisan lines" and gain support for their foreign policies.[37]

During the global war on terrorism, this high moral authority of religion crashed into an ideologically charged international crisis. Al-Qaeda's first attack against the United States was the coordinated strike on US embassies in East Africa in 1998 but, before that, it had released a declaration of war and fatwa explaining its grievances against the United States. This included specific complaints about US foreign policy, but also broader attacks on the United States' values and political system. This occurred alongside broader concerns that the US-led international order was under threat by religious extremism.

This became clear to US policymakers after 9/11. President Bush defined the global war on terrorism as a broader war of ideas.[38] According to Bush administration speechwriter Michael Gerson, he saw the struggle against "totalitarian perversions of Islam" as a struggle between idealism and cynicism.[39] Likewise, counterterrorism official Farah Pandith noted, "if we could get Muslims to perceive the United States differently, the thinking went, we would 'solve the extremism problem.'"[40] Muslim allies of the United States similarly saw al-Qaeda as an ideological threat to their rule. For example, when an al-Qaeda branch conducted a wave of attacks in Saudi Arabia in 2003, the Saudi regime treated it like a challenge to the religious bases of both the regime and society.[41]

The recognition of religion's importance continued into the Obama administration. While some criticized Obama for downplaying the ideological threat of al-Qaeda, he did acknowledge the "war of ideas" in his first international interview, noting al-Qaeda's ideas are "bankrupt."[42] And when ISIS emerged as a more serious threat than al-Qaeda, concerns about its extremism spreading and undermining liberal values continued. The Obama administration's strategy to defeat ISIS noted the threat had "perverted a religion into a dangerous ideology," while expert analyses of ISIS's transnational presence noted the need to combat its ideological appeal among disaffected members of Western society.[43]

68     **CHAPTER 3**

## US Religious Appeals in the Global War on Terrorism

Thus, the United States saw the global war on terrorism—and its extension against ISIS—as an ideological struggle against extremist threats to liberal democracy. It therefore turned to ideological tools to defeat terrorism alongside conventional military and economic policies. Due to the high moral authority of religion in the United States, these ideological tools focused on religious appeals, as US policymakers saw religion as significant and potent in political debates. We can see this across both the Bush and Obama administrations.

### THE BUSH ADMINISTRATION AND RELIGIOUS APPEALS

Bush-era counterterrorism efforts were marked by the global war on terrorism, a massive undertaking to disrupt al-Qaeda and undermine its support among Muslims. The most well-known initiatives were the invasion of Afghanistan after 9/11 to uproot al-Qaeda's leadership, and the ill-fated 2003 invasion of Iraq. US efforts also involved a variety of pressures on states to reform their counterterrorism policies in line with US initiatives.[44] But religious appeals were a crucial part of the global war on terrorism as well.

From its very beginning, President Bush and his advisers envisioned the struggle against al-Qaeda as broader than an effort to destroy one terrorist movement. They hoped to change the conditions that gave rise to al-Qaeda in the first place. This included promoting democracy throughout the Middle East and spurring economic development. But it also involved attention to counter what they saw as trends in Islam that led to many Muslims supporting groups like al-Qaeda. As the administration wrote in its 2002 National Security Strategy, one of their goals was to support "moderate and modern government, especially in the Muslim world, to ensure that the conditions and ideologies that promote terrorism do not find fertile ground in any nation."[45] The 2006 National Security Strategy echoed this point, declaring the United States would support "political reforms" that allow "peaceful Muslims to practice and interpret their faith," and that "responsible Islamic leaders need to denounce an ideology that distorts and exploits Islam."[46] Additionally, Bush used religious language in his speeches, such as when he argued the global war on terrorism was a "monumental struggle of good versus evil."[47]

Unlike some of the United States' Cold War-era appeals, these were not calls for Christians to unite in the face of the terrorist threat. In fact, it was in some ways the opposite; the Bush administration called on "moderate" Muslims to join with the United States and other nations to defeat religious extremists in their ranks. Bush recognized the risk of creating a religious war as the United States stepped up its global war on terrorism. Additionally, the Bush administration knew it needed the support of Muslim governments, which would be difficult if they or their publics saw the United States engaged in a war against Islam. As Michael Gerson noted, Bush felt he needed a "big speech" after the attacks "to explain the nature of the enemy and the new kind of war we're about to undertake."[48] Bush thus incorporated a discussion of Islam into his speeches on the global war on terrorism, emphasizing that "terrorists are traitors to their own faith, trying, in effect to hijack Islam itself."[49] Similarly, Bush announced he was appointing an envoy to the Organization of the Islamic Conference in a speech at the Washington Islamic Center: according to Bush speechwriter Matthew Latimer, this was "part of our effort to show that America was interested in greater dialogue and understanding with the Muslim world."[50]

Some of the Bush administration's strategy involved rhetorical appeals to moderate Muslims, and attempts to convince Muslims that the United States was on their side. As Farah Pandith noted, the "immediate response was a kinetic one" but the United States quickly began to think about how to "posture the conversation globally" as "al-Qaeda was using Islam . . . to recruit the next generation."[51] As a result, the United States tried to "push back against the al-Qaeda narrative" as well as al-Qaeda itself. Bush created the Greater Middle East Initiative, an attempt to promote freedom in the Middle East and undermine the allure of extremism.[52] The Bush administration also dispatched Karen Hughes on a public diplomacy tour of the Middle East to highlight commonalities with the United States. Additionally, the administration brought in an advertising executive to create a campaign featuring US Muslims.[53]

The United States took tangible steps to promote moderate Islam. The Bush administration tried to identify and support moderate Islamic actors US policymakers believed would be a positive influence on Muslims. As Eric Rosand, a former counterterrorism official, put it, "pretty much since 9/11 . . . the role of religion has been assumed to be" an important part of "policy and programmatic responses. . . . The idea was that if only we can get more religious leaders to speak out against the manipulation of Islam, and understand what Islam is and is not," the United States could undermine support for al-Qaeda.[54] As a result, the United States tried to get "countries across the Middle East and Africa" to place some "oversight" over their religious institutions, "direct them to become partners in the war on terror," and at times even "co-opt

70    CHAPTER 3

them to become advocates for peaceful Islam." Connie LaRossa, another former counterterrorism official, argued that America was "stunned by 9/11," especially the fact that it was carried about by a group with a "religious affiliation as its identity."[55] That "caused America to pause," and attempt to figure out "how do we as a society disassociate what they are identifying as their group identification from how we target them."

These are examples of religious appeals intended to effect international collective mobilization. The United States was not appealing to a specific religion in its struggle with al-Qaeda, but rather to a crosscutting element of religions: moderation. The Bush administration tried to frame the global war on terrorism as a struggle between moderate religious communities and the extremism of al-Qaeda: by appealing to "moderate Islam" they intended to strengthen moderate actors and convince Muslims that America was not their enemy. This included literal appeals, as well as support for moderate figures and pressure on Muslim states to reform their own approaches to Islam. The United States hoped that appealing to the desirability of moderation would convince these states to combat al-Qaeda. Moreover, these appeals were part of the US effort to craft a state and society alliance against al-Qaeda. Appeals to Muslim societies would hopefully soften their support for al-Qaeda, just as Cold War religious appeals were meant to increase wariness of communism among publics. And appeals to Muslim states were intended to draw them closer so they would coordinate their counterterrorism policies with the United States in its struggle with al-Qaeda.

Bush-era religious appeals were never a priority for the United States. They were perennially underfunded by the administration.[56] James Patton—a counterextremism expert who has worked closely with the US government—argued that many saw religion as "spiritual at best," and a "not so critical human activity when it came to political considerations."[57] And Pandith noted that while "we did not hold back militarily" in the war on terrorism, "we never stood up that sort of response" on the "ideological front."[58] As evidenced in their ignorance in works on the global war on terrorism, many security experts saw these religious appeals as tangential to the "more serious" efforts to combat al-Qaeda.

Despite this dismissive attitude, however, religious appeals were a persistent element in US policy that policymakers emphasized in their interactions with Muslim states. One counterterrorism expert noted the United States relied on moderate Islam promotion to such an extent that there was an "oversimplification in this response," with the United States turning to it because it was "expedient."[59] As they hoped to "build a global coalition against Islamist-inspired terrorism," many US policymakers thought "we should go to the heart of the Muslim world, speak to these Muslim majority countries," and "tap into religious institutions" to "speak out against this violence."[60]

Moreover, they were not just cynical instrumentalist ploys. President Bush's deep faith, and the importance of faith in US society and politics, inspired the appeals. Michael Gerson claimed that "every Christian believes there is a golden thread of purposes in their lives" and that Bush felt he was called by God in the wake of 9/11.[61] As Prodromou notes, 9/11 "crystallized the application of the president's personal theology" to US foreign policy.[62] Additionally, Bush's various pronouncements were "the fusion between the worldview of the New Religious Right and the secular neoconservative ideology."[63] Bettiza similarly discussed the connection between Bush's moderate Muslim promotion and broader efforts to "desecularize" US foreign policy.[64]

At the same time, these appeals were clearly a strategic effort. The Bush administration hoped they could advance US interests by undermining support for al-Qaeda. That is, they were a means to an end, not an end in themselves. Beyond expanding intelligence communities, the US government needed to make sure, as Pandith said, al-Qaeda was not "replenishing its armies."[65] This is where the religious appeals came in. The United States had to "engage with Muslim communities" to "build resilience" against extremism and "make sure we were building positive connectivities [sic] so the narrative of the al-Qaeda–US war with Islam was debunked." Likewise, one religious engagement expert noted that after 9/11, the US government initially approached religion as a "negative" disruptive force.[66] Over time, the Bush administration came to a more "nuanced understanding of religious actors" and saw religion as an ambivalent force that could be "instrumentalized."

## THE OBAMA ADMINISTRATION AND RELIGIOUS APPEALS

Barack Obama came to office with a healthy dose of suspicion for the Bush administration's foreign policy, especially its approach to the Middle East and counterterrorism. Obama hoped to rebrand the global war on terrorism with a focus on engaging Muslim communities. The Obama administration continued and expanded upon Bush administration efforts that came to be known as countering violent extremism (CVE). CVE emphasized working with social groups to prevent their members turning to al-Qaeda, and later ISIS. Religious appeals were a significant part of these efforts, as the United States attempted to engage with religious groups to spread their CVE message. The goal was partly to increase ties between the United States and Muslim communities

72    CHAPTER 3

around the world, establishing a state–society coalition that could undermine the appeal of al-Qaeda and ISIS. But the Obama administration also hoped its religious appeals would convince other states it was a credible partner in fighting terrorism without demonizing Muslim communities.

The approach of the Obama administration can be best seen in its 2010 National Security Strategy. The strategy emphasized the importance of "empowering communities to counter radicalization," and "developing new partnerships with Muslim communities around the world."[67] The Obama administration also adopted detailed strategies for religious engagement, which—as Bettiza noted—"explicitly recognized" the United States' "history" of engagement with religious figures, while working to "elevate" these initiatives.[68] This thus represented a moment of both "continuity and change": the Obama administration continued to recognize the importance of religion in US counterterrorism efforts even as it tried to distinguish itself from the Bush administration.[69]

As one Obama-era official noted, the focus on religious outreach "intensified once CVE became a thing," with many assuming religious engagement to "be the holy grail" for counterterrorism responses.[70] Likewise, Patton argued that "after ten years or so in Afghanistan and Iraq," the US government "started to realize that approaching religion as only a source of violence" was a problem.[71] As a result, there was a "transformation in the mindset," promoting more religious outreach. Others noted that Obama continued Bush's efforts but broadened them to allow "wider religious engagement."[72] To some this "shift from CT to CVE" involved a "more holistic look at drivers and preventers of violent extremism."[73]

Similarly, LaRossa noted that the Obama administration did not have a "lessened sense of security or priorities" on counterterrorism.[74] Instead, it was "more sensitive" to the way their policies had an effect on Muslim communities and made a more "conscientious effort to build a bridge" with Muslims in the midst of counterterrorism efforts. She said that the Obama administration was trying to pay more attention to the "vernacular they were using," and that ISIS and al-Qaeda were trying to "proliferate the notion that it was us versus them." So the Obama administration hoped to "counter that."

The Obama administration's use of religious engagement extended beyond counterterrorism. Peter Mandaville, an official in the Obama administration's Office of Religion and Global Affairs (based in the State Department), noted that they hoped to "move away from" and "de-emphasize security and terrorism": many "references to religion in diplomacy often function as a euphemism for conversations on Islam and security" and they wanted to change that.[75]

# US RELIGIOUS ENGAGEMENT IN THE WAR ON TERRORISM 73

Their goal was to "make the case for a broader play to be made with the intersection of religion and diplomacy" that would "transcend a narrow set of conversations about Islam."

The Obama administration's religious appeals took a variety of forms. The most notable was Obama's direct outreach to Muslims. In 2009, he gave a famous speech in Cairo. In it, Obama called for a "new beginning" between the United States and Muslims. Observers believed the speech was effective in recognizing the diversity of Muslims, acknowledging areas of disagreement with the United States, and pointing to new areas of cooperation.[76]

Other religious appeals were less public. The Obama administration attempted to engage directly with Muslim communities to undermine support for extremism. As Rosand put it, many US policymakers wanted to "engage with the mosques, because that's where the radicalization takes place."[77] Similarly, Seamus Hughes—who worked for the National Counterterrorism Center under Obama—noted numerous community engagement programs to prevent terrorist recruitment.[78] These would "rely heavily on religious outreach," such as work with mosques and Muslim community centers to figure out how extremist messaging "targeting people for recruitment." Examples included "community engagement briefings" that National Counterterrorism Center staff would give to Muslim organizations on warning signs of radicalization. They did so by having "community awareness meetings," connecting various counterterrorism bodies with Muslim communities to have "healthy thoughtful conversations along religious lines."[79]

There were also partnerships with Muslim countries. As one former counterterrorism official noted, the United States set up "messaging centers around the world" to "push back on propaganda about religion."[80] One example was a center Saudi Arabia launched with US help: this involved hiring a "US consulting firm" to run it, "looking at online ideologically and religious linked propaganda" to push back on extremist recruitment. Another program was the Mohammidiya Center in Morocco that focused on the "training of Imams in the country." One former counterterrorism official noted that Middle Eastern states "embraced" the United States' focus on religious engagement. There was also broader cooperation, with the United Nations accepting the importance of religious engagement, especially in the area of foreign fighter prevention.

As with the Bush administration, religious engagement and CVE were never priorities for the Obama administration. One expert argued that the administration failed to secure sufficient funding for religious outreach in CVE: as the expert said, it was something that "felt good but no one went to Congress

## 74    CHAPTER 3

for money."[81] Likewise, many counterterrorism professionals did not take religious engagement seriously as part of the struggle against al-Qaeda: according to one former counterterrorism official I interviewed, they saw it was "too soft, fluffy and amorphous," and that their reaction tended to be a series of "eye rolls."[82] Mandaville noted that while there was a "sense of a lot going on" in terms of religion in the administration, it did not seem to be "present in the day to day work" of most State Department offices.[83]

Yet, as with Bush, these efforts proliferated throughout the government and persisted throughout Obama's two terms. Eric Rosand, a counterterrorism and CVE official in the Obama administration who now runs an advocacy group focused on CVE, said religious engagement factored in a "fair bit" in Obama's strategy.[84] This was partly because of a "vague sense that Islam has some role" in extremism, which the United States had to address; it was also because many Muslim countries pointed to this approach as a useful one. Moreover, while domestic religious engagement programs tended to be poorly funded, the United States "pushed them internationally."

The persistence of these efforts was due in part to a general recognition in the administration that religion mattered. Obama continued to integrate faith communities into the US government, with extensive coordination in domestic affairs.[85] This extended to foreign policy: when discussing the Office of Religion and Global Affairs, John Kerry noted that "religious actors and institutions are playing an influential role in every region of the world and on nearly every issue central to U.S. foreign policy."[86] Several experts commented on this attitude. Some of the acceptance of religious engagement among both the United States and Muslim states was the recognition of growing social and demographic issues in Muslim states, so they had an incentive to address radicalization.[87] Other experts noted that governments "keep bumping up against" religion's importance "but don't know why or don't have the tools to figure out" how to effectively use it.[88] And Mandaville pointed out that even some regional State Department offices that were hesitant to expand their focus on religion still recognized its importance in their work.[89] Thus, there was a widespread acceptance of religion's importance in US politics, even among those who personally did not share this sentiment.

Yet, these remained strategic tools. Rosand argued that Muslim countries would point to religious engagement as a solution to extremism, so the United States would "jump on it as a way to partner with Muslim countries" and "deal with issues that were hard for the US government to deal with head-on."[90] That is, the Obama administration's religious engagement was not a principled expression of deep-seated religious motivations for policy.

# The Impact of US Religious Engagement

The United States drew on religious engagement during the global war on terrorism to build coalitions with Muslim states and societies. This had a noticeable impact on international relations. US religious engagement helped some Muslim states to justify working closely with the United States on counterterrorism. However, US efforts also led to some unintended effects. This included authoritarian Muslim states co-opting religious engagement for their own purposes and wasted resources due to uncertainty over the nature of religious engagement efforts.

## Conditions Influencing the Impact of US Religious Appeals

The United States launched its religious appeals during the global war on terrorism from a tricky position. First, its credibility on human rights—which Bush connected to his religious appeals—and Islamic arguments more specifically were lacking. The United States supported authoritarian regimes throughout the Cold War, so many saw the United States' professed championing of human rights as part of its religious engagement as suspect.[91] Moreover, the United States had little experience engaging with Muslims on religious issues. Previous attempts, such as the aforementioned "Islamic Pope," were ineffective.[92] Others, like US support for the mujahideen in the struggle against the Soviet invasion of Afghanistan, did not involve a deep knowledge of the religious issues involved or likely consequences.[93]

At the same time, Muslim states and societies faced a variety of material incentives to respond positively to US religious appeals and join its international coalition. Many Muslim states—from Egypt to Pakistan—were US allies. They thus had an interest in continuing to work with the United States in the global war on terrorism. States that had a more fraught relationship with the United States had an incentive to avoid antagonizing the United States on counterterrorism, especially after the invasion of Iraq. Muslim social groups around the world also had an incentive to work with the United States on counterterrorism. The United States made resources and training available to organizations that developed or implemented counterterrorism programs the United States saw as beneficial.

## US Religious Appeals' Impact

In line with these conditions, US religious appeals during the global war on terrorism had mixed impacts. They did manage to enable some coalition

76    **CHAPTER 3**

building to combat al-Qaeda and ISIS. However, the lack of US credibility led to some poorly implemented initiatives, while allowing authoritarian Muslim states to redirect the religious appeals toward their own interests.

## IMPACT OF BUSH ADMINISTRATION RELIGIOUS APPEALS

There were several beneficial effects of US religious appeals during the Bush era. Despite widespread opposition to the global war on terrorism, many Muslim states coordinated their counterterrorism policies closely with the United States. As I discussed in my previous book, numerous Muslim states cracked down on terrorist fundraising, arrested terrorist suspects, and participated in US intelligence-sharing operations in the struggle against al-Qaeda.[94] Many were also responsive to the religious elements of the global war on terrorism. States like the United Arab Emirates, previously a major counterterrorism concern, cracked down on terrorist financing and disrupted al-Qaeda sympathizers present in their territory. And Morocco developed and deployed counterextremism programs to undermine support for al-Qaeda.[95]

US religious appeals were not the reason for Muslim state cooperation with the global war on terrorism, but they helped ease some of the potential friction from US efforts. The United States asked a lot of Muslim states, involving both material and political costs. US efforts to avoid framing the global war on terrorism as a war with Islam arguably made it easier for Muslim states to cooperate; they could claim they were not turning on their fellow Muslims, only the extremists among them. For example, in a 2002 interview, King Abdullah of Jordan discussed his country's close cooperation with America in the war on terrorism, before noting that "I've always felt that it was never a struggle between East and West as most people understand it. There are those extremists that have used our religion to condone the killing of innocent people. And I think the 11th of September was a wake-up call to the Muslim masses that there are a bunch of extremists out there that have distorted our religion so badly, that we need to stand up and put a stop to this."[96] Thus, King Abdullah was able to draw on Bush's framing of the global war on terrorism as a religious struggle against extremism to justify his cooperation with the United States. Additionally, as one expert noted, it gave states that had experienced tense relationships with the United States—such as the United Arab Emirates—something concrete they could point to in order to gain favor with the United States.[97]

More broadly, some argue that these religious appeals prevented the global war on terrorism from becoming a war between the United States and Muslim societies. Bush's visit to the Washington, DC, Islamic Center and appeals

## US RELIGIOUS ENGAGEMENT IN THE WAR ON TERRORISM

to common religiosity precluded a "clash of civilizations" narrative that many feared. Muslims at the time noted that they were "grateful" about Bush's speech as they had been "feeling insecure in the wake of the attack."[98] Additionally, as Pandith discussed in her book, some of the local initiatives did succeed in strengthening anti-extremist voices. US efforts to create a network of activists "has had an important ripple effect through Muslim communities globally," with a "generation of young Muslims" trained to "to take on leadership roles in their communities."[99] Another program, Sisters against Violent Extremism, created "safety nets for kids: places where they can go to learn the truth about extremist ideology and explore their own cultural identities."[100]

But much of the impact from these arguably well-meaning religious appeals was negative. This was in part due to US unfamiliarity with these issues, and inability to tell if any of the appeals' effects were actually working. Some were wary of "finding moderate Muslims" to combat terrorism as it did not "take into account which religious actors have actual clout" and "radicalization's social aspect."[101] Similarly, Patton argued that the "narrative became that religion is an important driver of violence," pushing people to "extremes."[102] This led to an overemphasis on "Islamic extremism" as a problem. Pandith likewise noted that the Bush administration "initially miscalculated after 9/11 by only looking to Muslim religious leaders to influence their flock that al-Qaeda is bad."[103] Further work was needed to measure the impact of these messages. Thus, one could argue the Bush administration rushed into its outreach to "moderate Muslims" without clarifying what success would look like, leading to misdirected attention and resources.

US religious appeals also complicated relationships at the societal level. US policymakers hoped US religious appeals would endear the United States to Muslims around the world, as they would see the United States as a partner against a common foe. Likewise, they saw these appeals as a way to convince potential al-Qaeda supporters to turn on the group. But there is evidence that US Bush-era religious appeals worsened relations between the United States and Muslim societies. Many Muslims around the world interpreted US promotion of moderate Islam as a desire to change or control their religion.[104] LaRossa argued Bush's focus on Islam was counterproductive, as the US government was "reinforcing" the terrorist message that the United States was conducting a "war against Islam."[105] Additionally, the framing of "moderate Islam" was off-putting to many. Pandith discussed an initiative by the State Department that produced a magazine featuring US Muslims. Unfortunately, it backfired, as the US government "trotted out stereotypical Muslims as if they were zoo creatures . . . but mostly only succeeding in betraying ignorance and lack of respect for them."[106]

78    **CHAPTER 3**

There were also some unexpected effects of US religious appeals on Muslim states' behavior. Some states exploited calls for moderation as an opportunity to pursue Islamist political groups that opposed the regime. Claiming these groups were extremists and potential terrorist supporters, regimes could justify repression of political dissent through the same religious appeals the United States used. Egypt intensified surveillance and control of mosques, for example, under the guise of combating extremism.[107] Additionally, there were some concerns about the independence of the moderate Muslim voices the United States supported. As one expert noted, the model of "finding moderate Muslims" was "problematic because of the security agencies directing religious figures."[108]

## IMPACTS OF OBAMA-ERA RELIGIOUS ENGAGEMENT

There was a similar pattern in the Obama administration. Some useful effects occurred through the religious appeals. Muslim states that had previously been wary of moderate Islam promotion felt they needed to "be seen as doing something . . . beyond just harder security stuff" in response to the growing threat of ISIS: this drew them to the religious aspects of CVE.[109] Rosand noted that, whereas in the early years of the global war on terrorism, the United States "couldn't say anything about the role of Islam in connecting with terrorism" for fear of upsetting Muslim governments, now "all of a sudden" many "governments want to do this with us."[110] This "opened up opportunities," in turn, to "engage at the grass-roots level with religious communities." The Obama administration's work with majority-Muslim countries on religious engagement led some of these countries to focus on anti-extremist messaging centers.

In some ways, Obama's religious appeals made it easier to work with counterterrorism partners in other areas. Experts noted that some Muslim states expressed a desire for religious engagement to be part of their "partnership" with the United States on violent extremism and the United States, in return, "built up" what those states were doing.[111] Religious appeals thus may have led to a greater sense of trust and coordination on policy issues. Another expert noted that the religious elements of America's CVE policies under Obama "made it easier" to work with most Muslim states.[112] Likewise, the Office of Religion and Global Affairs worked with a diverse group of religious leaders and nongovernmental organizations in Nigeria to combat corruption. This resulted in religious leaders "as voices of moral authority" calling "Nigerians together to address this issue."[113] This got significant attention in the media in Nigeria and elsewhere, and US embassies in other countries used it as a model to begin similar conversations. Another Office of Religion and Global Affairs

# US RELIGIOUS ENGAGEMENT IN THE WAR ON TERRORISM

effort involved "engagement with religious leaders" around the "role of religious leaders in preventing violence during elections."[114] This helped "to support the integrity of the process, keeping things calm and peaceful."

These efforts also had positive effects at the social level. Hughes discussed a few positive outcomes of religious engagement in CVE efforts.[115] He pointed to a case in which two US teenagers tried to travel to Turkey to slip into Syria and join ISIS. After their father realized what was happening and informed the US government, US authorities were able to intervene and have them sent back. The family's imam then reached out to the National Counterterrorism Center to work together and prevent future such incidents. Similarly, a "peer to peer" network was set up, in which college students around the world attempted to develop programs to "counter recruitment," with the winners receiving a cash prize. As the expert noted, "every now and then a good one comes through." A lot of this, he said, involved "low-hanging fruit that actually does a good bit of work." One example involved helping bloggers in Indonesia who pushed back on extremist messaging with search engine optimization.

There was also some indication that religious engagement facilitated broader cooperation. For example, the Office of Religion and Global Affairs engaged with Brunei about its plan to implement *hudud* (conservative Islamic) punishments. This plan by Brunei led to some concern in the US Congress, which led to opposition to Brunei joining the Trans-Pacific Partnership. The Office of Religion and Global Affairs held a meeting of global Islamic scholars to meet with the religious and political establishment in Brunei and work out different "models for implementing shariah law."[116] This was a case of the United States "finding a way to allow the leadership of a country to avoid having to walk back a commitment to Shariah," but also avoiding "falling afoul of US human rights commitments" through religious engagement.

Just as with the Bush administration, however, there were many negative and unintended impacts from these religious appeals. One issue had to do with the uncertainty over whether any of them were working. A skeptical former counterterrorism official noted that because religious engagement programs "were an easy set of initiatives to develop," and because of the interest in partnering on them from Muslim countries, the US government "wasn't asking deep questions" and was "taking too much at face value."[117] As a result, it was not clear whether any of these initiatives undermined support for extremist groups. Additionally, Hughes noted that many of the people involved in religious outreach "didn't know the differences between conservative, liberal, or Salafi mosques," raising questions about who they engaged with and how effective it would be.[118] There was also little evidence that this approach worked. Rosand argued that many messaging campaigns were "ineffective and not well-resourced," but that

80     **CHAPTER 3**

they were "shiny objects with no 'oomph' to them."[119] As a result, they "don't actually do anything" besides "convince Western audiences that they are doing something." Similarly, some believe that "just educating young [people] about the ways of Islam is the solution" to extremism.

Many were specifically skeptical of the emphasis of engaging with "moderate" religious leaders. An Obama-era CVE official said they understood "why the government goes to religious leaders," as they were the "gatekeepers in the community": that being said, a "60 year old Imam who says [extremism] is wrong is not the one to connect with" to prevent radicalization.[120] They argued this may not "hurt" but "doesn't get to ISIS recruits," especially considering each Middle Eastern country's own "baggage" with human rights issues. While it "doesn't hurt to show pluralism in society, it's not going to stop a guy from getting on a plane" to join ISIS. Patton also noted that the United States "hasn't seen the benefits in the way it wishes it had" from engaging moderate religious actors.[121] Likewise, there was little evidence that the aforementioned messaging centers "were actually going to reduce extremist violence." Similarly, Patton noted that not all targets of religious outreach would "listen to moderate voices like the Marrakesh Declaration."[122] During the "2015–2016 CVE push" some policymakers wanted the Office of Religion and Global Affairs to emphasize that, but the office resisted as it thought that "religious scholars on US government platforms weren't going to be credible CVE voices." But this "CVE machinery . . . just wanted the name of sheikhs to be invited to talk about how bad ISIS was, and the importance of being moderate."

It is difficult to assess the impact of these initiatives. As one expert noted, with the "heavy focus of religion on programs for disengagement, there's little information on what the program constitutes, and what success is."[123] They noted the "methods we've used for measuring success aren't necessarily tailored well enough to what we're trying to measure." There may also be bigger issues with the nature of these initiatives' religious engagement. For example, Hughes argued that religious interpretation is "largely a settled point with ISIS folks; they are not looking for spiritual sanction" and think that their ideology is "justified" and a "settled question."[124]

This is not just a case of ineffective government policies, however. The desirability of religious engagement blinded US policymakers to some of these issues. As one expert put it, policymakers' interest in seeing religious engagement work caused them to "willfully or not choose to ignore evidence . . . and what's at root in violent extremism": religious engagement "makes sense for policymakers that the messages and propaganda is bad, and we have to do something about it," but "research show that's only a secondary issue."[125] As the same expert argued, "policymakers will rely on it" without "taking the time

# US RELIGIOUS ENGAGEMENT IN THE WAR ON TERRORISM

to study the evidence." With the emphasis on religious engagement there is a "temptation to entertain" CVE strategies focused on state-led anti-extremist messaging. This is not because people think it will be "successful [or] credible" but that it is "just an easy way to lubricate the bilateral relationship more broadly" with governments launching these initiatives. There's also a concern that these efforts will allow these governments to "displace onto Islam the blame for things going on in their own countries that are more properly understood as a by-product of the lack of accountable governance."

The desire to incorporate religion into CVE also redirected resources away from more productive areas. Rosand noted that many CVE efforts focused on an "implicit link between violent extremism" and religion, with religious engagement a "backdoor way to get there."[126] With time, counterterrorism experts realized that religious motivation was "disproportionate to the actual drivers" of extremism, with the focus on religion being "reductive." As a result, this emphasis "distracted a lot of these governments from doing the much harder work" required to "deal with radicalization." Rosand believes much of these efforts were "misguided, focusing on the wrong object," which "undermined our ability to actually deal with" the problem. The community is now "trying to put the genie back in the bottle," as "most people realize that religious engagement . . . is not insignificant, but is a much smaller piece of the solution than it's made out to be." In a way, however, he believes it is "almost too late," as religious engagement has now "become embedded in all the partnerships with other Muslim majority countries" and that it is hard to change that.

There was also concern that injecting religious engagement into counterterrorism would complicate the United States' international efforts. One former official noted a "certain amount of ambient hesitation" within the State Department about engaging with religion that was the result of a "wariness towards religion" and concern that efforts to expand their work in it would run afoul.[127] Another expert noted that US policymakers were "scared to death of touching religious issues, particularly with Islam" for fear of running afoul of US laws or antagonizing Muslim societies.[128] This wariness may have contributed to some negative impacts of the policies: "because of the sensitivities . . . the United States government has always had [when] dealing with religious issues," policymakers were more likely to back religious engagement strategies without analyzing their effectiveness. Similarly, because the "US was scared to touch" religious engagement but also "wants to touch it," it ended up being overly supportive of problematic religious engagement strategies. Patton noted that some US embassies "pushed back" on religious engagement programs, seeing them as "too sensitive" and dealing with "delicate issues" that could

## CHAPTER 3

upset bilateral relationships.[129] Generally, he argued, there is a "risk aversion in" the US government, as religious engagement "makes people nervous."

Others recognized the potential danger in basing US CVE on religious outreach. LaRossa noted the Obama administration often tried to "downplay the religious aspect" of their efforts; for example, they would often host interfaith roundtables instead of just focusing on Islam.[130] The "goal" was to "minimize the us versus them" element of counterterrorism. They worried that "highlighting religion would make things worse," and "play into terrorist narratives." She argued that when governments "create programs targeted towards Islamic communities only," this just "reinforces the terrorist mantra" of groups like ISIS and "strengthened their base." Instead, she believed religion should "only be used for the purposes of . . . bringing homogenous [sic] groups to a broad and wide issue."

Another area that undermined the impact of international religious engagement was, according to Hughes, the question of including Islamists. That is, US policymakers never resolved the question of "who do you engage with?"[131] As Hughes noted, Islamists "have the clout to be able to talk about why [extremism] is wrong," but there is a fear of "giving them validation for illiberal views." This is something the United States continues to "struggle with," as have other countries.

There is also some evidence that religious engagement efforts led to tensions with Muslim countries. The US experienced "some pushback" from the Saudi government on its criticism of its textbooks, while Pakistan was also wary of the aforementioned religious engagement programs.[132] Patton also noted the issues with religious engagement in Tunisia, as it increased tensions because of the "'hangover' from the Arab Spring" and any "engaging with Islamists was political suicide."[133] Hughes argued incorporating religious engagement into US relations with Oman and Yemen "made it harder" to cooperate on counterterrorism as "it put a lot more requirements with capabilities issues" when implementing counterterrorism programs.[134] Likewise, religious engagement with Tunisia complicated efforts to prevent radicalization, as its status as a "fledgling democracy" added "another layer on top of other issues" involved in counterterrorism cooperation.[135] And some states were wary of the US government and Western organizations "going in and meddling with religion," as they assumed such efforts were motivated by Christianity.[136]

Another unintended consequence of Obama-era religious appeals involved their misuse by other states. Specifically, states used this emphasis on religious engagement and tolerance to repress political dissent. The aforementioned messaging center in Saudi Arabia gave, according to one expert, the "impression that the Saudi fervently committed to this part of CVE, when it's really a big distraction from things they are doing in other parts of the world."[137] Additionally, counterterrorism experts noted that US religious engagement efforts allowed Muslim states to "show that they're committed to this agenda of CVE without having to deal with issues within their country" that contribute to extremism.[138] Likewise, a former Obama CVE expert said Middle Eastern states incorporated religious engagement into their counterterrorism policies with "Middle Eastern flair."[139] This led to an ambiguous situation in which their religious outreach programs were simultaneously "state control" over society, "cheap talk," and "credible" initiatives. There is also some skepticism of unintended "backfires" from these efforts. For example, some worried that Uzbekistan's efforts to promote moderate and tolerant Islam was really an effort to "construct religion in a particular way," which "leaves out others" and may "increase alienation and marginalization" thus "sowing the seeds of discontent."[140]

## Analysis

America used religious appeals to form an international coalition with Muslim states and societies against al-Qaeda and, later, ISIS. This was due to the combination of an ideologically charged threat and the moral authority of religion in US politics. Likewise, the combination of the lack of credibility and material incentives led to substantive but complicated impacts from US religious appeals.

First, religious appeals were an important part of US counterterrorism efforts. They persisted across two administrations, with policymakers recognizing their significance when building coalitions to defeat al-Qaeda and ISIS. But they saw this as one of several tools in the struggle against terrorism, rather than a means to spread US religious ideals.

This was due to the combination of the moral authority of religion in US politics and the nature of the international struggle it faced. Religious appeals across the Bush and Obama administrations reflected policymakers' perceptions of and assumptions about religion's significance in the world. Moreover, they saw al-Qaeda and ISIS as a threat to liberal democracy and international order. As a result, the United States turned to ideological tools alongside military and economic ones.

These religious appeals had a mixed impact. US religious appeals appeared to convince leaders of Muslim states that cooperating with the United States on counterterrorism was in their interest, in a way that they would not have been convinced if the United States had just relied on security explanations. Similarly, some of the religious engagement efforts under Obama seemed to

84    **CHAPTER 3**

resonate with domestic publics, leading to small-scale rejections of extremism. Yet, much of the impact was more complex than that. Neither Muslim states nor societies were completely convinced by US religious engagement, and thus the counterterrorism coalitions did not result in durable and unproblematic cooperation with the United States in the global war on terrorism.

This was due to the combination of low credibility and high material incentives producing a convenient alignment that complicated the impact of the religious appeals. Many Muslims were suspicious of US intentions, given its history of interactions with Muslim states. Additionally, the very nature of US religious appeals led to some concerns, as they were seen as attempts to interfere with Muslim communities. At the same time, the United States offered security to Muslim states and communities that it worked with, and they feared reprisals if they did not. Coalitions formed, but they were unsteady.

This case can also tell us something about why religious appeals produced these unintended effects. They seemed to arise from the novelty and complexity of religious discourse. US policymakers were unsure how best to assess and measure the impact of the appeals, while anxiety about religion's intensity led to wariness across governments. At the same time, the multivalent nature of religious discourse is what allowed authoritarian states to twist appeals to "moderation" to their own ends.

Counterarguments, in turn, were insufficient. First, the religion skeptic counterargument would require evidence that religious engagement was mere window dressing for more essential counterterrorism efforts involving military and economic tools. There is evidence that US religious engagement was not a priority, but little indication policymakers saw it as insignificant. Likewise, few of the experts and practitioners argued religious engagement was insubstantial or useless, despite their concerns about these programs. The religion skeptic argument thus fails in its claim that these religious appeals were not significant to the United States.

Similarly, the instrumentalist critique is a weak explanation that requires resorting to facile post hoc arguments. Religious appeals were clearly strategic: US policymakers saw them as a potentially beneficial tool in the fight against terrorism. But they did not appear out of thin air. Claims that they were "cynical" moves by leaders do not explain why the United States relied on them, or why other states and societies reacted to them. One could insist that US policymakers "didn't really care" about the religious appeals, or that Muslim states "just pretended" to accept them. We are unlikely to delve into policymakers' minds, however, and must focus on observable behavior, which suggests religious appeals' importance. An instrumentalist explanation, then, can tell us little of value.

The religion triumphalist explanation, however, is equally weak. There is little evidence that the United States' religious engagement during the global war on terrorism was an attempt to act on or spread its religious belief systems. Meanwhile, there was little evidence of widespread transformation of US–Muslim relations or internalization of anti-extremist messaging, undermining the religious triumphalist counterargument.

There are some caveats to these findings, but they do not harm my argument. The bulk of this analysis is based on interviews. There may be some concern about respondents' biases, and I do not have "hard data" on the impact of US religious appeals. As I note above, however, I was able to get candid takes on religious appeals' effects even from those who would be expected to have an interest in championing them, lessening concern about biases. In terms of objectively assessing their impact, firsthand experience by policymakers and practitioners is a useful gauge of a policy's effects. Additionally, these are US-based experts, rather than people in Muslim regimes or societies who were the target of US appeals. There may be some bias as a result. However, we would expect the bias to be in the direction of exaggerating religious appeals' impact, given their desirability among US policymakers. The fact that the experts I interviewed pointed instead to many concerns with religious engagement, despite generally being supportive of its use, actually means the possible bias strengthens my argument.

## Conclusion

The United States launched a massive military, bureaucratic, and diplomatic undertaking after the 9/11 attacks to destroy al-Qaeda and undermine its support around the world. One underappreciated aspect of this global war on terrorism was the religious appeals the United States used to try and form coalitions with Muslim states and societies. The United States first attempted to promote a moderate Islam and emphasize common religiosity with Muslim states, and later tried to engage with Muslim states and societies along religious lines and contest messaging by ISIS and al-Qaeda. Analyses of the global war on terrorism that ignore this aspect—and broader studies of US foreign policy that ignore or downplay the constant presence of religion—would be incomplete.

The evidence in this chapter, based on secondary studies and interviews with counterterrorism experts and practitioners, demonstrates the complicated role of religious appeals in power politics. The United States drew on religious appeals due to the moral authority of religion in its politics and the

## 86   CHAPTER 3

ideologically charged nature of the global war on terrorism. It was a less than credible voice on Islamic issues, however, but did provide material incentives to Muslim states and societies. As a result, its religious appeals generated convenient coalitions that altered behavior but led to some complications from uncertainty about the nature of the religious policies and the complexity of the religious messaging.

This chapter thus further rejects the religion skeptic counterargument, which would require ignoring the voluminous evidence about religious engagement's importance in US counterterrorism. It also, however, rejects those who would argue religion is transforming US foreign policy or international security issues. Religious appeals remained a strategic tool for the United States to draw on alongside more conventional policies. And the prominence of the unintended and complicated effects of the religious appeals would frustrate optimists about religion's impact on the international system.

This case provides a useful comparison to the Saudi case in the previous chapter. Despite vastly different socioeconomic and political conditions, both shared a high domestic religious moral authority and both faced an ideologically charged international crisis. We saw religious appeals in both cases. They varied, however, in their credibility and the material incentives involved, resulting in a different impact from the religious appeals. I extend this comparison further in the next chapter, which examines Russia's struggle with the West over its "near abroad."

# CHAPTER 4

# Russia

## Undermining Western Opposition to the *Russky Mir*

In March of 2014, Russia annexed Crimea, the Black Sea peninsula in Ukraine. The move by Russia was part of its broader effort to maintain control over what it saw as the *Russky Mir* or "Russian world." Interestingly, however, Putin drew on religious language to justify this action. He called Crimea Russia's "Temple Mount," referencing the sacred, and contested, site in Jerusalem.[1] This rhetoric was partly for domestic purposes, to justify his increasingly aggressive actions. But he also a had a more distant target: conservative forces in Western Europe and the United States who were increasingly supportive of Putin due to his apparent backing of "traditional values" and religious causes. Putin directed much of his religious rhetoric toward these audiences in the hope that they would undermine Western opposition to Russian policies.

As I will show in this chapter, these religious appeals are a substantive—if unwieldy—aspect of Russian foreign policy. Russia's religious appeals are tied to both the domestic and international context in which the Russian regime has been operating since 2012. The Russian Orthodox Church (ROC), weakened under decades of Communist rule, burst back into the public sphere in the 1990s. Russian politicians recognized its importance. Putin took this the furthest by establishing a reciprocally supportive relationship with the church. At the same time, Putin and many others in Russia viewed the West as an ideological foe focused on undermining Russia's influence in the post-Soviet

87

88    CHAPTER 4

"near abroad." These two conditions combined to make religious appeals a desirable tool to form Russia's international coalitions.

These religious appeals resonated with Western far-right audiences but failed to form the desired international coalition or undermine Western efforts to isolate Russia. Far-right groups saw Putin as a credible speaker on traditional values, and accordingly opposed tough stances toward Russia by their states. Sometimes this translated into political pressure or policy changes, but Western states generally held together in their opposition to Russia's aggression. Instead, his appeals seemed to primarily increase international tensions and Western suspicion of Russia.

I proceed in five sections. First, I discuss the debate over the role of religion in Russian foreign policy. After that, I discuss the conditions predicting Russia's use of religious appeals, and examples of such use. I then discuss conditions predicting the impact of these appeals and provide evidence for this before presenting an overall assessment and conclusion.

## The Debate over Religion in Russian Foreign Policy

As with the United States and Saudi Arabia, Russia is a typical case for both my argument and alternative explanations. Religion, primarily the ROC, plays a significant role in Russian domestic and foreign politics. At the same time, Russia remains a military power with significant influence over energy markets. One could therefore formulate both religion skeptic and religion triumphalist explanations for the role of religion in Russia's power political struggles with the West.

Russia has been a major topic in policy discussions since the fall of the Soviet Union. Predictably, much of this discussion focused on conventional security issues. Studies have analyzed the status of Russia's nuclear arsenal and doctrine.[2] Others have analyzed Russia's outreach to developing countries around the world.[3] Still others have looked into Russia's cyberwarfare efforts.[4] And some have discussed Russia's ability—or lack thereof—to confront the United States directly.[5]

Many studies on Russia's post-Cold War politics downplay the significance of religion. Security discussions of Russia recognize the threat its nonmilitary efforts pose, but often frame this in nonreligious terms. Many discuss Russia's appeals to values in terms of soft power, traditional values, or nationalism.[6] Moreover, some studies on Russian domestic politics present religion as irrelevant in current politics.[7]

Several scholars, however, recognize the importance of religion in Russia's contemporary domestic and foreign politics. Scholars have written on the resurgence of the ROC and the resulting rightward shift in Russian politics.[8] Others have discussed the intertwining of the ROC and the Russian state.[9] Several have specifically written on the use and influence of religion in Russian foreign policy.[10]

Thus, one could easily formulate both religion skeptic and religion triumphalist explanations for Russia's foreign policy in this case. One could argue Russia is primarily motivated by conventional security concerns: any appeals to religion are intended primarily for domestic audiences. Similarly, one could acknowledge Russia's ideological appeals but deny their connection to religion. Alternately, one could argue Putin's religious appeals represent the impact of a religious resurgence on Russia's foreign policy, which threatens to upend the international order.[11]

## Russia's Use of Religious Appeals in Its Struggle with the West

Putin's use of religious appeals occurred in the context of his increasing antagonism with the West, and his desire to maintain influence over the "near abroad." This arose due to the interaction between the high moral authority of religion in Russian politics and the ideologically charged natured of Russia's struggle with the West. In this section I demonstrate the presence of these two conditions, and the nature of Russia's religious appeals.

### Background: A Resurgent Russian Orthodox Faith and a Rising International Presence

This chapter deals specifically with Russia's post-2012 foreign policy focused on Western audiences, but this occurred amid growing Russian dissatisfaction with its place in the post-Cold War world. Russia, as the Soviet Union, reigned as one of the world's two superpowers throughout much of the twentieth century. The end of the Cold War and dissolution of the Soviet Union in the 1990s, however, caused significant disruptions in Russian politics and society. The Russian economy struggled to transition away from central planning, with rising corruption and inequality. Russia became a democracy, but with significant divisions between liberal and conservative voices. As I will discuss in the next section, the ROC reemerged as a powerful force in Russia, providing a moral center to the seeming chaos.

90     CHAPTER 4

After the Cold War it seemed possible that Russia would engage with and join the West, similar to Germany's integration after World War II. The United States and Russia signed the second Strategic Arms Reduction Treaty (START II) and worked together through the Nunn–Lugar Cooperative Threat Reduction program. Diplomats from each side frequently engaged with each other, forming a durable pattern of interactions some hoped would grow into deeper bonds.[12] Russia was brought into the G8 group of wealthy countries. And Russia's first post-Cold War president, Boris Yeltsin, got along well with Western leaders. Yeltsin described the signing of START II as "the treaty of hope," while observers noted Yeltsin and Bill Clinton were "friends with an easy rapport."[13]

Simmering issues remained, however, which would limit Russia's ties to the West. Russia feared the loss of influence that came with the end of the Soviet Union and resented the spread of the North Atlantic Treaty Organization (NATO) and the European Union (EU) into former communist states. Russia fought two brutal wars against breakaway factions in the province of Chechnya. And Yeltsin was succeeded by Vladimir Putin, a former KGB official who seemed to long for the lost glory of the Soviet Union.

Tensions increased into the twenty-first century, rising to outright hostility by Putin's third term as president in 2012. The United States worked with Russia on common areas of concern, such as counterterrorism. But Putin's increasing authoritarianism concerned Western audiences; this intensified after 2012, when protests broke out throughout Russia at his return to the presidency after serving as prime minister.[14] Meanwhile, Putin directed his foreign policy toward maintaining control over the "near abroad," states formerly under Soviet control or influence. He often justified this as defending the *Russky Mir*, or Russian-speaking world. Putin's frustration at former Soviet states' Western turn exploded into hostilities with the Russian war on Georgia in 2008 and Russia's subsequent ejection from the G8.[15] This pattern continued when Russia reacted to pro-Western protests in Ukraine by annexing Crimea and supporting breakaway provinces in the country's east, leading to Western sanctions against the country.[16] Putin was also aggressive toward other former Soviet states, and famously interfered in US elections in 2016.

## Conditions Predicting Russia's Use of Religious Appeals

First, religion has a high moral authority in post-Soviet Russia. Orthodox Christianity has been an important part of Russian politics for centuries, helping to define the Russian identity. Russian identity often involves the sense of Russia as the "third Rome," the heir to true Christianity following Rome and Byzantium.[17] The Crimean war of 1853 was partly a struggle over Russia's claim to be the protector of all Orthodox Christians.[18] In the 1800s, the tsar tied Orthodoxy to Russian nationalism, claiming that "a Russian, devoted to his fatherland, will be unwilling to surrender a single dogma of our Orthodox religion."[19] This can also be seen in contemporary Russia. Influential Russian Orthodox figures believed that Orthodox faith was the foundation of the post-Soviet Russian state. For example, in 1998, Metropolitan Kirill argued it "was orthodoxy that stood at the sources of Russian statehood."[20]

The Soviet Union tightly controlled the church, but the institution managed to persist.[21] After the end of the Soviet Union, a wave of piety swept over Russia. This began with Gorbachev's reforms, when he guaranteed religious freedom as part of his broader glasnost and perestroika.[22] Gorbachev also recognized the positive potential impact of religion, turning to religious leaders to mediate ethnic tensions that erupted with the breakup of the Soviet Union.[23] It continued with the new religion laws of post-Soviet Russia, which allowed the teaching of religion in schools, conscientious objection, and the registration of religious organizations and legal bodies.[24] A later law in 1997 established "managed pluralism," which granted significant privileges to "traditional" religious communities while marginalizing proselytizing organizations.[25] This unleashed long-suppressed religious sentiment.[26] Clerics became prominent voices in popular debates, while the media took a more favorable tone toward religion; the number of churches expanded, as did the number of Bibles imported into the country.[27]

The religious boom was not politically neutral, however; conservative voices dominated the new public religiosity.[28] Much of this came from the ROC, in which conservative voices had been ascendent.[29] Threatened by spreading religious pluralism after the end of the Soviet Union, the ROC believed conservative morality was the best way to revive Russia.[30] A 2000 statement by the ROC called for a religious revival and rejected Russia as a multiconfessional state.[31] Additionally, the church tried to ban foreign missionaries, and called for censorship of inappropriate content in media.[32]

Other groups mixed Russian nationalism with faith. What some call the "Eurasianist stands of Russian intellectual thought" emerged to focus on "collectivism, spiritualism, traditionalism and Orthodox Christianity" as a contrast to the West's "spiritually impoverished individualism and materialism."[33] One political movement called for the restoration of Christianity in Russian society to solve the problems it faced after the end of the Soviet Union.[34] Conservative nationalists hoped to maintain what they saw as proper Russian and Slav values, seeing Russia as defined by its Orthodox faith.[35]

Not all of this conservative activism reflected specific Orthodox beliefs. The ROC criticized liberalism in general, focusing on areas such as science, education,

## 92    CHAPTER 4

and homosexuality.[36] Conservatives in Russia base their views on Orthodoxy, but also argue they are appealing to traditional values common to all religions.[37] For example, the ROC called for limits on abortion, homosexuality, and art it found objectionable.[38]

Russian politicians embraced this piety, turning to the church for support and inspiration for domestic policies.[39] Politicians appealed to religious organizations and provided aid in order to gain their support.[40] For example, Yeltsin arranged for the ROC patriarch to bless him at his inauguration.[41] A 2010 law on social organizations led the state to work with religious groups to run orphanages, homeless shelters, and welfare programs.[42] And the ROC gained significant political influence: at one point, Patriarch Kirill called legislators to his office to oppose legislation that would introduce sex education into schools.[43]

This accelerated under Putin, with many viewing the current church–state relationship as a modern version of the "symphonia" that characterized historic relations between the Russian tsar and the church. Putin argued that "Orthodoxy was the most important, defining milestone in the fate of Russia . . . the source of [Russia's] statehood, great culture" and "national character."[44] Putin has worked with the ROC to limit foreign missionaries, while appealing to the need for a "spiritual Russia" in official pronouncements.[45] After the 2011–2012 protests, Putin turned to the ROC as a way to increase the legitimacy of his regime.[46] Some have noted Putin's "forays against homosexuality and his lengthy courting of the national church" as part of his broader authoritarian impulses.[47] Studies of the initial post-Soviet period foresaw this development, arguing that "tsarist power" was an "important component of national Orthodoxy," so attempts to "restore Orthodoxy" would also come to embrace state power.[48]

Russian Orthodox Christianity has also found a place in Russia's foreign policy. Some of this is connected to the ROC's extensive international activities. The ROC saw the loss of its parishes in Ukraine after the fall of the USSR as a "debacle," and pressured the president of the newly independent Ukraine not to establish an independent church.[49] The church also attempted to maintain influence over other former Soviet states, such as Moldova and Latvia.[50] The ROC frequently engages in public diplomacy, including calls to protect Orthodox Christians outside of Russia and dialogue with the Vatican.[51]

As with its domestic politics, religion has become a major part of Russia's foreign policy under Putin. One Ukrainian official noted, after a 2009 visit by Patriarch Kirill to the country, that the ROC was "being used as an instrument in the Kremlin's game."[52] Russia emphasized concern over Middle East Christians to justify its support for Syria's government and intervention there.[53] Russia also expressed concern for the treatment of Christians in Nigeria.[54] Russia has worked to reacquire ROC property in Western Europe lost after the Bolshevik Revolution: after one such effort in Italy succeeded, then president Medvedev noted it established a "deep connection between our cultures and people."[55] Russia has appealed to Slavic identity and Orthodox Christian values when reaching out to Belarus and Ukraine.[56] The Russian state supports ROC institutions in the Middle East and, in 2006, Putin pushed the foreign ministry to negotiate with Israel over the return of a historic Orthodox site in that country to the ROC. Meanwhile, other states have recognized this as a priority for Russia, as seen in 2007 when Jordan's King Abdullah granted the ROC a site on the Jordan river to build a church for Russian pilgrims.[57] Overall, Putin has "used ideology instrumentally, invoking Russian Orthodoxy and family as values as Russia became more estranged from the West."[58]

Beyond this, Russian Orthodox faith is an indelible part of Russia's vision for itself in the world. Many in Russia were unhappy with the end of the Soviet Union, as Russia's status in the world declined greatly.[59] Conservatives in Russia saw the country as exceptional in the international community, adopting an anti-Westernism.[60] Much of Russia's aggressive foreign policy involves overcoming its sense of inferiority by pointing to the uniqueness of Russian identity.[61] And Russia at times relies on the ROC for informal "track 2" diplomacy on contentious topics it does not want to address directly, such as international negotiations over South Ossetia and Palestine.[62]

Russian Orthodox Christianity is also part of the reason for Russia's emphasis on the "near abroad," its term for neighboring post-communist states. This is partly geopolitical, as Russia worried about its former clients aligning themselves with the West.[63] But it is also due to identity ties: some conservative nationalists also protested Russia for not doing enough to protect their ethnic kin in nearby countries.[64] As a result, Russia has based much of its foreign policy around the *Russky Mir* concept. This asserts identification between Russia and other states with ethnically Russian populations and is closely tied to common Orthodox bonds.[65]

Russia's Orthodox faith has also inspired Russian policy in international forums, particularly its attempts to promote what it calls "traditional values." Much of this involved an assertion of Russian values in contrast to those of the West.[66] In a 2008 speech to the United Nations (UN) Human Rights Council, Kirill pushed back on conventional definitions of human rights, arguing they had been used to undermine religious teachings.[67] The ROC and the Russian foreign ministry worked together to push "traditional" values in UN human rights discussions, which includes opposing lesbian, gay, bisexual, transgender, and queer/questioning (LGBTQ) protections and state involvement in family issues.[68] Russia has worked closely with states like Egypt to push conservative causes, and gained support from other developing countries for

## 94    CHAPTER 4

doing so; some have argued Russia is "taking over the traditionalist agenda" in international forums from Muslim states and the Vatican.[69]

The ROC has also become closely intertwined with the Russian military. The Russian regime has set up pro-government Orthodox militias, while Cossack regiment training includes Orthodox teachings.[70] The ROC discussed the Chechen wars as involving the "blood of new Russian martyrs," and churches were dedicated to soldiers who fought in them.[71] In 2002 Patriarch Alexey II consecrated a church at an office of the Federal Security Bureau, emphasizing the need to work together against threats to Russia's spiritual security.[72] ROC figures blessed military hardware, took part in military exercises, and provided guidance to officers.[73]

The increasing prominence of faith in Russian politics intertwines with the ideologically charged nature of its attempts to maintain influence over the "near abroad." Contemporary Russian foreign policy is marked by a "revival of Russian exceptionalism" and security concerns motivated by the fear of NATO expansion and losing influence in Ukraine.[74] Russia has been attempting to regain influence over its "near abroad" through international coalitions such as the customs union with Belarus and the Shanghai Cooperation Organization.[75] By the end of the Bush administration, Russian foreign policy was a "power-seeking enterprise . . . committed to rebuilding the country's military power, determined to maximize Russian influence in the post-Soviet space."[76] Putin's primary foreign policy goal was to "restore Russia's foreign policy autonomy and its great power status."[77]

Russia is not just trying to gain more prominence in the international community, however. It is pushing back on what it sees as the hegemonic liberal order centered on the United States. Some nationalists in Russia worried Western aid was meant to weaken Russia and limit its global power.[78] Conservative intellectuals who became prominent after the end of the Soviet Union saw Russia as the "harbinger of the coming . . . culture" that could reestablish traditional values.[79] Russian and ROC officials argue Russia is a distinct civilization, and Western values are a threat to its integrity.[80] Putin has echoed this: in 2014 he argued that "the people of Russia always ponder the higher moral predestination of the human being" while the West is focused on itself.[81] A February 2003 National Security Concept framed Russia as distinct from the West, and Russia has made similar pronouncements since Putin became president.[82] Russia is trying to undermine US dominance with outreach to states like Germany and Italy, opposition to the US invasion of Iraq, and summits with China.[83]

As Russia pushes back on US leadership, it has attempted to replace it as a global leader. Russia is trying to expand its "soft power" in the world to gain international support and increase its status.[84] Contemporary Russian foreign policy is a "reaction to Russians' perception that they have failed to achieve the desired recognition as an equal to the major powers."[85] Russian government and ROC officials have argued Russia can become a role model for the rest of the world on how to act based on traditional values, and save the West from its decline.[86] Russia has also appealed to Middle Eastern states unhappy with US leadership in order to gain influence.[87]

## Russia's Use of Religious Appeals

This combination of a high moral authority of religion in its politics and the ideologically charged nature of its struggle with the West led Russia to draw on religious appeals as a power political tool. That is, religious appeals are serious and strategic elements of Russian foreign policy intended to create an international coalition in support of its influence over the *Russky Mir*.

Several have noted Russia's outreach to right-wing forces. Russia launched a "PR offensive to win over support from conservatively minded governments and various political constituencies" in Europe.[88] Under Putin, Russia has established ties with Viktor Orbán—the far-right leader of Hungary—and far-right parties in Austria, Denmark, Bulgaria, and Greece. Russia has also worked with the United Kingdom Independence Party (UKIP) and France's National Front. Far-right support for Russia is partly due to the funding these groups receive, but it is also because Putin's rhetoric resonates with them.[89] Russia has organized homeschooling networks—drawing in many conservative Western nongovernmental organizations (NGOs)—and other networks emphasizing "traditional values" as well.[90]

Religion is an important element of these efforts. Russia has set up NGOs, which it uses in concert with the Foreign Ministry to reach out to publics around the world: many of these NGOs focus on unity among Russians outside of Russia.[91] Russia often explicitly emphasizes conservative and traditional values in this outreach.[92] And the aforementioned involvement of the ROC in Russian efforts in international forums is part of an attempt to insert Russia into European "conflicts over the right place of religion in the public sphere."[93] Additionally, Russia has gained support from many conservative Western NGOs as a result of its push for "traditional values" in international forums.[94]

Russia frequently used religious appeals in order to contrast itself with the US-led West. Some of this was an official part of Russian foreign policy. In 2014, the Kremlin issued a directive to "develop a set of measures to strengthen the coordination of activity in this area, based on the need to defend traditional values and humanitarian views" in Russia's information policy.[95] That is, Russia

## 96    CHAPTER 4

officially recognized the defense of traditional religious values as an important element of its rhetorical exchanges with other states.

Putin also works these appeals into his speeches. In a December 2013 speech, Putin pushed back on Western criticism of Russia's anti-LGBTQ laws, attacking the West for "treating good and evil equally": he argued that Russia's "traditional family values" were "the foundation of Russia's greatness and a bulwark against 'so-called tolerance.'"[96] Putin connected these appeals to calls for Ukraine to remain tied to Russia, as well as the customs union with Belarus and Kazakhstan.[97] Putin claimed that the "destruction of traditional values from above not only entails negative consequences for society, but is also inherently anti-democratic because it . . . runs counter to the will of the majority of people."[98] One report characterized his speech as painting "a picture of Russia as the world's last bastion against countries bent upon destroying traditional values."[99]

This can be seen at other points. In a 2015 interview, Putin discussed the role of values. He argued that "a great many nations and people in the world . . . are fully behind" Russia on its support for traditional values, and that even when leaders criticize Russia, their people support Putin.[100] Additionally, Putin contrasted this with attempts to impose values on others, assumedly an attack on Western support for human rights.[101] In a 2019 interview, Putin argued that "Western societies are rejecting liberal values" as they are "obsolete" and "traditional values are more stable and more important."[102] In response to claims that Russia was interfering in other states' politics, Putin instead argued that "liberal governments 'have not acted to reassure citizens,'" and connected this to concerns about refugees, "gender diversity and multiculturalism."[103] Thus, Putin's religious appeals are clearly connected to Russia's broader challenge to US dominance.

Putin has also tried to highlight how close he is to religious organizations and emphasize the common conservative values uniting believers in Russia and elsewhere. In a 2020 meeting with religious leaders, Putin argued that "forces seek to use [traditional values] in dirty political games."[104] Specifically, he was referring to Western states attempting to undermine what he sees as traditional values through policies like abortion rights and LGBTQ protections. He also noted that Russia has a "long tradition of respect for people of different ethnic and religious backgrounds and that tradition 'should be protected, strengthened and promoted.'"[105]

Putin also expressed concern about Christians in the Middle East. During a 2020 visit with Syrian president Bashar al-Assad, Putin visited the tomb of John the Baptist and the two leaders visited an Orthodox Cathedral together in Damascus.[106] In discussing the fight against rebels in Syria, Putin specifically noted the recapture of "historic Christian regions" that would allow "refugees of all faiths to return home." Putin also appealed beyond Christianity, vowing to restore holy sites of Syrian Muslims and Jews.[107] Additionally, Russian foreign policy experts have discussed the intervention as a strategy to "build a fortress for Syria's Christian, Druze and Alawite minorities" against ISIS.[108]

He used these concerns to explicitly draw a contrast with the West. Many Western Christians, particularly conservatives, worried that the war would destroy remaining Syrian Christians who had been under Assad's protection.[109] In 2013, Putin said that "we face a terrible tragedy of losing Christian presence" in the Middle East and that Russia "will not stand aside." Meanwhile, he argued, the West "tends to gloss over this phenomenon, if not enable it, through their inexplicable support for the Muslim Brotherhood in places like Egypt and in Syria by supporting the Islamist-dominated opposition."[110]

Putin has also used religious appeals to disrupt rival coalitions in the United States and Europe. Putin often appealed to US conservatives using the language of religious and "traditional values" to undermine support for his political rivals. During the 2016 election, he praised Trump, noting he represented the "working class" and the people who respect "traditional values."[111] In the wake of the 2016 election, Putin argued that most Americans share Russia's "traditional values."[112] He pushed back on criticism from President Obama, arguing that Republican support for Putin showed "that a significant portion of Americans shares the concerns and traditional values of Russians."[113]

Putin also presented Russia as a contrast to the United States. In his 2013 state of the nation address, which occurred during international criticism of Russia's hosting of the Winter Olympics, Putin "sought to cast Russia as the moral arbiter of the world" and criticized the United States' "non-traditional values."[114] He argued the West was involved in the "destruction of traditional values" that went against "the will of the people."[115]

Russia directed its appeals to Europe as well. One state-affiliated analyst presented a report in which he argued that "Europe and the United States have given up" on traditional values, but Putin "embodies that model that . . . is envied by many in the West."[116] Putin criticized the Austrian drag artist Conchita after she won the Eurovision Song Contest, arguing that it was "important to reaffirm traditional values": this followed the ROC's denunciation of the artist's win as "one more step in the rejection of the Christian identity of European culture."[117]

Putin has used appeals to traditional values to undermine critical voices in Europe, and back supportive ones. For example, he attacked European media for presenting a "distorted picture of what is going on to support entrenched interests," but praised an Italian paper, *La Stampa*, as a "model of traditional

98    CHAPTER 4

values."[118] In a 2021 interview, Russian foreign minister Sergei Lavrov argued that human rights as enshrined in the Universal Declaration of Human Rights did not extend to LGBTQ issues, which he described as "traditional values": he also warned Europe, specifically Poland, that it would experience disruption if it undermined those traditional values.[119] The Russian government helped to buy a plot of land for an Orthodox cathedral in Paris that also houses a Russian cultural center. Russia's ambassador to France celebrated the cathedral as proving "Russia is sacred and eternal." Russia also lobbied to have the ROC take control of a private Orthodox cemetery in Paris.[120]

Just as in the United States, Russia has backed far-right groups in Europe. The deputy leader of Putin's party reached out to Austrian far-right political forces, calling on partnership on economic issues, migration, and "supporting traditional values."[121] Putin welcomed Marine Le Pen to Moscow in 2013, and held a secret meeting between Putin's party, Geert Wilders, and Matteo Salvini.[122] In 2019, Russia invited far-right politicians from the UK, Poland, and other countries to speak to parliament: one speaker stated that he agreed with Putin that "liberalism was obsolete," and that Europe need to "end the new Cold War" and "embrace traditional values."[123] In 2015, Russia organized a conference for far-right groups from Europe and the United States that produced a resolution blaming the United States for the conflict with Ukraine and "deploring the erosion of traditional values in the West."[124]

# The Mixed Impact of Russia's Religious Appeals

Thus, Russia used religious appeals as a power political tool in its attempts to build an international coalition in the West in favor of its aggressive policies toward the *Russky Mir*. These appeals had significant impacts on international relations. Russia under Putin was a credible voice on religious issues, but target states had mixed material incentives concerning alignment with Russia. As a result, Russia was able to pull together some powerful political actors in an international coalition, but the overall result was to increase tensions over Russian policies. In this section, I first discuss the conditions affecting the impact of Russia's religious appeals before presenting and analyzing evidence of their impact.

## Conditions Affecting the Impact of Russia's Religious Appeals

The Russian situation was similar to that of the Saudis in the 1960s. Vladimir Putin was credible as a speaker on far-right religious causes. In the United

States, many conservatives saw Putin as "defending sovereign nationhood . . . and traditional values" against "multiculturalism" and "nontraditional sexual identity."[125] Prominent conservative Pat Buchanan called on Western conservatives to back Putin as a champion "against the militant secularism of a multicultural and transnational elite."[126] Steve Bannon spoke before a meeting of European conservatives, and argued that the West "should focus more on Putin's promotion of 'traditionalism' and values that support 'the underpinnings of nationalism.'"[127] And the number of US Republicans who saw Putin as very unfavorable went from 51 percent in 2014 to 10 percent in 2016.[128] Some have noted Buchanan's support for Putin was due to the view that Putin was "standing up for traditional values against Western cultural elites."[129] Similarly, evangelical leaders like Franklin Graham and Larry Jacobs backed Putin as he was "on our [*sic*] side in the war against secularism and sexual decadence," with some calling him a "moral compass."[130] There were some signs of US evangelicals "leaning on Russia for support" as a "model" to institute laws in line with conservative Christian values.[131]

There are numerous other examples of Putin's credibility on religious issues among US conservatives. Putin's ability to "portray himself as a defender of traditional social values," and as a "religiously devout alternative to Western countries" has "drawn praise" from "like-minded American activists."[132] For many US conservatives, Putin "personifies many of the qualities and attitudes that conservatives have desired in a president: a respect for traditional Christian values, a swelling nationalist pride and an aggressive posture toward foreign adversaries."[133] As one expert put it, Putin is the "true defender of Christian values," and the United States is the one that is "decadent."[134] Experts have argued that Putin's "religious, nationalist turn" inspired alt-right figures in the United States.[135] The president of the World Council of Families said that "the Russians might be the Christian saviors of the world," while others noted that they look to "Russia as having the potential to 'save' Western civilization."[136] Konstantin Malofeev, a Russian oligarch with ties to pro-Russian rebels in Ukraine, was also closely connected with US evangelicals.[137]

Just as in the United States, these efforts seemed to have resonated with far-right Europeans. One participant in the 2015 conference mentioned above said he saw the event as "pushing the fight back against liberalism" and "the destruction of traditional values including Christianity": he argued that "Russia is about tradition and Christianity."[138] One Russian analyst argued that "Putin embodies mostly the model that can be envied and is envied by many in the West," and that "in the eyes of millions of Europeans and Americans, Putin is the man who embodies those traditional and also conservative values."[139] Many populist parties in Europe see Putin as an "ally" because he shares their concern

## 100 CHAPTER 4

over immigration, globalization, and Islamic radicalism: they "perceive" his actions as a "defense for strong traditional values."[140] For example, a figure in Hungary's Jobbik Party argued that Russia "represents European values 'much better' than Europe itself" as Russia "preserves its traditions."[141]

Far-right observers have noted that the "alt-right has found a natural ally in Russia's current zeitgeist."[142] For example, one alt-right argued that "Russia is the leader of the free world right now," as Putin supports "nationalists around the world . . . while promoting traditional values."[143] Pegida, a German anti-immigration group, has waved signs saying "Putin, help us" in protests.[144] Meanwhile, Matteo Salvini of Italy's Northern League argued against sanctions on Russia, asking "why wage a commercial war on the main bulwark against the spread of . . . Islamic extremism?" And Nigel Farage, who was the leader of UKIP, called for unity with Putin as he was "actually on our side."[145] Tomas Vanas, a far-right Czech politician, said he stood with Putin to "resist 'the perverse liberal values of the Western world.'"[146]

Russian appeals have also resonated with some Orthodox figures. Priests in Moldova loyal to the ROC have blocked efforts to work with the West, while priests in Montenegro opposed calls to join NATO. A member of that community argued "they want to show that there is only one Russia, the Russia of Putin."[147] A pro-Russian priest in Moldova who opposed closer ties to the West argued that "the voice of the church and the voice of Russian politicians . . . are the same": he added that "Russia is the guardian of Christian values," while Europe "demands we play with our souls."[148]

Yet, the material incentives for target states were mixed. Russia has offered material support in addition to symbolic support to far-right forces. A nationalist party in Russia organized a 2015 conference that included many alt-right figures from the United States. One called the United States "the greatest enemy of tradition everywhere," while a Ku Klux Klan attorney also spoke.[149] Sputnik, a Russian state media service, has set up radio stations in the United States. They have given an outlet for "a cast of far-right conspiracy theorists, evangelical pastors and anti-Semites," and note that "the United States has become a different country that now looks down on traditional values."[150] Also, the World Congress of Families—an important evangelical backer of Russia—was formed through a partnership between US and Russian conservatives.[151] Russian forces helped fund France's National Front, and Moscow organized conferences for groups including neo-Nazis and US secessionists.[152] Russia is also an important provider of natural gas to much of Europe, leaving European states wary of challenging Russia too directly.

At the same time, European states are wary of Russia's growing influence and hope to maintain close ties with the United States. Some Western Euro-

## RUSSIA 101

pean states have been directly affected by Russian aggression, such as the assassination of a Russian dissident in London or the shooting down of a Dutch airliner by Russian-tied forces in Ukraine. Likewise, both France and the UK have been the targets of Russian disinformation campaigns during elections. Additionally, Western European states hoped to maintain the integrity of NATO, worrying greatly about the United States abandoning the alliance during the Trump presidency.[153] European states thus have significant incentives to resist Russia's religious appeals.

## Impacts of Russian Religious Appeals

Russia under Putin was thus a credible speaker on religious issues, but the targets of its religious appeals faced contrasting material incentives. Russia's religious appeals resonated with far-right groups in Europe and the United States, leading them to oppose harsh action on Russian policies: we see this most clearly in the case of the Russian annexation of Crimea. Yet, as states faced material disincentives to follow the urging of these far-right groups, these religious appeals also increased tensions over Russian policies.

### EXPECTED IMPACTS OF RUSSIAN RELIGIOUS APPEALS

Several observers have noted Putin-aligned far-right forces gave him political cover. After Russia invaded Ukraine and seized Crimea, Putin had "coalesced support from far-right forces across the West, ranging from white nationalists . . . to political groups bent on fracturing NATO and the European Union": this was partly due to the fact that Russia had "wrested control of the global Christian right from the U.S."[154] European far-right forces have tended to downplay Putin's aggressive actions such as the invasion of Ukraine. Observers noted European far-right forces saw Russia as "defending itself against globalism," rather than "committing aggression against Europe."[155]

One example is the UK's Nigel Farage. Nigel Farage said that the invasion of Crimea was an "understandable response to Western overreach." Furthermore, he argued the EU had "blood on its hands" over the fighting in Ukraine as it gave "false hope" to Ukrainians."[156] Farage persisted in this line of attack despite criticism, arguing that he had more respect for Putin than then UK prime minister David Cameron.[157] While Farage was never in UK leadership, there is evidence his views on Russia had some impact. After a debate with Liberal Democrats party leader Nick Clegg, 68 percent of British voters reported siding with Farage, including 77 percent of voters for the ruling Conservative party.[158] Additionally, UKIP members in the European Parliament—along with

102    **CHAPTER 4**

other far-right groups—voted against a resolution imposing sanctions on Russia.[159] And this was in the period in which mainstream UK parties were "rattled" by UKIP's apparent popularity.[160]

This was also apparent in Italy. Putin developed close ties with Italy's populist leader, Matteo Salvini, who accordingly argued for a resumption of regular ties between Russia and Europe.[161] Salvini was an "open admirer" of Putin.[162] Salvini also visited Crimea, arguing that its people have "chosen freely to remain with Russia" and that Italy and Europe "cannot conceive of sanctions against Russia."[163] As with other far-right groups, the Northern League pushed back on EU Russian policies in the European Parliament. Salvini swore that he would "start our battle for the recognition of Crimea and lifting anti-Russian sanctions."[164] Salvini also argued that Italy's support for EU sanctions would harm Italy's "national interests."[165]

There was a similar dynamic in France. An adviser to National Front leader Marine le Pen visited Crimea during its referendum to "confirm that the referendum was successful" and that turnout was very high. He called on Europe to be "pragmatic" and avoid falling into a "trap that has been laid by the United States" to split the EU and Russia.[166] Le Pen claimed that Putin's "courage, honesty and respect of identity and civilization" was absent in most of French politics, and called on France to abandon NATO and form an alliance with Russia.[167] She also criticized EU sanctions on Russia and France's suspension of arms sales to the country.[168]

As with UKIP, the National Front was not in a leadership position in France but did influence French and European politics. A National Front member in the European Parliament argued that "if I had been in Putin's shoes I would have done the same thing," and that Putin had been "very patient for 15 years": he claimed Putin had "no other choice" but to invade Ukraine, and called for "strategic aggression against Russia to stop."[169] Observers worried the National Front would work with other far-right groups in the European Parliament to form a "pro-Russia bloc."[170]

This extended to the United States. Shortly after the invasion of Crimea, Franklin Graham said that while the United States had held "the high moral ground," that status was now conferred on Russia.[171] Later that year, Graham helped organize a visit by a delegation of Russian Christian organizations with ties to Putin to meet with US evangelical organizations. During the trip, he noted that "as we find tensions increasing once again . . . it is vitally important that we try to build bridges of understanding and respect."[172]

Other US evangelical leaders advocated closer ties between Russia and the United States. Some publicly supported Russia in the face of criticism in the United States, while others openly called for the United States to work with

Russia. This included televangelist Jim Bakker, who saw Russia as an ally in the end times. Likewise, both Robert Jeffress and Jerry Falwell Jr. supported Trump's friendliness toward Putin.[173] Additionally, Brian Brown from the National Organization for Marriage visited Moscow in 2017 and discussed the "strong common bond with these countries of reverence and appreciation for the natural family."[174] Some critics of the United States' hostile stance toward Russia have pointed toward Putin's defense of Middle East Christians to call for supporting Russia's ties to Assad.[175]

While mainstream conservatives in the United States initially did not join in evangelical praise of Russia, this changed with the election of Donald Trump. During the Obama administration, many Republicans criticized Obama for not taking a stronger stance on Russia's annexation of Crimea.[176] Donald Trump, however, reflected evangelicals' positive attitude toward Putin. He praised Putin's attempts to get around US sanctions.[177] He also seemed to support Putin's invasion of Crimea and his influence over Ukraine. Trump was open to Russian control over Baltic states as well.[178] And he pushed back on the US government's attempts to investigate and punish Russia over its interference in the 2016 presidential election.[179] This permissive attitude spread to Republicans in general: Republican support for Putin rose from 12 percent to 32 percent between 2015 and 2017.[180]

The reasons for Trump's positive attitude toward Putin are unclear, but pro-Russian voices among evangelicals and other conservatives may have influenced his policies toward Russia. At the least they gave Trump political cover to express such views. Outspoken defenders of Putin such as Franklin Graham and Steven Bannon supported and were connected to the Trump administration. Evangelicals also formed a powerful constituency for Trump, helping to secure his victory in the 2016 election so he was less reliant on traditionally hawkish Republicans.[181] In return, Trump gave evangelicals significant access to his administration, and prioritized many of their concerns.[182]

This extended to foreign policy primarily through international religious freedom promotion. International religious freedom had been a priority for US evangelicals for years, and Trump promised to emphasize it once he came to office.[183] One of their primary concerns was the status of Middle East Christians, particularly those in Iraq and Syria who faced genocide under ISIS. Under pressure from evangelicals, the Trump administration controversially directed foreign aid toward Middle East Christians.[184] Russia was spared such attention, even though it had extensive restrictions on religious freedom in place such as the aforementioned restrictions on missionaries, a major concern for US evangelicals. It is very likely the lack of evangelical elites' pressure on Russia was related to their overall positive image of Putin. Given their influence over the

104 **CHAPTER 4**

Trump administration, these groups could have pushed for a harsher US stance on Russia over its religious freedom record. The support for Russia among many evangelical leaders, however, seemed to have spared him from this fate.

## DISRUPTIVE EFFECTS OF RUSSIAN RELIGIOUS APPEALS

There have been many effects from Russia's religious appeals, however, that have not been positive for Russia. One is an increased polarization, making it easier to critique far-right policies for their purported connection to Russia. A Polish opposition figure criticized the conservative Polish leader for meeting with Orbán and Salvini, arguing he was "implementing Putin's policy" and that "champagne corks may pop in the Kremlin."[185] Russia's hosting of an extremist conference led to greater scrutiny of Russia's ties to UK groups by the Foreign and Commonwealth Office.[186] When Putin attended the wedding of a far-right Austrian foreign minister, one expert claimed it made it harder for Austria to "look like an honest broker between Europe and Russia . . . Austria looks like a Trojan horse for Russian interests": likewise, an Austrian left-wing politician argued that "Putin is coming to overhaul EU sanctions with the help of the Austrian government."[187] And a Ukrainian member of parliament said "from now on, Austria can't be a mediator in Ukraine."[188] Danish far-right figure Anders Vistisen opposed Salvini's pro-Russian policies as he was "very concerned about Russian aggression."[189]

This shift was apparent in the United States as well. Democrats had previously been open to engagement in Russia, supportive of both Bill Clinton's and Barack Obama's outreach. As I noted, Republicans tended to be critical of such moves. Yet, Putin's interference in the 2016 election in favor of Trump, and Trump's clear bias toward Putin changed this situation. Democrats became very critical of Russia, and supportive of harsher sanctions on Russia's government.[190] Democrats also used connections to Russia as an attack line on Republicans and conservative activists.[191] Thus, Putin may have ensured future Democratic leaders will keep him at an arm's length, rather than trying to reset relations as Obama did.[192]

Western states have accordingly taken a harder stance against Russia. Obama came to office seeking a "reset" with Russia after tensions during the Bush administration. By the time of the 2016 election, however, Obama recognized Russia's international aggression and attempts at electoral interference, expanding sanctions on the country. The UK and other states condemned Russia after a dissident was poisoned by Russian agents in England.[193] German lawmakers and the European parliament have opposed the Nord Stream 2 pipeline connecting Russia with Germany.[194]

While some of this is conventional geopolitics, much relates to Russia's religious appeals. As Huseynov notes, "Russia's image suffers . . . from its controversial efforts to preserve its traditional influence" over its neighboring states.[195] As I noted earlier in the chapter, some Western concern over Russia had to do with its "soft power" efforts, which involved its appeals to "traditional values" and faith. This was also apparent in policy responses; for example, the Obama administration drew on Western identity and values in an attempt to form a coalition against Russia's Ukraine aggression.[196]

We can see some specific examples of this as well. In Latvia, a 2018 vote on whether or not to recognize Orthodox Christmas as an official holiday became heated due to concerns over Russian influence. One activist argued that this would "symbolically accept Latvia's membership in the 'canonical territory' of the Moscow Patriarchate" and be part of Russian attempts to "divide the world into zones of influence."[197] In 2020, an Estonian security expert analyzed a statement by Putin about the legacy of World War II, noting Putin's emphasis on the historical borders of the Orthodox Church, which included Estonia. The expert argued this represented a hostile intention by Putin.[198] When one ROC official discussed Russia's intervention in Syria as a holy war, Middle East Christians pushed back as ISIS used this to justify its attacks.[199]

## Analysis

This analysis shows Russia's religious appeals were a power political tool with unpredictable effects. The religious appeals were clearly significant and strategic efforts to build an international coalition. The effects were more subtle, but numerous pieces of evidence point to their complicating impact on anti-Russian coalitions, albeit with disruptive side effects for Russian foreign policy. Moreover, both the religion skeptic and religion triumphalist arguments were insufficient.

First, Russia's religious appeals are clearly strategic. While this was difficult to discern using the primary evidence, scholars of contemporary Russia have noted it. While Putin does seem to have some sincere faith, his appeals to Christianity are a political tool. Scholars have argued that Putin seems to have some sincere faith, but only turns to religious issues in his political rhetoric when it is necessary or convenient.[200] Others have noted the way his appeals to faith in Russian foreign policy are tied to broader geopolitical concerns.[201] Supporting

106   **CHAPTER 4**

the claim that they are strategic in nature, Putin's appeals to traditional values increased in response to political pressures.[202]

Russia's religious appeals are, at the same time, connected to the domestic and international ideological context. Russia's religious appeals occurred in the context of Putin's efforts to restore Russian power and challenge the US-led international order. This was more than just expanding political influence over countries such as Ukraine: it involved contestation over international norms concerning human rights and democracy. Putin's religious appeals were part of an attempt to push back on and change these values. Additionally, they were connected to the moral authority of religion in Russian politics. The post-Soviet resurgence of the Orthodox faith led religious figures and symbols to gain significant influence in Russian politics. This led Putin to draw on religious appeals while simultaneously ensuring he saw them as a viable option in domestic and international struggles.

Moreover, this was not just "cheap talk": Russia's religious appeals were serious efforts. Putin frequently connected them to broader political messages, such as the pro-European tilt of Ukraine or his desire to ensure a friendly US president. Additionally, they were integrated into Russia's broader foreign policy: policymakers, propaganda outlets, and state-aligned policy experts echoed Putin's rhetoric. Russia thus approached these religious appeals as a serious element of its power politics, alongside military threats, cyberattacks, or economic inducements.

The evidence for the religious appeals' effects is less clear than in the other cases, but we can point to their impacts. First, there is ample evidence that far-right groups in the United States and Europe backed Russia because of Putin's religious appeals and called for concrete policy changes as a result. Many organizations and national figures specifically noted Russia's defense of "traditional values." Additionally, they did not just praise Russia's domestic policies but called for closer ties between their states and Russia. Even when they did not explicitly call for such policy changes, they emphasized positive aspects of Russia in the midst of criticism of its foreign policies.

Second, these pro-Putin coalitions complicated Western responses to Russia. Groups like the UKIP and National Front dominated political discourse in their countries. Far-right parties in other countries complicated efforts to craft sanctions against Russia as they were "pivotal in national power-brokering."[203] Moreover, their presence in EU bodies made it harder for the EU to act decisively and in a united fashion. Finally, Donald Trump did not manage to withdraw from NATO, but he did raise significant doubts about the United States' reliability as an ally against Russia.

Additionally, Putin's religious appeals did seem to increase tensions surrounding Russian foreign policy. There was initial optimism about Western–Russian relations, even under Vladimir Putin. US President George W. Bush said he "looked [Putin] in the eye" and "got a sense for his soul" after a summit.[204] As I noted above, Obama attempted a reset with Russia over tense relations. German chancellor Angela Merkel attempted to engage with Putin even after the 2008 war with Georgia and the annexation of Crimea.[205] Western states eventually abandoned these efforts. We do not have clear evidence of policymakers and social groups expressing greater concern over Russia due to its religious appeals, but the ideological challenge from Russia seems to have prompted their actions.[206] This suggests the perceived threat would be lower—and tensions reduced—without the religious element to Russia's actions.

This case study can also provide further insight into the means through which religious appeals affect power politics. The clearest impact seems to arise from these appeals resonating with domestic audiences, specifically far-right groups. They then pressure their regimes to act in line with Russian preferences. We can also gain insight into the unintended impacts of religious appeals. Much of this had to do with the tendency of religious appeals to raise the stakes of an international crisis. The tensions that emerged were due to Western states feeling threatened by Putin's ideological challenge and direct address to domestic far-right groups. Additionally, there is some evidence that these religious appeals mattered due to the complexity of religious arguments. Putin could appeal to traditional Orthodox values in a way that also resonated with particularistic European nationalism and US conservative evangelicalism. Yet, he also lost control of the narrative. Far-right groups were at times criticized because of their support for Russia, with the ideological connections proving a hindrance to Russian influence.

Alternative explanations, in turn, were insufficient. The religion skeptic argument would need to find evidence that religious appeals were either absent or only used in unimportant aspects of Russian foreign policy. This was not the case. Additionally, there were noticeable effects from the religious appeals: this was not "cheap talk" that serious policymakers ignored. Yes, the effects were not exactly what Russia intended, but the religion skeptic argument would expect them to be insignificant. At the same time, religion triumphalist counterarguments would require evidence that Russia's religious appeals were the result of Russian foreign policymakers reflecting on their religious values and forming foreign policy in response. The religion triumphalist argument would struggle with this strategic use of religion and the unintended and mixed effects from religious appeals' use. We can thus reject the counterarguments.

108    **CHAPTER 4**

There are a few other alternative explanations we can also reject. Some may argue that the appeal to "traditional values" is not "really" religious. Indeed, this is the approach taken by some of the policy experts I discussed earlier in this chapter. But, as I have shown, Russia's traditional values are based on the prominence of its Orthodox faith. Similarly, the specific issues Russia discusses in the context of "traditional values" are those championed by conservative religious groups, such as opposition to LGBTQ equality or abortion. It is thus difficult to deny the religious element of these traditional values. Others may argue the reaction to Putin's outreach is based on political polarization. That is, conservative pro-Trump Christians in the United States supported Putin because Trump supported Putin. This explanation is limited because conservative Christian support predated Trump's presidency, while there was no similarly unifying far-right figure in Europe. Another concern may be the limited role of energy supplies in this analysis. I do acknowledge Russia's importance in energy markets, as part of the mixed material incentives Western states faced. However, it would be a stretch to reduce all far-right and conservative religious statements in support of Putin to his delivery of natural gas to their countries.

One final concern is valid. There is some indication that Russian religious appeals increased the extent to which religion was a part of political struggles. Instead of being focused on nuclear doctrine or oil politics, much of the debate over Russian policy involved its popularity among far-right groups. The debate thus shifted to include their religious arguments and concerns. That is, the appeals changed the religious conditions from which they emerged. I will discuss this possibility, and ways to address it, in the concluding chapter.

## Conclusion

As I write this chapter, Putin faces international condemnation for his invasion of Ukraine, and the prolonged and brutal war he is waging on that country. His religious appeals appear to have failed to translate into concrete support for this military action. It is thus difficult to assess the overall effect of Russia's religious appeals on Russia's power political goals. We can, however, say with confidence that these religious appeals are a serious part of Russian power politics. We can also point to their real, if unpredictable, impacts on international relations.

Skeptical attempts to dismiss their importance require ignoring the vast amount of evidence I presented above. Russia has integrated religious appeals into its foreign policy process and connected them to crucial security issues.

These generated support for Russian policies among far-right forces in the United States and Western Europe. Arguing they were inconsequential would require rejecting the significance of Putin's numerous statements, and all the sympathetic statements in response from the targets of these appeals.

That being said, it is not clear these religious appeals succeeded in their goals. While support for Russia has grown, many in Western Europe and the United States remain suspicious of Russia and its aggressive foreign policies. Some of this has to do with Russia's religious appeals themselves. The infusion of religion into already tense geopolitics increased the stakes of these struggles, making it harder for Putin to gather allies. Russia's religious appeals, then, may ironically undermine any gains Russia has made in expanding its influence.

As with my other case studies, advocates of religion's importance in international relations may be frustrated with this chapter. I did not present a "slam dunk" on religion's importance, instead suggesting its impacts may be mixed. Like the Saudi and US cases, this is due to the complex and dynamic nature of religion's impact on international relations. I will return to the implications of this finding for the study of religion and international relations in the concluding chapter. First, I will expand this analysis to other cases of religious appeals in power politics.

# CHAPTER 5

# Expanding the Analysis

The previous three chapters have shown that religious appeals can be a powerful but unwieldy tool in power politics. Saudi Arabia in the 1960s, the United States in the global war on terrorism, and Russia post-2012 all turned to religious appeals because of the high moral authority of religion in their politics and the ideologically charged nature of the international crisis they faced. They varied in their credibility and the material incentives facing their targets, producing a range of impacts on international relations. The evidence I found indicating the importance of these conditions, and their impact on power politics, strongly supports my theory.

Yet, these case studies do not exhaust all possibilities for the conditions I theorized. All three cases were examples of states using religious appeals. Examining cases in which states did not use religious appeals, even when one may expect them to do so, can demonstrate the importance of variations in my theorized conditions. Additionally, the cases were mostly intermediate examples of religious appeals' impact. Expanding the number of cases would test whether credibility and material incentives affect religious appeals' success or failure in mobilizing international coalition action. This chapter thus fills in the missing cells of my theory, improving its explanatory power (see tables 5.1a and 5.1b).[1]

I first discuss the negative cases. That is, do my theorized conditions explain when states do not use religious appeals? I demonstrate that Saudi Arabia did not use religious appeals in all international crises during the 1960s,

## EXPANDING THE ANALYSIS    111

*Table 5.1a*    Expanded tests of religious appeals and power politics

|  | MORAL AUTHORITY OF RELIGION | |
| --- | --- | --- |
| IDEOLOGICAL CRISIS | *HIGH* | *LOW* |
| *Yes* | **Saudi Arabia, 1960s; US, global war on terrorism; Russia, post-2012** | European states, global war on terrorism |
| *No* | Saudi Arabia, 1960s Bahrain tensions | Conventional geopolitics |

*Note:* Bolded entries are chapters in this book.

*Table 5.1b*    Expanded cases on the use of religious appeals

|  | MATERIAL INCENTIVES TO JOIN COALITION | |
| --- | --- | --- |
| CREDIBLE WIELDER | *YES* | *NO* |
| *Yes* | Iran and the Middle East; The Vatican and the Syrian civil war | **Saudi Arabia, 1960s; Russia and America/Western Europe** |
| *No* | **United States, global war on terrorism; China, Confucius Institutes and Belt and Road Initiative** | Iraq, Operation Desert Storm; Thai-Cambodia border dispute |

*Note:* Bolded entries are chapters in this book.

deploying them based on the ideological nature of the crisis. I also show that European states—for whom religion has a lower moral authority—did not rely as heavily on religious engagement in their counterterrorism policies. I then discuss the other examples of religious appeals' impact. I first discuss attempts to use religious appeals that failed: Saddam Hussein's Islamic appeals during Operation Desert Storm and Thai and Cambodian appeals to Buddhism during their border dispute. I then discuss two successful cases in which the wielder was credible and the targets had a material incentive to cooperate. One was Pope Francis's international mobilization against military action in Syria in 2013, and the other was Iran's formation of a revolutionary coalition in the Middle East after the 1979 revolution. I also provide an additional case to strengthen all cells of my typology: specifically, I discuss China's Confucian outreach as an example of low credibility and material incentives.

# Expanded Analysis: When States Use Religious Appeals

I first demonstrate that the moral authority of religion and ideological nature of international crises influences whether states use religious appeals in power

112    **CHAPTER 5**

politics. While there are numerous such cases, I return to cases I have already explored. During the 1960s, Saudi Arabia became involved in several crises that were less ideologically charged than its struggle with Egypt; as expected, the regime did not turn to religious appeals. Likewise, during the global war on terrorism, many European states faced a similar ideologically charged threat from al-Qaeda and ISIS. Yet, as religion had a lower moral authority in their politics, their counterterrorism efforts relied less on religious engagement than did those of the United States. I present each in this section, drawing in part on the primary research I conducted for the corresponding chapters.

## Saudi Arabia in the 1960s: No Religious Appeals When Is Not Ideologically Charged

The high moral authority of religion in Saudi Arabia's politics has been a constant throughout its history. This does not translate into a uniformly Islamic foreign policy, however. The extent to which Saudi Arabia has drawn on or mobilized Islam in its dealings with other states has varied greatly based on whether it faces an ideological challenge in a crisis.

We can see some of this in Saudi interactions with Iran during a tense episode over the independence of Bahrain.[2] Iran claimed the territory, while Saudi Arabia supported a referendum on the country's fate. This nearly erupted into conflict when Iranian forces seized Saudi workers on an oil rig in waters Iran claimed were disputed. The tensions threatened to derail relations between these two key US allies. Additionally, Iran cancelled a visit with the Saudis over what the shah called Saudi "teeth-baring."[3]

As they were geographically proximate states vying for regional influence, Saudi Arabia could have drawn on religious appeals in order to mobilize support among other states. It did not, however: Saudi officials instead used conventional diplomatic tools. For example, in a meeting between a US consulate official and a Saudi diplomat in January 1968, the Saudis referred to their "legal right" to continue drilling in the disputed waters.[4] Later that month, the US ambassador met with Rashad Pharaon, an adviser to King Faisal, and Ahmad Yamani, the minister of petroleum. In response to a US suggestion that Saudi Arabia issue conciliatory statements toward Iran, Pharaon said this was "fully in accord" with the Saudi government's "thinking," but the king could not "in dignity make [a] public statement" about the dispute.[5] These statements read more like conventional diplomatic wrangling than the Islamic appeals that suffused Saudi discourse on Egypt.

The tensions eventually died down through patient diplomacy. This included a meeting between Saudi officials and Manouchehr Eqbal, a former

EXPANDING THE ANALYSIS     113

Iranian prime minister who ran the national oil company. Eqbal worked with Saudi officials to negotiate an acceptable border, while Faisal—according to an August 1968 US memo—"made [a] favorable impression" on Eqbal by "describing the Communist threat" the two countries faced.[6]

A major difference between Egypt and Iran was the ideological nature of the challenge Saudi Arabia faced. Iran and Saudi Arabia were both allies of the United States, but they were bound by more than that. Both states were monarchies that opposed revolutionary movements; while Iran was majority Persian it did worry about Gamal Abdel Nasser Hussein's Arab nationalism due to its Arab minority. Thus, Saudi policymakers did not perceive a challenge to their regime or ideology when Iran raised antagonistic claims over Bahrain. As a result, the crisis did not become ideologically charged and Saudi policymakers likely saw little value in turning to religious appeals in order to undermine Iran's position.

## European States in the Global War on Terrorism: No Religious Appeals with a Low Religious Moral Authority

European states' behavior during the global war on terrorism diverged from that of the United States. This is due partly to the differing moral authority of religion in many of these states. While Western European and Scandinavian countries are historically Christian, and many still have established churches, the level of public religiosity is very low.[7] Accordingly, religion has less of an impact on politics and society in these countries.[8]

These states' ambivalence toward religion is apparent in their approach to their Muslim minorities. Many did little to help these populations integrate into society or express their faith publicly, while at times there were high profile efforts to remove religious expression from the public square, which tended to have the biggest impact on Muslims.[9] This combination of marginalization and limited religious expression led to significant grievances among many Muslims in Europe, leading some of them to embrace extremism.[10]

This situation influenced these states' counterterrorism strategies. Many European states did "securitize" their Muslim populations, viewing them as potential counterterrorism threats.[11] But they did not turn to religion as a tool to combat terrorism to the same extent as the United States. European counterterrorism discourse tends to focus on poverty and social alienation, while US discourse focuses more directly on Islamist ideology: the EU also emphasizes the importance of changing foreign policies in order to address Muslim grievances, rather than engaging in Islamic debates—as seen in US discourse.[12]

114    **CHAPTER 5**

Additionally, even after the EU began to address religion as a potential aspect of countering violent extremism, it "remains an elusive topic in institutional documents . . . political discourse and policy instruments." This has led to a "hollowing of religion" in European counterterrorism efforts.[13] This is apparent when reviewing official documents. The 2020 EU counterterrorism agenda emphasized combating extremist ideologies online and supporting local communities but did not specifically point to religious engagement as a tool to do so.[14] A 2015 counterterrorism strategy had a similar focus.[15]

Several of the experts I interviewed for the US chapter suggested this situation has to do with European discomfort with the role of religion in politics and statecraft. One expert noted that the UK's Prevent countering violent extremism program "seesawed back and forth" over whether to engage with Islamist groups due to concerns over their clash with "British values."[16] Another noted that the United States was "ahead of the curve" on religious engagement as a way to combat extremism, while European states "had differences in how they understood the threat" and did less to engage with Muslim communities.[17]

There are a few exceptions to this, although they prove the rule. One expert pointed to engagement with faith-based organizations among Muslim communities in the Western Balkans as an important part of countering violent extremism efforts.[18] As a result, this was the "only region where there was an emphasis on faith-based organizations as distinct from civil society." Yet, this region is distinct from much of the rest of Europe for the prominent role Islam plays in its politics.[19] Likewise, another expert noted that Hungary was eager to "jump on board" with religious freedom promotion when it is framed in the context of Christian persecution.[20] Hungary under Viktor Orban is likewise unique for its fusion of right-wing Christian beliefs and political authority. Finally, Mohammed el-Sannousi noted that US Offices of International Religious Freedom and Religion and Global Affairs efforts inspired European countries to set up their own offices for religious freedom and religious dialogue.[21] These efforts, however, were separate from security policies in these states.

## Expanded Analysis: When Religious Appeals Have an Impact

Thus, in line with my theory, variations in the moral authority of religion and ideological nature of crises influence whether states use religious appeals in power politics. My theory similarly explains the range of impacts of these religious appeals on power politics. While I am not relying on a strict case comparison in this book, these additional cases can further demonstrate the

## EXPANDING THE ANALYSIS    115

plausibility of my theory by providing more evidence that would be unlikely if I was wrong. First, I provide two cases of failed attempts that correspond with low credibility and few material incentives: Saddam Hussein's attempts to rally support in Operation Desert Storm, and the Thai-Cambodian border dispute. Next I provide two successful cases that corresponded to high credibility and material incentives: the Vatican's intervention against military action in Syria in 2013, and Iran's post-1979 Middle East influence. Finally, I provide one additional case of low credibility and material incentives, as that category was underrepresented in the main cases: China's Confucius Institutions and the Belt and Road Initiative (BRI).

## Failed Attempts: Low Credibility and Lacking Material Incentives

There are many failed instances of countries appealing to religion in order to gain support in international crises. While their attempts at collective mobilization did not fail *because* the religious appeals were unsuccessful, the lack of impact from the religious appeals contributed to the ultimate failure. I provide two cases that vary greatly but share the conditions I theorized for such unsuccessful attempts: Saddam Hussein's efforts to organize Muslim states in opposition to Operation Desert Storm, and rival Thai and Cambodian efforts to frame their border dispute in religious terms in order to gain international support.

### Saddam Hussein and Operation Desert Storm

In the 1990s, a dominant Saudi Arabia faced a new challenger—Iraq. Saudi Arabia had been supportive of Iraq throughout the 1980s as it was fighting another Saudi rival, the Islamic Republic of Iran. But Iraq's leader, Saddam Hussein, was a secular Arab nationalist who repressed Islamic activism at home. He also desired a larger leadership role in the region. After the Iran–Iraq War ended in stalemate, Hussein hoped to capitalize on his regional prestige and revive his economy by seizing Kuwait and its significant oil wealth. His invasion of the country—a mutual neighbor with Saudi Arabia—threatened the Saudis, who worried Hussein may have designs on their territory and that his control of Kuwait would, in the words of a Saudi royal, threaten "the independence of Saudi Arabia, and indeed the whole Arab Gulf."[22]

The Saudis responded by requesting help from the United States, but also by countering Iraq's invasion—and Hussein's popularity—with religious appeals. Saudi Arabia requested US troops deploy to Saudi soil: this was controversial

116    **CHAPTER 5**

due to the presence of Islam's holiest sites in this territory and the fact that Saudi Arabia was asking for help from an outside power to defeat someone many in the region saw a hero. In response, Saudi Arabia's most senior Islamic cleric issued a fatwa calling Saddam Hussein the "enemy of God," and defined the struggle with him as a holy one; Saudi Arabia had also issued an earlier fatwa authorizing the presence of non-Muslim forces in the country.[23]

Iraq countered with Islamic appeals of its own. Hussein had already issued an Islamic challenge to Saudi Arabia, organizing a gathering of Islamic clerics who denounced Saudi Arabia's ties to the United States.[24] As the crisis progressed, he presented himself as a defender of Islam and the Arab people. He compared himself to Saladin, the Crusades-era Islamic leader.[25] And, after the war, he built mosques throughout Iraq to demonstrate his Islamic credentials, including the "Mother of all battles" mosque with missile-shaped minarets.[26]

Yet, Iraq was unable to turn regional states against Saudi Arabia. The United States decided to intervene in support of Saudi Arabia, and the UN Security Council authorized a military mission. The US-led coalition included states from around the world, including most states in the Middle East. The only regional entities to support Iraq were Jordan and the Palestine Liberation Organization (PLO), although most believe their support had little to do with Islam. The PLO's support was likely motivated by Saddam's antagonistic stance toward Israel and his support for the organization.[27] Jordan's support was more complicated, a combination of fear of Iraqi attacks and the popularity of Saddam Hussein in Jordan, especially among Palestinians.[28] The latter may have been due to his religious appeals, although his earlier stance as an Arab nationalist seems to have had more of an effect. Either way, Jordan only refrained from joining the US coalition: it did not come to Iraq's aid. The coalition easily defeated Iraqi forces in Kuwait.

The failure of Iraq's religious appeals corresponded to its low credibility and the material disincentives for states to join its coalition. Saddam Hussein had repressed Islamists in his country as a threat to his rule and out of fear of the Shia majority's ties with Iran. It is therefore unlikely Muslim audiences saw him as an authentic champion of Islamic causes, whatever their concerns about Saudi ties to the United States. In addition to this, the recent end of the Cold War left the United States as the remaining world superpower. Middle Eastern states thus had an incentive to get on the United States' good side and avoid antagonizing it. These material disincentives combined with Hussein's low credibility to limit the impact of his religious appeals.

It should be noted, however, that Iraq's status increased while Saudi Arabia faced intensified criticism for its failure to live up to Arab and Islamic standards. The continued unpopularity of the United States and the punishing

EXPANDING THE ANALYSIS     117

sanctions on Iraq burnished Hussein's image as an Arab champion standing up to outside aggressors. His symbolic support for Islam granted him some religious appeal: as one supportive Islamic cleric later said, Hussein was "the symbol of belief for all Muslims."[29] Meanwhile, Saudi Arabia faced fierce criticism from domestic Islamic reformists as well as transnational militant groups like the newly formed al-Qaeda. Some of this was due to its attempted religious defense of its policies.[30] This made the Saudis wary of crossing Hussein, such as when the United States sought Saudi support for missile strikes against Iraq in the late 1990s.[31] This case raises some questions about the longer-term impact of religious appeals, and their ability to shift the nature of political discourse, which I will address in the conclusion.

## PREAH VIHEAR TEMPLE DISPUTE

Another example of a failed religious appeal came from a long-running border dispute between Thailand and Cambodia.[32] As part of its colonial project in Southeast Asia, France forced Siam to sign a treaty establishing the border with what was then French Indochina. Siam (now Thailand) later attempted to change this agreement, but the French refused. When Cambodia became independent, these borders persisted. However, Thailand occupied a disputed area, the Preah Vihear Temple. This temple was built by the Khmer Empire. It was initially a Hindu site but was later converted to a Buddhist temple. In the 1960s, the International Court of Justice (ICJ) ruled that the site belonged to Cambodia: Thailand handed it over, but kept control of the adjacent land.[33]

The uneasy truce broke down in the early 2000s. In 2002, Cambodia nominated the temple for designation as a UN Educational, Scientific, and Cultural Organization (UNESCO) World Heritage site, with the site receiving this designation—as a Cambodian property—in 2008.[34] This set off protests in Thailand, which spread into the temple complex. By 2011, growing tensions led to an outbreak of hostilities along the now militarized border.[35] These tensions were accompanied by protests on both sides that included Buddhist rituals. The Cambodian first lady led a ritual on the temple grounds: Thai soldiers, in turn, feared the rituals were directed toward them and nationalist Thai political parties held rival rituals.[36] Thailand appealed for support from the Association of Southeast Asian Nations (ASEAN), but that body initially remained passive in the conflict and later attempted a neutral mediation.[37] Each country also appealed to international bodies for support: Cambodia called on the UN Security Council to act against Thailand, while Thailand petitioned the ICJ to change its 1962 ruling.[38] Neither were successful, and the ICJ eventually negotiated a ceasefire between the two countries.[39]

## 118    CHAPTER 5

While this differs from the use of religion in other cases in this book, we can approach it as a failed use of religious appeals during power politics. The fighting was not over religion, but each side appealed to their own religious traditions and connections to the temple as they tried to gain an edge over their rival and gain international support. Other Buddhist states—and international cultural bodies like UNESCO—did not see either of them as credible defenders of their religious tradition, however. Moreover, regional states had little material incentive to involve themselves in this border dispute. The religious appeals thus failed to mobilize international collective action.

The states were not directly appealing to religion when asking for help: instead they were asking for international and regional support in defense of their religion-related claims. This difference in the nature of religious appeals may raise some questions about my focus in this book. All other cases involve Abrahamic religions, specifically Christianity and Islam. This may suggest that religious appeals work or manifest differently across different religious traditions. I will discuss this further in the conclusion.

## Successful Attempts: High Credibility and Material Incentives

Examples of completely successful religious appeals in power politics are rare. As I will further discuss in the next chapter, the complex and unintended effects of religious appeals tend to override their expected effects. Yet, we can find a few examples that correspond to my theorized conditions. One is the Vatican's opposition to military action against Syria during its civil war. The other is postrevolutionary Iran's ability to craft a coalition in the Middle East, partly through appealing to shared faith.

### Pope Francis and the Syrian Civil War

Pope Francis assumed office in 2013 as the world faced a host of problems. He worked quickly to address them, calling on states to fight poverty, attempting to soothe polarization over cultural issues, and generally increasing the prominence of the Vatican among Catholics and non-Catholics alike. He also became involved in international power politics through his intervention in the Syrian civil war. Depending on one's perspective, this is either a case of a successful mobilization of an international coalition for peace, or a successful demobilization of an international coalition meant to punish Syria's government for its human rights abuses.

By 2013, the Syrian civil war had raged for two years. Beginning with Arab Spring protests that spread and became violent, the country was torn apart by competing rebel groups, the Syrian government, and eventually ISIS. As rebel groups gained ground on the Syrian government, Syrian president Bashar al-Assad turned to more brutal means of controlling the country. This included the August 2013 chemical weapons attack on rebel-held areas outside of Damascus: the attack—with the nerve agent sarin—led to between 200 and 1,200 deaths. This crossed the "red line" President Obama claimed would necessitate US action, and the United States and France began discussing a potential military action against Syria.

Pope Francis loudly opposed such an action.[40] He addressed world leaders at the G20, imploring them to pursue a negotiated settlement instead of war.[41] He called for a cease-fire, delivery of humanitarian aid, and an end to any support for rebel groups.[42] He also explicitly connected this to the Catholic faith, organizing peace vigils at the Vatican and incorporating it into his Christmas message.[43] Ultimately, Assad was spared. Popular opposition to international action, combined with wariness among US and other leaders of getting involved in another prolonged conflict in the Middle East, led to continued support for a peace process. Unfortunately, this meant the civil war continued for several more years, culminating effectively in Assad's victory.

This successful use of religious appeals to mobilize an international coalition against military action—or break up a military coalition, an ambiguity I will discuss below—relates to the conditions I theorized for religious appeals' impacts. Even early in his reign, Pope Francis was incredibly popular with people of all faiths. Many saw him as a consistent and deep voice on religious affairs.[44] His religious appeals thus had significant credibility. Additionally, there were clear material incentives for states to back down from military action in Syria. Western publics were not enthusiastic about getting further involved in the Middle East: additionally, Syria's government was backed by both Iran and Russia, raising the risk of broader hostilities.[45] These two factors combined to leave Pope Francis's appeals effective.

However, this does raise some ambiguity about the impacts of religious appeals. That is, while I use Goddard and Nexon's typology of integrating and fragmenting goals in power politics, in practice it can be hard to differentiate between the two.[46] A religious appeal may simultaneously integrate a coalition and fragment rival groupings. In the Syria case, Pope Francis was both building a coalition opposed to intervention while breaking apart the coalition forming to launch an intervention. I will address the implications of this in the conclusion.

120    **CHAPTER 5**

## Iran and the Middle East

Postrevolutionary Iran is another example of religious appeals successfully crafting international coalitions. Prior to the Iranian revolution, Iran had aligned with the United States. When the shah was removed from power and the Islamic republic established, Iranian leaders began issuing appeals for regional and global groups to join them in their revolutionary cause. As Roy noted, Islamist ideologues in Iran saw "the Shiite community in the way Marx thought of the proletariat: a particular group that brings about the emancipation of all humanity."[47]

Despite the strain the new Islamic republic was under, thanks to Iraq's invasion and the long Iran–Iraq War, Iran was able to form a regional coalition. Moreover, this was partly due to these religious appeals. Syria aligned itself with Iran both materially and religiously: the Syrian regime had Iranian religious authorities declare Syrian Alawites as Shia in order to deepen their ties.[48] This persisted through the Arab Spring and the Syrian civil war, with Iranian forces helping to support Syria's government. Shia populations in Saudi Arabia and Bahrain rose up in protest against their Sunni rulers in response to Iranian calls.[49] Iran also backed Hizballah in Lebanon and Hamas in the Palestinian territories: despite the latter being Sunni, they shared an opposition to Israel both of which framed in religious terms.[50] Moreover, Iran's outreach to Shia groups beyond these militants has led it to successfully "[integrate] foreign Shiite minorities under the guidance of the imam."[51] Iran's regional coalition broadened after the US invasion of Iraq, when newly powerful Shia political forces—initially directed by their religious leaders—granted Iran significant influence over the country.[52]

This corresponds to Iran's credibility and the material incentives it provided to coalition partners. Ayatollah Ruholla Khomeini was popular among Shia around the world for his activism against the Shah: he became a symbol of the revolution, increasing his appeal. This was only strengthened when Iran fought Iraq to a cease-fire, which the Iranian regime described as a religious conflict.[53] Islamic appeals from Iran were thus more credible than those from Saddam Hussein's Iraq. At the same time, regional states and nonstate actors had a material incentive to work with Iran. Iran was relatively powerful, able to support states like Syria that had been dependent on Soviet aid. Iran could also provide material and logistical backing to terrorist groups like Hamas and Hizballah. The combination of the two contributed to Iran's religious appeals—intended to form a revolutionary regional coalition with Iran as its leader—resonating with domestic audiences and convincing leaders to align themselves with Iran.

I should note that, even in this successful case, the use of religious appeals may have backfired on Iran. Its initial success in prompting protests among Shia populations led these regimes to crack down even harder on their societies. Iranian religious appeals intensified the United States' sense of threat from Iran, contributing to their long antagonistic relationship. And it has caused Saudi Arabia to fear any apparent gain by Iran, leading the Saudis to form a counterrevolutionary coalition to undermine Iranian influence. Moreover, some experts have argued that, despite the universal nature of Iran's revolutionary claims, its impact has been limited to Shia societies.[54]

## Intermediate Case: Low Credibility and Material Incentives

While I am not attempting to provide a comprehensive overview of them in this book, I do want to sufficiently cover each category of religious appeals' impacts. As we only have one case of religious appeals' intermediate impacts from low credibility and material incentives, I provide another one here to further strengthen my argument. Specifically, I discuss China's efforts to build support for its BRI through its Confucius Institutes.

China's BRI is an infrastructure investment project that has become a major part of China's regional diplomacy.[55] Xi Jinping, general secretary of the Chinese Communist Party, announced the initiative in 2013 as a network of transportation and energy routes through former Soviet republics and into South and Southeast Asia. Over sixty countries have signed on to various infrastructure projects China is funding. While China has attempted to present this initiative as one of mutual gain, many other countries have been wary of China's intention. India and Japan both worry about China's growing regional influence and have attempted to provide an alternative to Chinese resources. States outside the region, such as the United States and France, have warned others of China's aggressive intentions and attempted to draw states away from China such as through the Trans-Pacific Partnership.

One of the means through which China has attempted to mobilize international support for the BRI is appeals to its Confucian heritage. While China is officially a nonreligious state, it has accepted Confucianism as an important part of its heritage. Accordingly, it has turned to Confucianism and other elements of Chinese culture as part of its push for the BRI. For example, in May 2021, China released a new edition of Confucius's sayings in the language of several countries that are part of the BRI.[56] China has also drawn on its Confucius Institute program to expand support for the BRI. China began funding Confucius Institutes in 2004: these centers worked with universities around

## 122    CHAPTER 5

the world to provide Mandarin language instruction and resources for the study of China. China views these as a way to expand its "soft power," by increasing interest in Chinese culture and history.[57] There is also some evidence that China has directed this program toward mobilizing support for the BRI. Some have noted the Confucius Institutes may help overcome language barriers, while another study found that Confucius Institutes eased the adoption of BRI initiatives.[58] Indeed, official Chinese government conferences for BRI participants include discussions of the important role Confucius Institutes are expected to play in this initiative.[59]

The combination of potential BRI funding and the resources made available by the Confucius Institutes has led many states to sign on to these programs, but the ideological aspect of China's efforts and China's broader credibility have raised concerns. The spread of the Confucius Institutes has occurred in the context of China's aggressiveness on the South China Sea and Taiwan, as well as continued human rights abuses. These human rights issues include its widespread religious repression targeting Uighur Muslims, Christians, and new religious groups like the Falun Gong. Accordingly, many worry that China will use Confucius Institutes to undermine opposition to its domestic and foreign policies.[60] The US government has acted on these concerns, denying funding to US universities that host Confucius Institutes without sufficient oversight.[61] Some have accused Australian universities of limiting free speech in order to maintain ties with Chinese funders.[62] And Germany's education ministry called for an end to cooperation with the program.[63]

I would argue that this is a similar situation as US religious engagement during the global war on terrorism. In both cases, there were significant material incentives to go along with the collective mobilization. China is providing both academic research and infrastructure funds to states that cooperate with its international efforts. However, China is not a credible actor when it comes to religious and philosophical engagement and harmony. This is due to its domestic policies—China is one of the most religiously repressive states in the world—and its increasingly aggressive foreign policies. As a result, any apparent coalition it formed proved to be shaky. Moreover, China's attempt to use religious appeals to build international support backfired, as the ideological underpinnings of its investment and educational aid increased international wariness and opened up China to critiques over its record.

This case thus provides further support for my theory. When states use religious appeals in power politics that involve low credibility but material incentives, they produce weak coalitions and can easily lose control of the religious narrative. This case, like the others I discussed in this chapter, may raise some additional questions for my theory, however. As with the Thai-Cambodian border dispute, it raises questions about the extent to which religious appeals function similarly outside of non-Abrahamic contexts. Moreover, the possibility that China's international efforts may have gone more smoothly if framed merely as economic interactions—rather than ideological partnerships—reinforces my theme of unintended consequences of religious appeals. I will address both of these in the next chapter.

## Conclusion

This chapter strengthened support for my theory by demonstrating that it holds up beyond my three main cases. The use of religious appeals varied based on the conditions I theorized: the moral authority of religion and the ideologically charged nature of international crises. When Saudi Arabia faced a nonideological crisis over the independence of Bahrain, it relied on conventional statecraft not Islamic appeals. And when European states with a low moral authority of religion crafted counterterrorism policies in response to al-Qaeda, they did not emphasize religious engagement to the same extent as did the United States. The impacts of religious appeals also depended on the conditions I emphasize: the credibility of the wielder and the material incentives facing the targets. In both Iraq's Islamic appeals during Operation Desert Storm and the Thai-Cambodian border crisis, the states launching religious appeals had little credibility and there was little incentive for other states to join them. They thus failed. By contrast, in both the Vatican's intervention in the Syrian civil war and Iran's Middle East influence, the Vatican and Iran had greater credibility and offered material incentives to the targets of their appeals. These appeals succeeded in organizing collective action. Finally, China's establishment of Confucius Institutes to support its BRI had a moderate impact: China offered material incentives to states that cooperated with it, but its low credibility on religious issues led to charges of hypocrisy and backlash.

These cases further highlighted a theme throughout this book. Religious appeals may seem easier, cheaper, and even more morally satisfying tools in power politics than military threats or economic coercion. They tend to slip out of their wielders' control, however, causing as many problems as they solve. I will explore the implications of this aspect of religious appeals in the next, and concluding, chapter.

# Conclusion

## How We Can Better Study and Leverage Religion in International Relations

In *Monty Python and the Holy Grail*, King Arthur and his knights did manage to defeat their foe—the Rabbit of Caerbannog—with the holy hand grenade of Antioch. But this did not solve all their problems: they soon faced a greater monster and a series of puzzles. The police then arrested them for creating a disturbance. Their turn to religion as a tool in their struggle was an unwieldy solution, as they lacked an understanding of the broader religious issues into which they were wading.

This may be pushing the metaphor a bit too far—and Monty Python fans may debate my interpretation of this scene—but states that have turned to religious appeals in power politics have experienced similar fates. Saudi Arabia managed to unsettle Egypt and other Arab nationalist states, but failed to form its Islamic Pact, instead intensifying hostilities in the Middle East. The United States eased coordination of international counterterrorism efforts with its religious engagement during the global war on terrorism, but wariness of US intentions remained while it wasted resources on unfamiliar programs. And Russia managed to gain support from far-right forces in Europe and the United States, which pressured their governments to allow Russia's aggressive policies toward its "near abroad." But, in the process, Russia increased hostility to its actions, hardening some states' stances.

Clearly, religious appeals are a useful but complicated tool in international power politics. Just like a holy hand grenade, when tossed into a tense situation they have an impact, but it is hard to predict where the shrapnel will land. In this concluding chapter I draw together the observations from the case studies to demonstrate this. I then apply these findings to a set of more current events and discuss the book's broader theoretical and policy implications.

## Validating My Theory of Religious Appeals' Nature and Impact

The starting point for this book is the observation that states frequently draw on religious appeals as a tool in power politics: the attempt to form or break apart international coalitions during an international crisis. States believe (or hope) that incorporating religion into their foreign policy can help them gain allies in international struggles. States are not attempting to spread their religious ideals and values. Instead, it is an intentional deployment of religion as an instrument of power in power politics.

The case selection in this book validates the conditions I theorized as affecting states' use of religious appeals. The first is the moral authority of religion in a state's politics. When religion has a higher moral authority, political debates revolve around religion and religious arguments resonate with domestic audiences. Moreover, leaders more frequently turn to religion to justify their policies and are more likely to see religion as a useful political tool. The second is the nature of the international crisis a state is facing. When a state faces an ideologically charged crisis, their own ideology and identity are threatened as well as their material interests, and they are more likely to incorporate ideological appeals into their struggles with rival states. When both conditions are present, these ideological appeals take the form of religious appeals meant to mobilize friendly coalitions or break apart rival ones. I demonstrated that these religious appeals were serious and strategic foreign policy tools that corresponded to these conditions across the case studies. Saudi Arabia, the United States, and Russia—despite being very different in many areas—all drew on religious appeals under these conditions. Policymakers viewed them as a potentially valuable foreign policy tool, even though they were connected to the importance of religion in their societies. Moreover, when one of these conditions was absent, states did not use religious appeals in their foreign policy. In the case of both Saudi tensions with Iran over Bahrain and the European response to 9/11, the absence of both a high moral authority for religion and an ideologically charged crisis led states to adopt alternate power political tools to religious appeals.

The cases also varied on the conditions I theorized as influencing the impact of religious appeals—while the within-case analysis demonstrated the

126    CONCLUSION

mechanisms through which religious appeals mattered—validating this part of my theory as well. The first is the credibility of the state wielding the religious appeals. The second is the material incentives facing the targets of the appeals. When both are present, the appeals resonate with their target, which is encouraged to join the wielder's coalition. When both are absent, the appeals are overridden by other priorities. The intermediate conditions have more complicated effects: a credible wielder and targets facing material disincentives lead to generally intensified international tensions, while material incentives combined with a wielder lacking credibility lead to convenient alignment and a possible loss of control over the religious discourse.

We saw this play out in the case studies. Saudi Arabia in the 1960s was credible on Islamic issues, but target states faced material incentives to avoid antagonizing Egypt. As a result, the Islamic Pact did not come together, but states in the region generally grew more tense and wary in the run-up to the Six-Day War. The United States in the global war on terrorism lacked credibility on religious engagement with Muslims, but both Muslim states and societies had an incentive to work with the United States. There was thus some cooperation on counterterrorism, but general unfamiliarity with the nature and impact of US-led programs even as some authoritarian states adopted US religious rhetoric for their own purposes. And Russia was credible in its appeals to "traditional values," but its targets faced mixed material incentives. While Russia generated some support for its actions, it also antagonized foes.

The additional shorter cases I explored further validated my theory. During Operation Desert Storm, Saddam Hussein appealed to Islam to counter the US-led coalition against his invasion of Kuwait. Likewise, during the Thai-Cambodian border dispute, both states attempted to frame their desired control of a disputed Buddhist temple as a religious issue in order to gain international support. Both failed due to a lack of credibility and material incentives. By contrast, Iran managed to form a coalition in the Middle East by issuing revolutionary Islamic appeals. Likewise, the Vatican successfully opposed an incipient military coalition against Syria after its chemical attacks on civilians by appealing to religious values. In both cases the credibility of the state issuing the appeals and the material incentives that accompanied it led to the success of the international collective mobilization. Finally, the case of China's Confucius Institutes—one means through which it has attempted to build international support for its Belt and Road Initiative—further demonstrates the intermediate case of low credibility with material incentives. While several states have responded positively to Chinese outreach, its lack of credibility has also opened it up to backlash and charges of hypocrisy.

Alternative explanations for the nature and impact of religious appeals in power politics are insufficient. The religion skeptic argument would be unable to explain all the evidence of states adopting religious appeals as a serious foreign policy tool, or the noticeable impact they had on the relevant international crises. Some may shift to an instrumentalist critique, that leaders did not "really" believe in these religious appeals. As I have discussed in each chapter, however, this counterargument is incoherent. Alternately, such skeptics could claim the impacts I found from religious appeals were not significant enough to indicate their importance: I will address this below. At the same time, my findings also undermine the religion triumphalist counterargument. These religious appeals were strategic tools, just like conventional military or economic instruments. They do not represent the transformation of states' foreign policy due to rising religiosity. Likewise, their complex and mixed effects also indicate that these religious appeals are not overriding material concerns in international relations.

These findings provide broader insight into how we should study the primary countries I analyzed in this book. Religion—in the form of religious appeals—has clearly served as a foreign policy tool for the United States, Russia, and Saudi Arabia. Even though its effects are often unintended, the impacts we see from these religious appeals mean analyses of these countries that ignore religion are faulty. In fact, I would argue that it is because religious appeals' impacts are often unpredictable that scholars and policy experts should always address them in their analyses of these states. Despite the costs it incurs, states keep turning to religion as a tool in power politics and we must understand that.

Additionally, religious appeals will be a significant aspect of power politics beyond these cases, with specifics mattering based on the conditions I theorized. That is, this is not just a story about Saudi Arabia, Russia, and the United States. The fact that the mechanisms I theorized were present across diverse conditions, and held up when briefly examining other cases, indicates this is a generalizable relationship. While few would deny that religion matters in international relations, this book should push back on those who would confine it to "low priority" issues or "cheap talk." States will draw on religious appeals as a significant part of their power political efforts, and this can have real impacts on the world. Rather than debating whether religion matters, scholars and policymakers should pay attention to the moral authority of religion in states and the ideological nature of a crisis to predict whether religious appeals will be involved. Likewise, they should look at the credibility of the state issuing the appeals and the material incentives facing the targets to determine their impact.

This book can also tell us something about what effects we are most likely to see from states' use of religious appeals. This is a preliminary takeaway, as

128    CONCLUSION

I did not conduct an exhaustive study of all uses of religious appeals in power politics. But based on the cases analyzed, religious appeals primarily resonate with domestic audiences, who then pressure their leaders to act in line with the policies of the state wielding the appeals. They do not appear to persuade leaders. In both the Saudi and Russian cases, the religious appeals provoked reactions among domestic publics, while leaders generally remained unconvinced. The situation was a little less clear in the US case. US religious appeals did seem to persuade social groups to cooperate with the United States. Muslim leaders, in turn, seemed attracted to US appeals because of the potential they had to defuse and control domestic opposition.

I can also cautiously conclude that religious appeals' primary impact is unintended, rather than beneficial to the wielder. While there were some intended impacts in each case, much of the effect involved heightened tensions, opaque policy formulations, and uncertainty over the nature of the appeals. The qualitative nature of this book is not intended to assess the balance between intended and unintended effects, but in each case the overall impact of religious appeals seemed to be disruptive. There were a few examples of successful uses, but it will be rare to find the perfect combination of religious credibility and positive material incentives. Thus, most religious appeals we observe as part of power politics will be unwieldy and complex.

## Broader Implications

This book can also provide broader implications. First, it can apply to more current events than those I discuss in this book. Second, it can speak both to the broader study of religion and international relations, and efforts to integrate ideas and rhetoric into mainstream security studies. For the former, my findings can reinvigorate the research program by providing guidelines for a more dynamic approach to religion and international relations. For the latter, it can provide an additional example of the importance of ideas and rhetoric, while also prodding scholars to broaden their sense of how ideas and rhetoric matter by returning to classical realist insights about the complex nature of ideals in international relations. My theory does raise a few questions, however, which further research can address.

### Extending the Timeline of the Case Studies

The in-depth case studies allowed me to test my theory's validity, demonstrating the nature and significance of religious appeals in power politics. The ad-

## RELIGION IN INTERNATIONAL RELATIONS 129

ditional minor cases further demonstrated the generalizability of these results. I can further demonstrate this, and the relevance of my theory to current events, by looking at more recent episodes from each of the main case studies. Specifically, I will address the weaponization of international religious freedom (IRF) promotion under the US Trump administration, Saudi Arabia's counterrevolutionary mobilization under Mohammed bin Salman, and Russia's 2022 invasion of Ukraine. In each of these, I will demonstrate the use of religious appeals, and their varying and complicated effects.

After its relative marginalization through the previous two administrations, Donald Trump seemingly made IRF a key part of his foreign policy. The US IRF effort began with the 1999 International Religious Freedom Act that set up an ambassador-level office in the State Department and a governmental watchdog agency, the US Commission on International Religious Freedom (USCIRF). Yet, it was a relatively minor part of US foreign policy throughout the Bush and Obama administrations. The Trump administration, however—via Vice President Mike Pence—promised to make IRF a priority for US foreign policy and granted evangelicals access to his administration and its IRF apparatus.[1]

This led to several concrete changes in US foreign policy focused on building international coalitions to defend religious freedom. The United States appointed former senator Sam Brownback as its ambassador for IRF. Brownback's office organized an International Religious Freedom Summit that included a manifesto in defense of religious freedom many states and social organizations signed.[2] Additionally, high-profile evangelical figures—some part of USCIRF—have organized delegations to Egypt and Saudi Arabia: these states claimed to promote moderation but remained authoritarian with horrible religious freedom records.

Problems emerged due to the issues with the Trump administration's credibility on this issue, however. There was a clear incompatibility between this IRF promotion and Trump's rhetoric on Muslims. Additionally, the delegations to Egypt and Saudi Arabia praised these countries' support for religious freedom, undermining Trump administration credibility on religious issues.[3] This has led to the expected problems with the use of religious appeals in this context. Many of the IRF policies the United States pushed threatened to actually make religious tensions worse, such as its direction of aid specifically to Middle East Christians.[4] And religious freedom—which was initially a bipartisan issue in the United States—has become more partisan, making it harder to craft a similar broad coalition in the future.[5]

The importance of religious appeals continued in Saudi Arabia. Mohammed bin Salman, as crown prince and effective ruler of Saudi Arabia, oversaw

130   CONCLUSION

a similar shift in the country's approach to religion. Mohammed bin Salman established Vision 2030, a plan to transform the Saudi economy and society. This included diversifying the Saudi economy away from a reliance on oil. It also included social reforms, such as expanding entertainment opportunities, women's rights, and tourism. Mohammed bin Salman did not loosen the regime's hold over the country, however: instead, he cracked down on political dissent and potential rivals within the royal family.[6] He leveraged this into greater connections with the United States as a force for "moderation," as I discussed above.

This occurred during the Arab Spring, however, in which protests shook long-standing regimes and seemed to favor revolutionary Islamists the Saudi regime feared. As a result, Mohammed bin Salman also attempted to set up an international coalition of counterrevolutionary conservative states and undermine revolutionary forces. Saudi Arabia drew closer to other conservative monarchies, such as Jordan and Morocco, with these states exploring membership in the Saudi-led Gulf Cooperation Council.[7] Saudi Arabia also organized a blockade of Qatar in an attempt to rein in that state's tolerance of revolutionary actors and friendliness with Iran. Additionally, Saudi Arabia intervened in Arab Spring turmoil to keep Islamists out of power, including in Egyptian elections, the Syrian civil war, and the Yemeni civil war. The latter became a proxy war between Saudi Arabia and Iran and a humanitarian disaster.

The complex incentives facing Middle Eastern states and Mohammed bin Salman's low credibility on religious issues complicated the impact of these religious appeals. Unlike in the 1960s, the dividing line in Arab Spring-era Middle East politics was not Islamic versus secular but revolutionary versus conservative. The fact that Saudi Arabia was on the latter side, while many Islamists groups were on the former, made it hard for Mohammed bin Salman to gain the same amount of regional prestige as did King Faisal. Meanwhile, Iran, Qatar, and Turkey were also supporting Islamic movements in some form or another. Thus, while Saudi Arabia provided resources to conservative forces, revolutionary groups had an alternate patron. This situation led to a tense and unsettled region. Saudi Arabia managed to form an international coalition, but it was unable to undermine revolutionary movements or their backers. For example, the blockade of Qatar eventually broke down without achieving its stated goals. And the Saudi intervention in Yemen led to a prolonged war that attracted international condemnation and led to a string of attacks on Saudi targets. Additionally, current Saudi politics demonstrate the long-term negative impacts of religious appeals, as Saudi support for political Islam beginning in the 1960s led to the rise of extremist movements that have plagued the country since.

Finally, Russia's religious appeals faced a major test with its 2022 invasion of Ukraine.[8] Russia stated motivations involved "de-Nazifying" Ukraine and preventing it from formally aligning itself with the West.[9] There may also have been a healthy dose of misperception about Russian capabilities and Ukraine's willingness to fight. Additionally, Putin tied the war to his earlier religious rhetoric on Ukraine, pointing to the two countries' historic ties.[10] ROC figures also backed the war in religious terms.[11] The motivation was likely a mix of these, but the war was a chance for Russia's coalition of supporters in the West to stop their governments from taking action on Russia's war.

Yet, the patterns that were coming together with Russia's aggressive appeals to traditional values and attempts to claim authority over Orthodoxy became even more apparent with this war. Some did speak up in support of Russia: both Nigel Farage in Britain and Tucker Carlson in the United States defended Russia and criticized efforts to stop him.[12] Yet, most of the reaction was negative. Many Orthodox voices around the world criticized the invasion, with some Russian Orthodox churches outside of Russia cutting their ties with the ROC.[13] Those Western voices who did support Russia's invasion failed to stop a counter-coalition from forming—led by the Biden administration in the United States—which imposed severe sanctions on the Russian economy. Russia's coalition thus fell apart.

I would argue, however, that this presents not the ineffectiveness of religious appeals but their unpredictable nature. In a way, Russia may have been better off without drawing on the religious appeals. Years of Putin framing his domestic and foreign policies as a revival of "traditional values" and an assault on Western liberalism left many convinced Putin had expansive plans and poses an ideological threat to the West. It thus became harder for Putin to frame the invasion as a discrete action meant to influence Ukraine's alignment, not the beginning of a broader campaign. As a result, the United States took a hard-line stance on Putin's invasion—imposing sanctions and providing arms to Ukraine—while Europe was similarly united in its opposition.

## Reinvigorating the Study of Religion and International Relations

Beyond explaining current events, my findings can also tell us more about how to move the study of religion and international relations forward. The research program on religion and international relations is simultaneously exciting and frustrating. Those arguing for religion's importance managed to overcome mainstream international relations' hostility to and ignorance of religion as a force in international relations. Few now deny that it matters. But this research

132   CONCLUSION

program tends to focus only on a subset of topics in international relations and struggles to engage with the broader field. My approach and findings in this book can provide a set of guidelines to move the study of religion and international relations forward.

I should note that research into religion and international relations has made amazing progress, given this program barely existed two decades ago. Early works presented foundational ideas and generated frameworks for further research on this topic.[14] Research on religion and conflict has uncovered the nuanced ways religion matters in terrorism, civil war, and state repression.[15] Others have demonstrated religion's impact on conflict resolution and peacebuilding.[16] Finally, significant studies have analyzed the shifting border between religion and secularism in the modern international system as well as the tendency of states to "securitize" religious minorities as threats.[17]

Yet, this research program has struggled to influence broader scholarly and policy debates. Some of this is an issue of emphasis. Much work on religion and international relations has looked outside of core security concerns. Granted, this has broadened understandings of what matters in international relations and demonstrated religion's importance. But, by failing to confront these core security issues—like power politics—we marginalize ourselves in the subfield.

However, it goes deeper than that: limitations arise from *how* we study religion. Most studies of religion and international relations approach it as a set of beliefs that guide behavior. That is, most approach religious beliefs and identities as influences on the actions leaders and groups takes. Additionally, studies posit religion as so powerful that it overrides material influences. To be fair, this can be seen in much of my own work. I included religion in analyses as a fixed influence on behavior that I hypothesized would matter more than conventional influences.[18]

Many scholars have noted this as a problem. Pragmatically, it can be difficult to draw a direct line from religious beliefs to political behavior, and scholars have struggled to find clear cases of religion influencing core areas of international relations such as war.[19] Theoretically, treating religion as an inspiring belief system risks ignoring the dynamic nature of religious politics and its complex relationship with material forces.[20]

Moreover, others have adopted such an approach to the study of religion and international relations. Some scholars have approached religion as a set of practices and discourses as much as ideas.[21] Several empirical studies have taken this approach. A study of religious advocacy framed it as "a set of advocacy practices that become the standard tools" for humanitarian actors.[22] Likewise, a study on the roots of religious extremism emphasized blocked ambition among clerical networks, rather than shifting beliefs alone.[23]

## RELIGION IN INTERNATIONAL RELATIONS          133

Yet, the research program has not systematized these studies in order to address the above theoretical concerns. In order for the study of religion and international relations to move forward, scholars must therefore shift our theoretical focus. We should study religion as a tool or interaction rather than a belief or motivation. It did not really matter to my theory whether Vladimir Putin is truly concerned about the sanctity of the ROC, or King Faisal truly wanted all Muslims to unite against secularism. What mattered was that their interactions with other states involved appeals to religion. Other studies should follow this approach to expand the areas in which we can identify religion's impact and deepen our understanding of religion's complexity. The edited volume on religious soft power I discussed earlier in this book, as well as the theoretical takeaways I presented with Bettiza in that volume, are valuable guidelines for such studies.[24]

## Broadening the Study of Ideas in Security Studies

In addition to addressing issues in the study of religion and international relations, this book can also broaden security studies by demonstrating the importance of ideas, rhetoric, and legitimacy. It provides an additional example of rhetoric's importance. It can also push the study of rhetoric and legitimation to take religion more seriously and expand research beyond clear-cut cases of ideas' beneficial effects. Finally, it can allow for greater dialogue with mainstream security studies.

First, this book strengthens the claim that rhetoric and ideas matter in international security. Many of the works I drew on for my theory demonstrated the way policymakers justify their behavior is often as important as the manner in which they deploy their material resources. This book provides another example for this research, thus making it harder for mainstream security studies to focus only on states' rational calculations of material self-interest.

Second, this book can expand such work in international relations. One way it can do this is by encouraging further attention to religion. Most constructivist-inspired work focuses on secular values and concerns. This may be due to biases of scholars, the Western focus of much of this research, or uncertainty in how to address the complexities of religion. Whatever the reason, it is not inevitable. Indeed, Daniel Nexon—who developed the framework on power politics with Stacie Goddard I used in this book—attempted to provide some guidelines for demystifying the study of religion in international relations.[25] This book can demonstrate how to extend work on rhetoric and ideas to religious appeals, strengthening work in this area. Future works on power politics may need to address this.

134    CONCLUSION

Moreover, this book points to the importance of the *process* of power politics as much as the outcome. Goddard and Nexon's framework I use in this book focuses on whether instruments of power integrate or fragment international collective action. The cases in this book, however, demonstrate that the most interesting elements of power politics occur through states' attempts to influence collective action. Additionally, much of policymakers' day-to-day work involves these processes rather than the creation or dissolution of coalitions. Finally, the cases in this book suggest that integration and fragmentation of international collective mobilization can occur simultaneously. Expanding research to focus on this process would increase its richness and policy relevance.

Additionally, this book encourages research on rhetoric in international relations to look beyond clear and beneficial impacts of ideas and rhetoric. This tendency limits the number of cases such scholars can point to in order to support their arguments and makes it easier for skeptics to undermine the importance of ideas and values by pointing to the many cases in which they do not have their intended effect. As we have seen in this book, however, religious appeals intensified tensions and even convenient alignment with wielders' coalitions affected state behavior. It would be a mistake to ignore such phenomena.

This brings us to the final way this book can expand our understanding of ideas in international relations: allowing for greater dialogue across security studies. With the end of the paradigm wars, scholars arguing from a rationalist and materialist foundation rarely engage with scholars focusing on ideas and values. While the paradigm wars grew tedious, at least realist scholars felt compelled to raise and reject constructivist counterarguments, and vice versa. Much current research involves narrower debates. For example, rationalist studies tend to only engage with other rationalist studies while ignoring those focused on ideas and culture. I suspect some of this has to do with a divide in the way scholars approach ideas. Ideas seem to either have purposive and intended impacts on international relations or they are tangential to what really matters. If we formally introduce an intermediate category of effects—like I did here—it may be easier for both sides to find common ground.

## Suggestions for Future Research

Thus, this book provides several implications for the future of the study of both religion and international relations and security studies. Here I present specific suggestions for moving both of these areas forward. First, the study of religion and international relations should follow other work in international relations and adopt a relational framework. As Jackson and Nexon have discussed, there is a move in post-constructivist work away from conceiving of social forces as a driver of international relations. Instead, social forces are the products of actors' behavior, with the focus of analyses the interactions among actors rather than their ideas or the conditions in which they operate.[26] Some studies on religion and international relations have adopted this approach.[27] Research on religion and international relations could more explicitly adopt a relational approach to religion and international relations. For example, a follow-on study to this book could address one of the uncertainties I encountered in the case studies: the way interactions between states and social groups change the salience of religious arguments in international relations.

For those desiring a quantitative approach to the issues I study in this book, scholars could turn to network analysis. While conventional regressions are useful in many contexts, they may not capture the dynamic aspect of religious appeals. Network analysis, however, may. Network analysis looks at the interactions among states and nonstate actors, rather than state-level characteristics alone. It includes descriptive measures of the nature of networks or states' roles and statuses in a network. It can also explain the emergence of networks. Numerous studies in international relations have drawn on this tool to provide a more dynamic analysis of important topics.[28] There have been few examples of studies on religion and international relations applying this approach, although I have suggested it as a potentially useful tool in other works.[29] Future studies could treat religious appeals and other such religious interactions between states as edges in a network, analyzing how they grant certain states influence and transform or provoke international crises.

Network analysis could also be of use to new research on power politics. Network analysis could demonstrate the nature of states' interconnections and means through which states gain influence over others. It could also provide a richer set of data than static alliance or conflict measures, allowing for an analysis of the process of power politics I discussed above. Some works have already turned to this tool—both formally and informally—in order to study international hierarchy and reputation.[30] Future works could extend this to the study of how states create coalitions and even break apart rival groupings. One challenge both uses of network analysis may run into is finding sufficient data, but I have addressed this and presented options in other work.[31] Specifically, machine-generated event datasets allow for more fine-grained data on states' interactions than existing alliance, trade, or diplomatic representation data.

Theoretically, this book can demonstrate the relevance of classical realism. International relations scholars periodically return to this tradition as a way to broaden the relevance of modern rationalist–materialist approaches to realism. As Nexon and I argued, many scholars are overly optimistic about classical realism's ability to analyze religion and other ideational aspects of international

## 136    CONCLUSION

relations.[32] Yet, it does provide more room to study such things than either contemporary realism—which is overly materialistic—or constructivism, which tends to be overly optimistic.[33] Several classical realists argued that ideas and beliefs mattered in international relations. However, they claimed that they mattered as a disruptive force, which states can either use for their own purposes or use without realizing the negative impacts such ideals will have.

We can see this most clearly in Niebuhr's work. In *The Irony of American History*, Rienhold Niebuhr surveyed elements of US culture and history that drive it to, often inappropriately, chase ideals in its foreign policy. Niebuhr focuses on irony, the situation in which "virtue becomes vice through some hidden defect in the virtue."[34] This, he argues, is too often the case. Despite the United States' good intentions, we often create problems for both ourselves and the world due to these idealistic policies slipping out of our control. The United States was "involved in irony because so many of [its] dreams . . . have been cruelly refuted by history": yet, "the irony is increased by the frantic efforts of our idealists to escape this hard reality."[35] Moreover, these problematic aspects of the United States' foreign policies arise from its own virtues. As Niebuhr put it, "the irony in our historic situation is derived from the extravagant emphasis in our culture upon the value and dignity of the individual."[36] Thus, the apparent virtues of the United States cause problems when applied to international relations due to the complexity of the world.

My work on religious appeals is an example of Niebuhr's conception of "irony," and can provide an example for future such works in this area. States used religious appeals to draw on their values while advancing their interests. Yet, this appeal to deep-seated values seems to cause more problems for states than it solves. This could expand beyond the study of religion and international relations. The ironic impact of ideals in power politics falls between the intended and beneficial impacts constructivists theorize, and the tangential and minimal impact modern realists point to. Indeed, some have attempted to expand our understanding of security issues in this manner.[37] Studies could more explicitly use this classical realist framework to explore other cases of states trying to use ideas and values in their foreign policy.

## Other Questions

This book does leave several questions unanswered. Some of these I can address, but others may require further research. First, as I discussed in the previous chapter, the religious appeals I discussed in this book primarily involve Christianity and Islam. This raises a question over whether this phenomenon is confined to Abrahamic religions. "Eastern" religions may not function in the same way as Abrahamic religions, and it is a problem to conflate them under one category. At the same time, forces of globalization and colonialism have standardized religions along Western lines, and certain modern phenomena—such as fundamentalism—seem to occur across all faiths.[38] I would thus argue that religious appeals can serve as a foreign policy tool for any religion but admit that this is up for debate.

Some may also object that religious appeals did not lead to any "real" impacts. That is, they did not start a war or create a formal alliance. Mainstream security studies tends to focus on concrete, material changes in behavior while rejecting more subtle or perceptual phenomena and dynamic aspects of international relations. For example, in their critique of soft balancing, Lieber and Alexander dismissed potential incidents as "diplomatic friction."[39] While their critique of soft balancing was apt, their dismissal of one of the most common elements of international relations seems shortsighted. This greatly limits what international relations scholarship can explain. It also limits its applicability to policymakers, most of whose time is not spent starting wars or creating alliances. Security studies scholars need to broaden their perspective of the world. Some of this is the goal of Goddard, MacDonald, and Nexon's work on power politics.[40] The adoption of network analysis I discuss above is a similar move, emphasizing the importance of changes in connections among states, and intangible measures like centrality or brokerage. Ideally these two developments can work together to demonstrate the importance of the sort of outcomes I found in this book.

Another concern has to do with the possibility of religious appeals changing the nature of discourse and international relations itself. That is, do religious appeals change politics rather than just reflecting existing debates? One could argue that religious appeals are transforming the international context in which they are involved, rather than merely having an impact on states in certain contexts. This makes it harder to isolate their effects. Religious appeals may also increase the domestic moral authority of religion, both in the wielder and target states. One critique of my argument, then, is that it does not go far enough in capturing the dynamic nature of religious appeals in power politics.

I think this is valid, but it is also not a problem for my theory. Such shifts in political discourse and identity occur over long time periods, while my focus here is on the use of religious appeals in a specific interstate crisis. I would argue that religious appeals must be stable in order to have an impact on international relations. But longer term changes will occur. We can see this with Saudi Arabia.

138    CONCLUSION

While Saudi attempts to form an Islamic Pact failed, Egypt's President Nasser's loss in the Six-Day War created an opportunity to Saudi Arabia to expand its influence. Part of this involved its ideological appeal, with political Islam replacing pan-Arabism in the region by the 1970s. Future research could look at the longer-term impacts of the use of religious appeals.

Some may be concerned about the US focus of my case studies. The United States was the topic of one case study and was a major part in the other case studies. In part this is inescapable, as the United States has been the leading world power since World War II. It was also strategic. Part of my goal in this book is to demonstrate to the academic and policy security community that religious appeals are essential to their efforts to understand and defend world order. Focusing on issues of concern to the United States is one way to do this. It is possible that religious appeals functioned differently in different eras or regions. A study focusing just on the global south, for example, may reveal interesting dynamics.

Others may worry about my qualitative evidence. Unlike much work in security studies—indeed, unlike most of my other work—this book relies on case studies rather than regression analyses or survey experiments. I believe qualitative methods are best suited to capturing the richness of religious appeals in power politics, as well as developing this still novel theory. Using this book as a baseline, however, one could develop a quantitative analysis on the impact of religious appeals on collective mobilization.

By contrast, some may claim I am too positivist in my approach. While I do conduct in-depth qualitative analyses of these cases, the goal is to test the validity of my theorized conditions. This may be too close to a variable-based research design for some, who would prefer an interpretive study that does not impose theoretical priors on the investigation. I would argue this goes too far in the opposite direction from a quantitative study. One of the issues with some work on religion in international relations has been its hesitance to develop a generalizable theory about the way religion affects the world. This contrasts with works inspired by constructivism, which have maintained their richness while combining it with theoretical rigor. Postmodern scholars of religion and international relations should explore whether it is necessary to abandon conventional social scientific precepts in order to study this topic, and whether doing so contributes to the marginalization of the research program.

Finally, many of my claims are admittedly broad, albeit backed up by extensive secondary research. Each of the elements of my theory could easily be its own theory. This was necessary in order to synthesize various strands of research and make the generalizable theory about religious appeals in power politics. However, future research could easily focus on each of these claims.

## Policy Implications

In addition to this book's scholarly implications, I can also provide suggestions to policymakers on how to approach religious appeals as a potential tool in power politics. Lepgold and Nincic, in their work on policy relevance in international relations scholarship, argued a study is "policy-relevant if it addresses the instruments, contexts, and/or consequences of policy."[41] That is clearly the case with this book. Religious appeals are often an ineffective tool, but this is *because* of religion's importance. Calls to abandon them in favor of alternative foreign policy tools would be faulty. Instead, policymakers should draw lessons from my findings on the conditions affecting religious appeals' impact. They should expand credibility on religious issues and leverage these to craft more modest religious appeals. They should also disrupt rival coalitions by launching disruptive religious appeals and undermining rival credibility. Both, however, require expanded religious literacy in foreign policy apparatuses. I direct this section toward US policy audiences, but it could easily be adapted for other audiences.

## Why We Cannot Abandon Religious Appeals

The overall takeaway for policymakers is that religious appeals in power politics rarely work out as intended because of the sway religion holds over societies around the world. That is, attempts to incorporate religion into foreign policy are often ineffective, not because religion does not matter but because *it matters too much*. This pushes back on those who argue foreign policy should focus only on material interests. But it does align with contemporary foreign policy realists who call for modesty in the ambitions of the United States and other states.

Based on my book's findings, then, one could argue for the United States to stop using religious appeals in its foreign policy. Religious appeals represent the United States' naivete and grand ambitions. The United States risks repeating the same mistakes Niebuhr warned about early in the Cold War. Instead, policymakers should focus only on the United States' core interests—not values—and only use concrete and measurable instruments of power.

There are a few issues for such calls for restraint, though. First, these initiatives are relatively cheap. Yes, one of the downsides of religious appeals is that they cause states to misdirect resources. However, the resources misdirected still pale in comparison to the amount spent (and wasted) on military equipment. One F-35 fighter jet could translate into over a hundred well-funded, multiyear religious initiatives. If the United States was more careful about these initiatives—as I will discuss below—the relative amount of funds required to promote them are negligible.

140 **CONCLUSION**

Second, even if the United States stops drawing on religious appeals, others will continue to do so, and the United States must be prepared to counter them. Russia will draw on religious appeals in its aggressive foreign policy. Iran will invoke religious legitimacy when criticizing the United States. And China will keep funding Confucius Institutes or newer equivalents as part of its soft power strategy. Policymakers need to devote attention and resources to understanding how these appeals work and how best to limit their impact.

Finally, abandoning religious appeals would cause the United States to miss out on an opportunity to leverage the growing importance of religion. It is undeniable that religion plays a huge role in people's lives around the world. Ignoring this would be the equivalent of ignoring a new fuel source for naval vessels. Even if the United States adopts a more restrained foreign policy, policymakers must still engage with other states and societies. Understanding how religious appeals work will facilitate this.

If religious appeals are an unwieldy tool we cannot abandon, what is the alternative? The first step, following the foreign policy realists, is to keep any goals modest. Many of the unintended effects had to do with an overly optimistic assessment of the impact of religious appeals. In the 1960s, Saudi Arabia tried to craft a grand anti-Nasser alliance along Islamic lines and ended up antagonizing both Nasser and the United States. After 9/11, the United States tried to promote "moderate Islam" and religious engagement in order to create a global coalition against al-Qaeda and ISIS. This led to suspicion among many Muslims about the United States' true agenda. Instead of trying to transform the world, the United States should craft a series of discrete actionable policy instruments.

Moreover, some of religious appeals' negative implications only became apparent after some time. For example, Saudi Arabia's efforts to build an Islamic Pact helped keep pressure on Nasser, which contributed to his material and ideological defeat in the Six-Day War. But Saudi Arabia's subsequent ideological dominance created many issues for the regime, including revolutionary challengers like the Islamic Republic of Iran and groups like al-Qaeda that attacked the regime for not living up to its Islamic standards. If states are constrained and moderate in their religious appeals, there is less of a chance of them leading to a series of unintended effects that will create a dangerous situation in the future.

## Altering US Credibility and Material Incentives on Religious Issues

In terms of a positive foreign policy suggestion, policymakers should leverage the main findings of this book concerning the conditions under which religious appeals are likely to have an impact. The issues the United States ran into with religious engagement during the global war on terrorism arose from its lack of credibility on Islamic issues. The United States may never be seen as a reliable voice in Islamic debates, but steps like the Biden administration's appointment of an American of Muslim faith as IRF ambassador will help. So will steps domestically to protect the civil rights of non-Christian minorities. The United States may not be able to credibly intervene in internal debates of non-Christian religions, but it could present itself as a champion of a positive secularism that respects religious difference and expression.

The United States would have an easier job affecting the material incentives of states targeted by the religious appeals. Offering aid and trade deals to states, and grants to social organizations, could give these targets an incentive to join in the international coalitions the United States is attempting to form. As we saw with the global war on terrorism this may end up with complicated results. However, if US policymakers are modest in their goals—sticking to areas the United States could plausibly engage on—and combine that with broader attempts to improve US credibility, the unintended effects may be limited.

Some readers may see a similarity between my call to increase US credibility on religious issues and the idea of "soft power." As defined by Nye, soft power is the ability to get other states to want what you want, rather than coercing them to do what you want.[42] Nye proposed having a vibrant and attractive culture combined with a public diplomacy campaign to increase awareness of a country's desirable qualities as steps to expand soft power. One can think of this element of my argument as a specific form of soft power, in line with the idea of "religious soft power" that Mandaville and Hamid discussed.[43] Indeed, I contributed work to their project on attempts to use religion as a soft power resource in the United States and Russia.[44] However, as I discussed in other work, soft power is best defined as a passive and diffuse foreign policy tool.[45] Active uses of cultural and symbolic resources are a different policy tool. The increased credibility on religious issues I call for here is only the first step in the use of religious appeals, so the idea of soft power alone would not be sufficient. Instead, this enhanced credibility or soft power would increase the likelihood of religious appeals succeeding.

## Exploiting the Unintended Effects of Rivals' Religious Appeals

Thus, one way to translate this book's findings into policy advice is to improve US credibility and thus the effectiveness of its religious appeals. Another is to leverage the unintended impacts of religious appeals to undermine other states' efforts to use them. Looking at the Saudi and Russian cases, their religious

142    CONCLUSION

appeals seemed to primarily disrupt regular international relations due to concerns over their impact and the motivations behind them. This limited their intended impact. If, however, these states *intended* to increase uncertainty in international relations, these instruments would have been effective. In the US context, if the United States was facing a rival coalition, policymakers could direct religious appeals at state and societies that were not completely on board with the coalition. This would be unlikely to break apart the coalition, but it could lead to some fraying at the edges. Some of this was apparent in the ability of US religious appeals after 9/11 to facilitate Muslim opposition to al-Qaeda. Additionally, the United States could increase material disincentives of the religious appeals' targets. That is, if we offered aid or threatened retaliation to states for joining the rival coalition, this could create a situation like that of the Middle East in the 1960s. Even a credible voice on religious issues would be unable to overcome these material incentives and would instead face a more unsettled and hostile international situation.

Likewise, policymakers can exploit the tendency of religious discourse to be turned back on its wielder. Examples of the former include the United States' "moderation versus extremism" framing after 9/11, or its attempt to frame the Cold War as one between atheism and faith. These fell prey to the unintended effects of religious appeals. Authoritarian states in the Middle East redefined religious moderation to justify repression. Critics of Vladimir Putin pointed to religious faith and identity to rally opposition to his hostile policies. That is, they were able to use the very same religious discourse that produced the appeals to push back on them.

Policymakers could exploit the conditions affecting the impact of religious appeals to make it more likely such redirection occurs. Remember this was most likely in cases when a state of low credibility used religious appeals, resulting in convenient alignment with its coalition. In concrete terms, this would mean responding to hostile religious appeals by countering their point using equally religious terminology. For example, one could respond to Russia's invocations of traditional values, the importance of faith, and cross-cultural engagement by pointing to Russia's poor religious freedom record. Russia has severely restricted Western missionary groups' ability to operate since the 1990s, and recently banned the Jehovah's Witnesses. Realizing that Russia's definition of traditional values would not include their organizations and beliefs may dampen Western evangelicals' support for Putin. Similarly, Egypt's Nasser worried about Saudi Arabia's Islamic Pact in the 1960s and moved to shore up his Arab nationalist credentials in order to undermine Faisal's appeal. It may have been more useful to point out the depth of Egypt's own faith. While the state was officially secular, it housed Islam's most important university—al-

Azhar—whose judgments were as influential among Muslims as King Faisal's pronouncements.

## Expanding Religious Literacy in Foreign Policy

Both of these initiatives, however—small-scale religious engagement and disruptive religious appeals—depend on a religiously literate foreign policy apparatus. Many ineffective religious initiatives come from staff not fully understanding the issues with which they are dealing. As part of the effort to use religious appeals effectively in power politics, then, the United States should rejuvenate its ability to understand and act on religious issues.

One important step is reviving the Office of Religion and Global Affairs, ensuring it can incorporate religion and religious literacy into all areas of US foreign policy.[46] The Trump administration technically maintained the Obama administration's important role for religion in US foreign policy through the prominence of the International Religious Freedom office. Yet, Trump also gutted the Office of Religion and Global Affairs, and undermined IRF's credibility through its embrace of authoritarian states and anti-Muslim statements. Another step would be to continue existing programs, such as religious training in the State Department's Foreign Service Institute and faith-based partnerships in USAID (United States Agency for International Development). Finally, policymakers should attempt to restore the initial bipartisan promise of religious freedom promotion, demonstrating the importance of this issue in advancing US national security.[47]

# A Final Warning

Both scholars and policymakers may prefer more concrete takeaways from this book. Is religion a significant and impactful element of international relations or not? Are religious appeals a positive and effective potential foreign policy tool, or are they ineffective and a waste of time? Unfortunately, part of what makes religion such an important part of international relations is this ambiguity. Attempts to ignore this have led to many of the problems I discussed. Instead, we should aspire to constantly recognize and adapt to this complex situation.

Niebuhr provides guidance on this point. In the conclusion to *The Irony of American History*, he argued that "consciousness of an ironic situation tends to dissolve it . . . into pure despair or hatred."[48] Americans are growing tired of policing and managing the world's problems, realizing the grand ambitions

144　　**CONCLUSION**

of earlier eras led only to exhaustion and destruction. They are close to recognizing the irony Niebuhr warned about decades ago, which—despite the dreams of those calling for restraint—may lead to nihilistic or apathetic foreign policies. Instead, as Moore said in his work calling for a "Niebuhrian international relations," it is "these paradoxes and contradictions that Niebuhr found so important . . . things from which he urged us all not to run, uncomfortable though they might make us."[49] Policymakers should work to instill a "sense of an ultimate judgment upon our . . . actions" to "create an awareness of our own pretensions of wisdom."[50] In such a way, the "irony would . . . dissolve into an experience of contrition," allowing for religious appeals that are engaged but modest.[51] Hopefully the analysis and policy recommendations this book provides can contribute to this endeavor.

# NOTES

## Introduction

1. T. Gilliam and T. Jones, "Monty Python and the Holy Grail," (EMI Films, 1975).

2. The author would like to thank Ron Hassner for this simile.

3. Quoted in R. E. Hassner, *Religion on the Battlefield* (Ithaca, NY: Cornell University Press, 2016), 9.

4. S. E. Goddard and D. H. Nexon, "The Dynamics of Global Power Politics: A Framework for Analysis," *Journal of Global Security Studies* 1, no. 1 (2016): 6.

5. M. Albright, *The Mighty and the Almighty: Reflections on America, God and World Affairs* (New York: Harper, 2006), 11.

6. Albright, *Mighty and the Almighty*, 66.

7. George W. Bush, "Remarks Prior to Discussions with King Abdullah II of Jordan and an Exchange with Reporters" news release, 28 September, 2001, https://www.presidency.ucsb.edu/documents/remarks-prior-discussions-with-king-abdullah-ii-jordan-and-exchange-with-reporters-2.

8. J. Lieberman, "The Theological Iron Curtain: A Foreign Policy Strategy for Engaging the Muslim World," *National Interest* 73 (2003): 5–9.

9. W. I. Hitchcock, "The President Who Made Billy Graham 'America's Pastor,'" *Washington Post*, 28 February 2018; K. Gradert and J. Strasburg, "Billy Graham, Cold Warrior for God," *New York Times*, 23 February 2018.

10. J. Kerry, "We Ignore the Global Impact of Religion at Our Peril," *America*, 2 September 2015.

11. E. Green, "Protecting Religious Freedom Is a Foreign-Policy Priority of the Trump Administration," *Atlantic*, 12 May 2017.

12. Y. al Otaiba, "A Vision for a Moderate Muslim World" *Foreign Policy*, 2 December 2015.

13. R. Sinai, "Saddam's Goal to Be Like Saladin, Nasser," *Associated Press*, 17 February 1991.

14. "Arabs Must Follow Saladin's Example to Capture Jerusalem: Iraq," *Agence France Presse*, 2 October 2000.

15. D. Philpott, "Has the Study of Global Politics Found Religion?" *Annual Review of Political Science* 12 (2009): 183–202; E. S. Hurd, "The Political Authority of Secularism in International Relations," *European Journal of International Relations* 10, no. 2 (2004): 235–262; A. C. Stepan, "Religion, Democracy, and the 'Twin Tolerations,'" *Journal of Democracy* 11, no. 4 (2000): 37–57.

16. J. Fox, *A World Survey of Religion and the State* (New York: Cambridge University Press, 2008); J. Casanova, *Public Religions in the Modern World* (Chicago: University of Chicago Press, 1994).

17. K. J. Alexander, "The Impact of Religious Commitment on Patterns of Interstate Conflict," *Journal of Global Security Studies* 4, no. 1 (2017): 271–287; D. Philpott, "The Religious Roots of Modern International Relations," *World Politics* 52, no. 2 (2000): 206–245; P. S. Henne, *Islamic Politics, Muslim States and Counterterrorism Tensions* (New York: Cambridge University Press, 2017); S. Hoeber Rudolph, "Introduction: Religion, States and Transnational Civil Society," in *Transnational Religions and Fading States*, ed. S. Hoeber and J. P. Rudolph (Boulder, CO: Westview Press, 1997), 1–26; T. Banchoff, *Embryo Politics: Ethics and Policy in Atlantic Democracies* (Ithaca, NY: Cornell University Press, 2011); J. Haynes, *Religion, Politics and International Relations: Selected Essays* (New York: Routledge, 2011).

18. Banchoff, *Embryo Politics*; T. B. Schwarz, *Faith-Based Organizations in Transnational Peacebuilding* (Lanham, MD: Rowman and Littlefield, 2018); J. Haynes, *Faith-Based Organizations at the United Nations* (New York: Palgrave Macmillan, 2014); T. Kayaoglu, *The Organization of Islamic Cooperation: Politics, Problems, and Potential* (New York: Routledge, 2017).

19. J. C. Agensky, "Dr Livingstone, I Presume? Evangelicals, Africa and Faith-Based Humanitarianism," *Global Society* 27, no. 4 (2013): 1–21; J. C. Agensky, "Evangelical Globalism and the Internationalization of Sudan's Second Civil War," *Cambridge Review of International Affairs* 33, no. 2 (2019): 274–293.

20. P. S. Henne, "The Ancient Fire: Religion and Suicide Terrorism," *Terrorism and Political Violence* 24, no. 1 (2012): 38–60; P. S. Henne, "The Two Swords: Religion–State Connections and Interstate Conflict," *Journal of Peace Research* 49, no. 6 (2012): 753–768; P. S. Henne and Jason Klocek, "Taming the Gods: How Religious Conflict Shapes Religious Repression," *Journal of Conflict Resolution* 63, no. 1 (2019): 112–138; P. S. Henne, N. Saiya, and A. W. Hand, "Weapon of the Strong? Government Support for Religion and Majoritarian Terrorism" (International Studies Association, Toronto, Canada, 2019); M. Basedau, B. Pfieffer, and J. Vullers, "Bad Religion? Religion, Collective Action, and the Onset of Armed Conflict in Developing Countries," *Journal of Conflict Resolution* 60, no. 2 (2016): 226–255; J. Fox, "The Increasing Role of Religion in State Failure: 1960 to 2004," *Terrorism and Political Violence* 19, no. 3 (2007): 395–414; I. Svensson, "Fighting with Faith: Religion and Conflict Resolution in Civil Wars," *Journal of Conflict Resolution* 51, no. 6 (2007): 930–949; I. de Soysa and R. Nordas, "Islam's Bloody Innards? Religion and Political Terror, 1980–2000," *International Studies Quarterly* 51 (2007): 927–943; M. Duffy Toft, "Getting Religion? The Puzzling Case of Islam and Civil War," *International Security* 31, no. 4 (2007): 97–131; R. E. Hassner, "To Halve and to Hold: Conflicts Over Sacred Space and the Problem of Indivisibility," *Security Studies* 12, no. 4 (2003): 1–33.

21. D. Johnston and C. Sampson, "Introduction: Beyond Power Politics," in *Religion, the Missing Dimension of Statecraft*, ed. D. Johnston and C. Sampson (New York: Oxford University Press, 1994), 8–34.

22. S. E. Goddard, *When Right Makes Might: Rising Powers and World Order* (Ithaca, NY: Cornell University Press, 2018), 20.

23. This term comes from A. Grzymala-Busse, *Nations under God: How Churches Use Moral Authority to Influence Policy* (Princeton, NJ: Princeton University Press, 2015).

24. T. Farr, *World of Faith and Freedom: Why International Religious Liberty Is Vital to American National Security* (New York: Oxford University Press, 2008).

25. S. Thomas, *The Global Resurgence of Religion and the Transformation of International Relations: The Struggle for the Soul of the Twenty-First Century* (New York: Palgrave Macmillan, 2005).

26. D. Philpott, "The Challenge of September 11 to Secularism in International Relations," *World Politics* 55, no. 2 (2002): 66–95; K. D. Wald and C. Wilcox, "Getting Religion: Has Political Science Rediscovered the Faith Factor?" *American Political Science Review* 100, no. 4 (2006): 523–529; Philpott, "Has the Study"; R. Seiple and D. R. Hoover, eds., *Religion and Security: The New Nexus in International Relations* (Lanham, MD: Rowman and Littlefield, 2004).

27. J. Snyder, ed., *Religion and International Relations Theory* (New York: Columbia University Press, 2011); T. S. Shah, A. Stepan, and M. Duffy Toft, eds., *Rethinking Religion and World Affairs* (New York: Oxford University Press, 2012); T. A. Byrnes and P. J. Katzenstein, eds., *Religion in an Expanding Europe* (New York: Cambridge University Press, 2006).

28. P. S. Henne, *The Geopolitics of Faith: Religious Soft Power in Russian and U.S. Foreign Policy* (Washington, DC: Brookings Institute / Berkley Center for Religion, Peace and World Affairs, 6 June 2019); P. S. Henne, *Economic Integration and Political Reconciliation in Iraq* (Washington, DC: Center for American Progress, 2018); P. S. Henne, S. Hudgins, and T. Shah, *Religious Freedom and Violent Religious Extremism: A Sourcebook* (Washington, DC: Berkley Center for Religion, Peace and World Affair's Religious Freedom Project, 2012); "Latest Trends in Religious Restrictions and Hostilities: Overall Decline in Social Hostilities in 2013, Though Harassment of Jews Worldwide Reached a Seven-Year High" (Pew Research Center, Washington, DC, 26 February 2015).

29. J. Bethke Elshtain, "Military Intervention and Justice as Equal Regard," in *Religion and Security: The New Nexus in International Relations*, ed. R. Seiple and D. R. Hoover (Lanham, MD: Rowman and Littlefield, 2004), 116.

30. Farr, *World of Faith*; T. F. Farr, "Diplomacy in an Age of Faith: Religious Freedom and National Security," *Foreign Affairs* 87, no. 2 (March / April 2008): 122–124.

31. R. E. Hassner, "Religious Intelligence," *Terrorism and Political Violence* 23, no. 5 (2011): 684–710.

32. J. S. Nye Jr., "Soft Power," *Foreign Policy* 80 (Autumn 1990): 153–171.

33. P. S. Henne, "What We Talk About When We Talk About Soft Power," *International Studies Perspectives* 23, no. 1 (2022): 94–111.

34. Henne, "What We Talk About."

35. P. Mandaville and S. Hamid, *Islam as Statecraft: How Governments Use Religion in Foreign Policy* (Washington, DC: Brookings Institute, 2018); P. Mandaville, ed., *The Geopolitics of Religious Soft Power: How States Use Religion in Foreign Policy* (New York: Oxford University Press, 2022).

## 1. Why, How, and When Religious Appeals Matter in Power Politics

1. Goddard, *When Right Makes Might*, 12.

2. Goddard, *When Right Makes Might*, 13.

3. Goddard, *When Right Makes Might*, 14.

148 **NOTES TO PAGES 15–17**

4. S. E. Goddard and R. R. Krebs, "Rhetoric, Legitimation and Grand Strategy," *Security Studies* 24 (2015): 5–36.

5. J. Fox and S. Sandler, *Bringing Religion into International Relations* (New York: Palgrave Macmillan, 2004); N. Sandal and J. Fox, *Religion in International Relations Theory: Interactions and Possibilities* (New York: Routledge, 2013).

6. Goddard and Nexon, "Dynamics of Global Power," 6.

7. Goddard and Krebs, "Rhetoric, Legitimation and Grand Strategy," 6.

8. Goddard, *When Right Makes Might*, 23.

9. J. W. Busby, *Moral Movements and Foreign Policy* (New York: Cambridge University Press, 2010), 39–40.

10. V. Pouliot, *International Security in Practice: The Politics of NATO–Russia Diplomacy* (New York: Cambridge University Press, 2010).

11. M. E. Keck and K. Sikkink, *Activists Beyond Borders: Advocacy Networks in International Politics* (Ithaca, NY: Cornell University Press, 1998); C. Bob, *Rights as Weapons: Instruments of Conflict, Tools of Power* (Princeton, NJ: Princeton University Press, 2019).

12. P. T. Jackson, *Civilizing the Enemy: German Reconstruction and the Invention of the West* (Ann Arbor: University of Michigan Press, 2006), 31; R. R. Krebs and P. T. Jackson, "Twisting Tongues and Twisting Arms: The Power of Political Rhetoric," *European Journal of International Relations* 13, no. 1 (2007): 35–66; R. R. Krebs and J. K. Lobasz, "Fixing the Meaning of 9/11: Hegemony, Coercion, and the Road to War in Iraq," *Security Studies* 16, no. 3 (2007): 409–451.

13. S. M. Walt, *Taming American Power: The Global Response to US Primacy* (New York: W. W. Norton, 2004).

14. J. M. Owen IV, *The Clash of Ideas in World Politics: Transnational Networks, States, and Regime Change, 1510–2010* (Princeton, NJ: Princeton University Press, 2010); Jackson, *Civilizing the Enemy*.

15. R. B. Hall, "Moral Authority as a Power Resource," *International Organization* 51, no. 3 (1997): 591–622; Keck and Sikkink, *Activists Beyond Borders*; Walt, *Taming American Power*; Krebs and Jackson, "Twisting Tongues and Twisting Arms"; Pouliot, *International Security in Practice*; J. Mitzen, "Illusion or Intention: Talking Grand Strategy into Existence," *Security Studies* 24 (2015): 61–94; Goddard, *When Right Makes Might*.

16. Keck and Sikkink, *Activists Beyond Borders*; Busby, *Moral Movements*.

17. Grzymala-Busse, *Nations under God*, 55–56.

18. R. S. Appleby, "Building Sustainable Peace: The Roles of Local and Transnational Religious Actors," in *Religious Pluralism, Globalization and World Politics*, ed. T. Banchoff (New York: Oxford University Press, 2008), 125–155; A. Kaya and A. Tecmen, "Europe versus Islam? Right-Wing Populist Discourse and the Construction of a Civilized Identity," *Review of Faith and International Affairs* 17, no. 1 (2019): 49–64; P. Kratochvil, "Religion as a Weapon: Invoking Religion in Secularized Societies," *Review of Faith and International Affairs* 17, no. 1 (2019): 78–88; D. T. Buckley, "Religious Elite Cues, Internal Division, and the Impact of Pope Francis' Laudato Si'," *Politics and Religion* 15 (2022): 1–33.

19. R. E. Hassner, *War on Sacred Grounds* (Ithaca, NY: Cornell University Press, 2009), 96.

20. A. E. Ozturk, *Religion, Identity and Power: Turkey and the Balkans in the Twenty-First Century* (Edinburgh, UK: Edinburgh University Press, 2021); M. A. Tabaar, *Religious Statecraft: The Politics of Islam in Iran* (New York: Columbia University Press, 2019).

21. P. Stamatov, *The Origins of Global Humanitarianism: Religion, Empires and Advocacy* (New York: Cambridge University Press, 2013); Agensky, "Evangelical Globalism"; Haynes, *Religion, Politics.*

22. M. Bar-Maoz, "On Religion and the Politics of Security: How Religion's Involvement in Domestic Politics Affects National Securitymaking," *Review of Faith and International Affairs* 16, no. 2 (2018): 36–49; Mandaville and Hamid, *Islam as Statecraft*; Henne, *Islamic Politics.*

23. D. H. Nexon, *The Struggle for Power in Early Modern Europe: Religious Conflict, Dynastic Empires and International Change* (Princeton, NJ: Princeton University Press, 2009); G. Bettiza, *Finding Faith in Foreign Policy: Religion and American Diplomacy in a Postsecular World* (New York: Oxford University Press, 2019).

24. Ozturk, *Religion, Identity and Power.*

25. Bettiza, *Finding Faith*; Stamatov, *Origins of Global Humanitarianism*; Buckley, "Religious Elite Cues."

26. Kratochvil, "Religion as a Weapon"; T. Banchoff, "Religious Pluralism and the Politics of a Global Cloning Ban," in *Religious Pluralism, Globalization and World Politics*, ed. T. Banchoff. (New York: Oxford University Press, 2008), 276; M. Barbato, "A State, a Diplomat, and a Transnational Church: The Multi-Layered Actorness of the Holy See," *Perspectives* 21, no. 2 (2013): 27–48; J. Troy, "'The Pope's Own Hand Outstretched': Holy See Diplomacy as a Hybrid Mode of Diplomatic Agency," *British Journal of Politics and International Relations* 20, no. 3 (2018): 521–539; N. Sandal, "Religious Actors as Epistemic Communities in Conflict Transformation: The Cases of South Africa and Northern Ireland," *Review of International Studies* 37, no. 3 (2011): 929–949; Hassner, *War on Sacred Grounds.*

27. Bar-Maoz, "On Religion"; Hassner, *War on Sacred Grounds.*

28. Buckley, "Religious Elite Cues"; M. Darwich and T. Fakhoury, "Casting the Other as an Existential Threat: The Securitisation of Sectarianism in the International Relations of the Syria Crisis," *Global Discourse* 6, no. 4 (2016): 712–732; R. P. Burge and P. A. Djupe, "Religious Authority in a Democratic Society: Clergy and Citizen Evidence from a New Measure," *Politics and Religion* 15 (2022): 169–196; S. Kettell and P. A. Djupe, "Do Religious Justifications Distort Policy Debates? Some Empirics on the Case for Public Reason," *Politics and Religion* 13, no. 3 (2020): 517–543.

29. Kratochvil, "Religion as a Weapon," 79.

30. Ozturk, *Religion, Identity and Power*, 12.

31. T. G. Jelen and C. Wilcox, "Religion: The One, the Few and the Many," in *Religion and Politics in Comparative Perspective: The One, the Few and the Many*, ed. T. G. Jelen and C. Wilcox (New York: Cambridge University Press, 2002), 1–27.

32. Grzymala-Busse, *Nations under God.*

33. Casanova, *Public Religions*; A. Gill, *The Political Origins of Religious Liberty* (New York: Cambridge University Press, 2008).

34. T. Banchoff, ed., *Religious Pluralism, Globalization and World Politics* (New York: Oxford University Press, 2008).

35. Kratochvil, "Religion as a Weapon."

36. Gill, *Political Origins*; B. J. Grim and R. Finke, *The Price of Freedom Denied: Religious Persecution and Conflict in the Twenty-First Century* (New York: Cambridge University Press, 2011).

150    **NOTES TO PAGES 19–24**

37. R. S. Appleby, *The Ambivalence of the Sacred* (Lanham, MD: Rowman and Littlefield, 2000); D. Philpott, "Explaining the Political Ambivalence of Religion," *American Political Science Review* 101, no. 3 (2007): 505–525.

38. Rudolph, "Introduction."

39. Philpott, "Religious Roots"; Haynes, *Religion, Politics and International Relations.*

40. M. Juergensmeyer, *Terror in the Mind of God: The Global Rise of Religious Violence* (Berkeley: University of California Press, 2003).

41. Hassner, *War on Sacred Grounds*; M. Horowitz, "Long Time Going: Religion and the Duration of Crusading," *International Security* 34, no. 2 (2009): 162–193.

42. K. Waltz, *Theory of International Politics* (Reading, MA: Addison-Wesley, 1979).

43. N. Deitelhoff and L. Zimmerman, "Norms under Challenge: Unpacking the Dynamics of Norm Robustness," *Journal of Global Security Studies* 4, no. 1 (2019): 2–17; E. K. Wilson, "Beyond Dualism: Expanded Understandings of Religion and Global Justice," *International Studies Quarterly* 54, no. 3 (2010): 733–754.

44. Banchoff, *Embryo Politics*; Haynes, *Faith-Based Organizations*; Schwarz, *Faith-Based Organizations.*

45. Philpott, "Challenge of September 11."

46. Farr, *World of Faith.*

47. Grzymala-Busse, *Nations under God*, 40.

48. Gill, *Political Origins*; A. Sarkissian, *The Varieties of Religious Repression: Why Governments Restrict Religion* (New York: Oxford University Press, 2015).

49. Philpott, "Explaining the Political Ambivalence"; Grim and Finke, *Price of Freedom Denied*; Henne, *Islamic Politics, Muslim States.*

50. Grzymala-Busse, *Nations under God.* 9.

51. Casanova, *Public Religions*; K. A. Appiah, "Causes of Quarrel: What's Special about Religious Disputes?" in *Religious Pluralism, Globalization, and World Politics*, ed. T. Banchoff (New York: Oxford University Press, 2008), 41–65; Buckley, "Religious Elite Cues."

52. K. R. Dark, "Large-Scale Religious Change and World Politics," in *Religion in International Relations*, ed. K. R. Dark. (New York: St. Martin's Press, 2000), 50–82.

53. J. Casanova, "Globalizing Catholicism and the Return to a 'Universal' Church," in *Transnational Religion and Fading States*, ed. S. H. Rudolph and J. Piscatori (Boulder, CO: Westview Press, 1997), 121–143; Rudolph, "Introduction"; T. Banchoff, "Introduction: Religious Pluralism in World Affairs," in *Religious Pluralism, Globalization, and World Politics*, ed. T. Banchoff. (New York: Oxford University Press, 2008), 3–41.

54. Henne, "Two Swords"; P. S. Henne, "The Domestic Politics of International Religious Defamation," *Politics and Religion* 6, no. 3 (2013): 512–537; Henne, *Islamic Politics, Muslim States*; P. S. Henne, *The Geopolitics of Faith: Religious Soft Power in Russian and U.S. Foreign Policy* (Washington, DC: Berkley Center for Religion, Peace and World Affairs / Brookings Institution, 2019); J. Fox and N. Sandal, "State Religious Exclusivity and International Crises between 1990 and 2002," in *Religion, Identity and Global Governance: Theory, Evidence, and Practice*, ed. P. James (Toronto: University of Toronto Press, 2010); Alexander, "Impact of Religious Commitment"; E. J. Powell, *Islamic Law and International Law* (New York: Oxford University Press, 2020).

55. B. Buzan, *From International to World Society? English School Theory and the Social Structure of Globalisation* (New York: Cambridge University Press, 2004); B. Buzan and O. Wæver, *Regions and Powers: The Structure of International Security* (New York: Cam-

bridge University Press, 2003); F. G. Gause III, *The International Relations of the Persian Gulf* (New York: Cambridge University Press, 2010).

56. F. B. Adamson, "Global Liberalism versus Political Islam: Competing Ideological Frameworks in International Politics," *International Studies Review* 7 (2005): 547–569; Henne, *Islamic Politics, Muslim States*.

57. Philpott, "Religious Roots"; Nexon, *Struggle for Power*; W. T. Te Brake, *Religious War and Religious Peace in Early Modern Europe* (New York: Cambridge University Press, 2017).

58. Owen, *Clash of Ideas*; J. M. Owen IV, "Springs and Their Offspring: The International Consequences of Domestic Uprisings," *European Journal of International Security* 1, no. 1 (2016): 49–72.

59. F. G. Gause III, "Balancing What? Threat Perception and Alliance Choice in the Gulf," *Security Studies* 13, no. 2 (2004): 273–305; L. Rubin, *Islam in the Balance: Ideational Threats in Arab Politics* (Stanford, CA: Stanford University Press, 2014).

60. Owen, *Clash of Ideas*.

61. J. Mitzen, "Ontological Security in World Politics: State Identity and the Security Dilemma," *European Journal of International Relations* 12, no. 3 (2006).

62. Hassner, *Religion on the Battlefield*.

63. Grzymala-Busse, *Nations under God*; Kratochvil, "Religion as a Weapon."

64. Sandal, "Religious Actors"; Barbato, "A State, a Diplomat"; Troy, "The Pope's Own Hand."

65. Busby, *Moral Movements*.

66. Goddard, *When Right Makes Might*.

67. Philpott, "Religious Roots"; Gill, *Political Origins*; Henne, *Islamic Politics, Muslim States*.

68. Goddard and Krebs, "Rhetoric, Legitimation and Grand Strategy," 15–16.

69. B. Shaffer, ed., *The Limits of Culture: Islam and Foreign Policy* (Cambridge, MA: MIT Press, 2006).

70. S. M. Walt, *The Origins of Alliances* (Ithaca, NY: Cornell University Press, 1987); B. Shaffer, "Introduction: The Limits of Culture," in *The Limits of Culture: Islam and Foreign Policy*, ed. B. Shaffer (Cambridge, MA: MIT Press, 2006), 1–26.

71. R. L. Schweller, "Unanswered Threats: A Neoclassical Realist Theory of Underbalancing," *International Security* 29, no. 2 (2004): 159–201; C. Dueck, *Reluctant Crusaders: Power, Culture, and Change in American Grand Strategy* (Princeton, NJ: Princeton University Press, 2006); E. N. Resnick, "Strange Bedfellows: U.S Bargaining Behavior with Allies of Convenience," *International Security* 35, no. 3 (2010/2011): 144–184; K. Narizny, "On Systemic Paradigms and Domestic Politics. A Critique of the Newest Realism," *International Security* 42, no. 2 (2017): 155–190.

72. M. Mattes and M. Rodríguez, "Autocracies and International Cooperation," *International Studies Quarterly* 58, no. 3 (2014): 527–538; G. Jackson, "The Showdown That Wasn't: U.S.–Israeli Relations and American Domestic Politics, 1973–75," *International Security* 39, no. 4 (2015): 130–169.

73. D. Reiter, "Learning, Realism and Alliances: The Weight of the Shadow of the Past," *World Politics* 46, no. 4 (1994): 490–526; B. A. Leeds, "Alliance Reliability in Times of War: Explaining State Decisions to Violate Treaties," *International Organization* 57, no. 4 (2003): 801–827; B. A. Leeds and B. Savun, "Terminating Alliances: Why Do States Abrogate Agreements?" *Journal of Politics* 69, no. 4 (2007): 1118–1132; M. J. C. Crescenzi, J. D.

Kathman, K. B. Kleinberg, and R. M. Wood, "Reliability, Reputation, and Alliance Formation," *International Studies Quarterly* 56, no. 2 (2012): 259–274; M. Mattes, "Reputation, Symmetry, and Alliance Design," *International Organization* 66, no. 4 (2012): 679–707; E. Gartzke and A. Weisiger, "Fading Friendships: Alliances, Affinities and the Activation of International Identities," *British Journal of Political Science* 43, no. 1 (2013): 25–52; M. E. Henke, "Buying Allies: Payment Practices in Multilateral Military Coalition-Building," *International Security* 43, no. 4 (2019): 128–162.

74. Goddard and Krebs, "Rhetoric, Legitimation and Grand Strategy," 15.

75. Dark, "Large-Scale Religious Change"; Thomas, *Global Resurgence*; S. P. Huntington, *The Clash of Civilizations and the Remaking of World Order* (New York: Simon and Schuster, 1996); E. Henderson and R. Tucker, "Clear and Present Strangers: The Clash of Civilizations and International Conflict," *International Studies Quarterly* 45 (2001): 317–338; G. Chiozza, "Is There a Clash of Civilizations? Evidence from Patterns of International Conflict Involvement, 1946–1997," *Journal of Peace Research* 39, no. 6 (2002): 711–734; E. Gartzke and K. S. Gleditsch, "Identity and Conflict: Ties That Bind and Differences That Divide," *European Journal of International Relations* 12, no. 1 (2006): 53–87.

76. D. Collier, H. E. Brady, and J. Seawright, "Sources of Leverage in Causal Inference: Toward an Alternative View of Methodology," in *Rethinking Social Inquiry: Diverse Tools, Shared Standards*, ed. H. E. Brady and D. Collier (Lanham, MD: Rowman and Littlefield, 2010), 184.

77. Collier, Brady, and Seawright, "Sources of Leverage"; D. McAdam, S. Tarrow, and C. Tilly, *Dynamics of Contention* (New York: Cambridge University Press, 2001); A. George and A. Bennett, *Case Studies and Theory Development in the Social Sciences* (Cambridge, MA: MIT Press, 2005).

78. Collier, Brady, and Seawright, "Sources of Leverage"; George and Bennett, *Case Studies*, 132.

79. Jackson, *Civilizing the Enemy*; Te Brake, *Religious War*; Pouliot, *International Security in Practice*; A. Acharya, "How Ideas Spread: Whose Norms Matter? Norm Localization and Institutional Change in Asian Regionalism," *International Organization* 58, no. 2 (2004): 239–275; Owen, *Clash of Ideas*; Schwarz, *Faith-Based Organizations*; Bettiza, *Finding Faith*; Bob, *Rights as Weapons*.

80. Collier, Brady, and Seawright, "Sources of Leverage"; George and Bennett, *Case Studies*.

81. Acharya, "How Ideas Spread"; Owen, *Clash of Ideas*; Pouliot, *International Security in Practice*; A. Zarakol, *After Defeat: How the East Learned to Live with the West* (New York: Cambridge University Press, 2011).

82. J. Seawright and J. Gerring, "Case Selection Techniques in Case Study Research: A Menu of Qualitative and Quantitative Options," *Political Research Quarterly* 61, no. 2 (2008): 294–308.

83. J. Renshon, *Fighting for Status: Hierarchy and Conflict in World Politics* (Princeton, NJ: Princeton University Press, 2017); Goddard, *When Right Makes Might*; M. Murray, *The Struggle for Recognition in International Relations: Status, Revisionism and Rising Powers* (New York: Oxford University Press, 2019).

84. Busby, *Moral Movements*.

85. A. Curanovic, *The Religious Factor in Russia's Foreign Policy* (London: Routledge, 2014); Haynes, *Faith-Based Organizations*; Bettiza, *Finding Faith*; Tabaar, *Religious Statecraft*.

86. Hassner, *War on Sacred Grounds*; A. Phillips, *War, Religion and Empire: The Transformation of International Orders* (New York: Cambridge University Press, 2011); Te Brake, *Religious War*; Schwarz, *Faith-Based Organizations*.

87. Hassner, *Religion on the Battlefield*.

88. A. Bennett and J. Checkel, "Process Tracing: From Philosophical Roots to Best Practices," in *Process Tracing: From Metaphor to Analytic Tool*, ed. A. Bennett and J. Checkel (New York: Cambridge University Press, 2014), 7.

89. Bennett and Checkel, "Process Tracing," 16.

90. A. Bennett, "Process Tracing and Causal Inference," in *Rethinking Social Inquiry: Diverse Tools, Shared Standards*, ed. H. Brady and D. Collier (Lanham, MD: Rowman and Littlefield, 2010), 210–211. Bennett, following Van Evera, refers to these types of tests as "hoop tests," "smoking gun tests," and "doubly decisive tests."

91. I. S. Lustick, "History, Historiography, and Political Science: Multiple Historical Records and the Problem of Selection Bias," *American Political Science Review* 90, no. 3 (1996): 605–617; C. Thies, "A Pragmatic Guide to Qualitative Historical Analysis in the Study of International Relations," *International Studies Perspectives* 3 (2002): 351–372. Grzymala-Busse makes a similar point in her use of diverse data. Grzymala-Busse, *Nations under God*, 59.

92. See S. Van Evera, *Guide to Methods for Students of Political Science* (Ithaca: Cornell University Press, 1997).

## 2. Religious Appeals in a Middle East Rivalry

1. Box 155, envelope 6, document 115, LBJ Presidential Library, Austin, Texas. I will reference all subsequent archival records using the format: 155/6/115.

2. 155/7/24.

3. J. A. Kechichian, *Faysal: Saudi Arabia's King for All Seasons* (Gainesville, FL: University of Florida Press, 2008), 191.

4. S. M. Hersh, "King's Ransom: How Vulnerable Are the Saudi Royals?" *New Yorker*, 14 October 2001.

5. J. Feltman et al., *The New Geopolitics of the Middle East: America's Role in a Changing Region*, ed. B. Jones (Washington, DC: Brookings Institute, 2019).

6. S. Mabon, *Saudi Arabia and Iran: The Struggle to Shape the Middle East* (London: Foreign Policy Center, 2018).

7. C. Fraser, "In Defense of Allah's Realm: Religion and Statecraft in Saudi Foreign Policy," in *Transnational Religion and Fading States*, ed. S. H. Rudolph and J. P. Piscatori (Boulder, CO: Westview Press, 1997), 212–243.

8. M. D. Toft, D. Philpott, and T. S. Shah, *God's Century: Resurgent Religion and Global Politics* (New York: W. W. Norton, 2011); Thomas, *Global Resurgence*.

9. Rubin, *Islam in the Balance*; Mandaville and Hamid, *Islam as Statecraft*; Gause, "Balancing What?"

10. R. Bronson, *Thicker Than Oil: America's Uneasy Partnership with Saudi Arabia* (New York: Oxford University Press, 2006).

11. Bronson, *Thicker Than Oil*.

12. T. Matthiessen, "Saudi Arabia and the Cold War," in *Salman's Legacy: The Dilemmas of a New Era in Saudi Arabia*, ed. M. al-Rasheed (New York: Oxford University Press, 2018), 217–235, 218.

## NOTES TO PAGES 38–43

13. M. B. Oren, *Six Days of War: June 1967 and the Making of the Modern Middle East* (Novato, CA: Presidio Press, 2003).

14. M. al-Rasheed, *Contesting the Saudi State: Islamic Voices from a New Generation* (New York: Cambridge University Press, 2007), 34. Al-Rasheed refers to these practices specifically as "mechanisms."

15. M. al-Rasheed, *A History of Saudi Arabia*, 2nd ed. (New York: Cambridge University Press, 2010), 67.

16. Bronson, *Thicker Than Oil*, 195.

17. Fraser, "In Defense of Allah's Realm," 224.

18. F. G. Gause III, *Saudi–Yemen Relations: Domestic Structures and Foreign Influences* (New York: Columbia University Press, 1990), 221.

19. Gause, *Saudi–Yemen Relations*; Matthiessen, "Saudi Arabia," 222.

20. M. N. Barnett, *Dialogues in Arab Politics: Negotiations in International Order* (New York: Columbia University Press, 1998), 1–2.

21. W. Quandt, *Peace Process: American Diplomacy and the Arab–Israeli Conflict since 1967* (Washington, DC: Brookings Institution, 1993); N. N. Ayubi, *Over-Stating the Arab State: Politics and Society in the Middle East* (London: I. B. Taurus, 1995).

22. Al-Rasheed, *History of Saudi Arabia*, 119.

23. Bronson, *Thicker Than Oil*, 70.

24. Gause, *Saudi–Yemen Relations*; Matthiessen, "Saudi Arabia," 222.

25. 155/2/78.

26. 155/3/167a.

27. 155/1/3.

28. 155/1/3.

29. 155/1/3.

30. 155/6/115.

31. 155/3/155.

32. 155/3/141a.

33. 155/1/35.

34. A. Vassiliev, *King Faisal of Saudi Arabia: Personality, Faith and Times* (London: Saqi Books, 2012), 338.

35. D. E. Long, "King Faisal's World View," in *King Faisal and the Modernisation of Saudi Arabia*, ed. W. A. Beling (London: Croom Helm, 1980), 173–184, 179.

36. A. M. Sindi, "King Faisal and Pan-Islamism," in Beling, *King Faisal*, 184–202, 189.

37. 155/7/24.

38. 155/7/24.

39. 155/1/35.

40. 155/2/112.

41. 155/2/112.

42. 155/3/166a.

43. 155/3/166a.

44. 155/3/167a.

45. 155/1/3.

46. 155/1/4.

47. 155/1/10.

48. 155/1/10.

NOTES TO PAGES 43–47    155

49. 155/1/8.

50. 155/1/8.

51. 155/2/105.

52. 155/1/19.

53. 155/1/6.

54. 155/1/6.

55. 155/1/7.

56. 155/2/89.

57. 155/1/52.

58. 155/5/94a.

59. Vassiliev, *King Faisal*, 340.

60. Vassiliev, *King Faisal*, 297.

61. 155/1/27.

62. 155/1/37.

63. 155/1/37.

64. 155/2/71.

65. 155/2/71.

66. 155/2/101a.

67. Al-Rasheed, *History of Saudi Arabia*, 119.

68. S. Coll, *Ghost Wars: The Secret History of the CIA, Afghanistan and Bin Ladin, from the Soviet Invasion to September 10, 2011* (New York: Penguin Press, 2004), 77.

69. Matthiessen, "Saudi Arabia," 223.

70. V. Nasr, *The Shia Revival: How Conflicts within Islam Will Shape the Future* (New York: W. W. Norton, 2006).

71. Al-Rasheed, *History of Saudi Arabia*, 78, 102.

72. R. Hunter, *A Box of Rain: Lyrics, 1965–1993* (New York: Viking, 1990).

73. J. D. Singer, "Reconstructing the Correlates of War Dataset on Material Capabilities of States, 1816–1985," *International Interactions* 14 (1987): 115–132.

74. A. Dawisha, *Arab Nationalism in the Twentieth Century: From Triumph to Despair* (Princeton, NJ: Princeton University Press, 2016), 250.

75. Oren, *Six Days of War*, 14–15.

76. M. C. Hudson, *Arab Politics: The Search for Legitimacy* (New Haven, CT: Yale University Press, 1977); C. Ryan, *Inter-Arab Alliances: Regime Security and Jordanian Foreign Policy* (Gainesville: University Press of Florida, 2009), 214.

77. 155/3/161a.

78. Vassiliev, *King Faisal*, 341.

79. 159/2/153.

80. 159/2/160b.

81. TASS Version, Moscow TASS International Service, 15 May 1967, available through the Foreign Broadcast Information Service via Readex.

82. 159-2/2/103.

83. "Cairo Criticizes U.K. Labor Stand on Aden," Cairo Domestic Service, 3 March 1967, available through the Foreign Broadcast Information Service via Readex.

84. "Faysal Travels as Agent of Imperialism," Cairo Domestic Service, 30 August 1966, available through the Foreign Broadcast Information Service via Readex.

85. "Haykal Rips Husayn, See Arab Unity Failing," Cairo Domestic Service, 10 June 1966, available through the Foreign Broadcast Information Service via Readex.

## NOTES TO PAGES 47–49

86. "Further Comment," Cairo Domestic Service, 20 June 1966, available through the Foreign Broadcast Information Service via Readex.

87. "Press Comment," Cairo Domestic Service, 3 August 1966, available through the Foreign Broadcast Information Service via Readex; "British Iranian Arms Deal Seen as Plot," Cairo Domestic Service, 27 August 1966, available through the Foreign Broadcast Information Service via Readex.

88. "Faysal Is Trying to Revive the Baghdad Pact," Cairo Domestic Service, 6 September 1966, available through the Foreign Broadcast Information Service via Readex.

89. "McNamara Statements on Arab East Criticized," Cairo Voice of the Arabs, 30 April 1967, available through the Foreign Broadcast Information Service via Readex.

90. "Al-Ahram Discusses King Faysal's U.S. Trip," Cairo Domestic Service, 21 June 1966, available through the Foreign Broadcast Information Service via Readex.

91. 155/7/24.

92. 159-2/2/96.

93. 159/2/153.

94. S. K. Aburish, *Nasser: The Last Arab* (New York, St. Martin's Press, 2004), 156, 233.

95. Nasir, 18 February interview by Iraqi newsmen, Baghdad Domestic Service, 20 February 1966.

96. 155/2/77.

97. Vassiliev, *King Faisal*, 341.

98. Sindi, "King Faisal," 188–189.

99. Faysal Shah plot to share Arab oil wealth, *Damascuc Domestic Service*, 23 June 1966, available through the Foreign Broadcast Information Service via Readex.

100. "Press Comment," *Cairo Domestic Service*, 2 October 1966, available through the Foreign Broadcast Information Service via Readex.

101. "Radio Hits U.S. Arms in 'Certain Arab State,'" Damascus Domestic Service, 12 January 1966, available through the Foreign Broadcast Information Service via Readex.

102. "Chief of State Speaks on Evacuation Day," Damascus Domestic Service, 17 April 1967, available through the Foreign Broadcast Information Service via Readex.

103. "Defense Minister: We Shall Never Accept Peace," Damascus Domestic Service, 24 May 1966, available through the Foreign Broadcast Information Service via Readex.

104. "All Socialist Forces Will Fight on Arab Side," Damascus Domestic Service, 30 May 1966, available through the Foreign Broadcast Information Service via Readex.

105. "Sunay Visit Seen Part of Imperialist Plot," Radio Peyk-e-Iran, 6 October 1966, available through the Foreign Broadcast Information Service via Readex.

106. "June Communist Statement on Need for Unity," Voice of the Iraqi People (Clandestine), 5 July 1966, available through the Foreign Broadcast Information Service via Readex.

107. "Chairman Says PLO Was Meant to Be Permanent," Cairo Voice of Palestine, 27 May 1966, available through the Foreign Broadcast Information Service via Readex.

108. "Trade Union Statement on Imperialist Threat," Damascus Domestic Service, 6 June 1966, available through the Foreign Broadcast Information Service via Readex.

109. "Ath-Thawrah Sees Faysal-al-Bazzaz Link," Damascus Domestic Service, 6 July 1966, available through the Foreign Broadcast Information Service via Readex.

110. "Solidarity Conference Frames Resolutions," Damascus Domestic Service, 19 January 1967, available through the Foreign Broadcast Information Service via Readex.

NOTES TO PAGES 49–52 157

111. "Free Bahrainis Issue Transitional Demands," Damascus Domestic Service, 21 March 1966, available through the Foreign Broadcast Information Service via Readex.

112. "Statement After April Arab Communists' Meeting," Moscow, 26 May 1966, available through the Foreign Broadcast Information Service via Readex.

113. "Arab Lawyers Group Issues Resolutions," Cairo Domestic Service, 19 September 1966, available through the Foreign Broadcast Information Service via Readex.

114. Sindi, "King Faisal," 188.

115. 155/7/24.

116. 136/5/270.

117. Vassiliev, *King Faisal*, 341.

118. Vassiliev, *King Faisal*, 341.

119. Vassiliev, *King Faisal*, 341.

120. 136/3/64.

121. 136/4/135.

122. 136/2/62.

123. 136/3/164.

124. "Shah's Support of Islamic Alliance Assailed," Damascus Domestic Service, 24 June 1966, available through the Foreign Broadcast Information Service via Readex.

125. "Faysal, Shah Plot to Share Arab Gulf Wealth," Damascus Domestic Service, 23 June 1966, available through the Foreign Broadcast Information Service via Readex.

126. "Joint Session of Parliament," Teheran Domestic Service, 13 September 1965, available through the Foreign Broadcast Information Service via Readex.

127. "Joint Communique," Teheran Domestic Service, 14 December 1965, available through the Foreign Broadcast Information Service via Readex.

128. "Kayhan Excoriates Nasir for Speech on Yemen," Teheran Domestic Service, 5 May 1966, available through the Foreign Broadcast Information Service via Readex.

129. "Kuwait Is Deporting All Progressive Arabs," Damascus Domestic Service, 29 August 1966, available through the Foreign Broadcast Information Service via Readex.

130. "Ummah Party Leader Backs Islamic Summit," Rabat Morocco Domestic, 6 February 1966, available through the Foreign Broadcast Information Service via Readex.

131. "Speeches at Banquet," Rabat Domestic Service, 5 September 1966, available through the Foreign Broadcast Information Service via Readex.

132. 155/3/152.

133. 155/3/169.

134. 155/4/170.

135. 155/4/184.

136. 155/3/169k.

137. 155/3/169k.

138. 155/3/169g.

139. 155/10/35a.

140. 155/2/139.

141. 155/4/174.

142. 155/6/186.

143. 155/4/172.

144. 155/6/115.

145. 160/2/62.

146. 155/3/169a.

## NOTES TO PAGES 53–62

147. 155/7/24.

148. 146/7/6.

149. 147/1/3.

150. 146/4/7.

151. 146/4/18.

152. 146/7/25.

153. 146/7/35.

154. 147/4/56.

155. 146/4/101a.

156. "Husayn Dispatches Yemeni Peace Proposals," Amman Domestic Service, 13 June 1965, available through the Foreign Broadcast Information Service via Readex.

157. "As Battle Nears, Arab Good Will Should Prevail," Amman Domestic Service, 23 August 1966, available through the Foreign Broadcast Information Service via Readex.

158. "Saudi Arabia, Jordan Issue Joint Communique," Riyadh Domestic Service, 2 February 1966, available through the Foreign Broadcast Information Service via Readex.

159. "Relations with Saudis," Amman Domestic, 19 April 1966, available through the Foreign Broadcast Information Service via Readex.

160. "King Husayn Comments on Middle East Problems," Amman Domestic Service, 5 October 1966, available through the Foreign Broadcast Information Service via Readex.

161. 136/4/128.

162. 136/4/242a.

163. 137/6/166.

164. 136/4/135.

165. 136/4/222.

166. 137/7/22.

167. 136/3/206.

168. 136/3/206.

169. 136/1/16.

170. 136/1/16.

171. 146/7/43.

172. 137/6/166.

173. Matthiessen, "Saudi Arabia," 225.

174. Gause, *International Relations*, 1.

175. Oren, *Six Days of War*.

## 3. US Religious Engagement in the Global War on Terrorism

1. Walt, *Taming American Power*; R. Kagan, *Dangerous Nation: America's Foreign Policy from Its Earliest Days to the Dawn of the Twentieth Century* (New York: Vintage, 2007); W. McDougall, *Promised Land, Crusader State: The American Encounter with the World since 1776* (Boston, MA: Mariner Books, 1998); Dueck, *Reluctant Crusaders*.

2. J. Mearsheimer, *The Tragedy of Great Power Politics* (New York: W. W. Norton, 2001); R. J. Lieber, *The American Era: Power and Strategy for the 21st Century* (New York: Cambridge University Press, 2007).

3. Lieber, *American Era*; C. A. Kupchan, *The End of the American Era: U.S. Foreign Policy and the Geopolitics of the Twentieth Century* (New York, Random House, 2002).

NOTES TO PAGES 63–65    159

4. Walt, *Taming American Power*; M. Finnemore, "Legitimacy, Hypocrisy, and the Social Structure of Unipolarity: Why Being a Unipole Isn't All It's Cracked Up to Be," *World Politics* 61, no. 1 (2009): 58–85; J. S. Nye Jr., *The Paradox of American Power* (New York: Oxford University Press, 2002).

5. P. Bergen, *The Longest War: The Enduring Conflict between Al-Qaeda and America* (New York: Free Press, 2011); L. Wright, *The Terror Years: From Al-Qaeda to the Islamic State* (New York: Alfred A. Knopf, 2016); J. E. Owens and J. W. Dumbrell, eds., *America's War on Terrorism: New Dimensions in US Government and National Security* (Lanham, MD: Lexington, 2008); M. Ayoob and E. Ugur, eds., *Assessing the War on Terror* (Boulder, CO: Lynne Rienner, 2013); E. H. Prodromou, "U.S. Foreign Policy and Global Religious Pluralism," in Banchoff, *Religious Pluralism*.

6. W. R. Mead, "God's Country?" in *Rethinking Religion and World Affairs*, ed. T. S. Shah, A. Stepan, and M. D. Toft (New York: Oxford University Press, 2012), 247–262; McDougall, *Promised Land*; Bettiza, *Finding Faith*; P. S. Henne and G. Bettiza, "Geopolitical Grand Narratives, Religious Outreach, and Religious Soft Power in US Foreign Policy," in *The Geopolitics of Religious Soft Power: How States Use Religion in Foreign Policy*, ed. P. Mandaville (New York: Oxford University Press, 2023); D. Kirby, "Religion and the Cold War: An Introduction," in *Religion and the Cold War*, ed. D. Kirby (New York: Palgrave Macmillan, 2003), 1–23; W. Inboden, *Religion and American Foreign Policy, 1945–1960: The Soul of Containment* (New York: Cambridge University Press, 2008); A. Preston, *Sword of the Spirit, Shield of Faith: Religion in American War and Diplomacy* (New York: Alfred A. Knopf, 2012); Haynes, *Religion, Politics*.

7. Albright, *Mighty and the Almighty*.

8. W. Ochsenwald, "Saudi Arabia and the Islamic Revival," *International Journal of Middle East Studies* 13, no. 3 (1981): 271–286; A. Haris, "The Role of Muslims in the Struggle against Violent Extremist Ideology in Indonesia," *Connections* 5, no. 4 (2006): 157–166; A. Etzioni, "Leveraging Islam," *National Interest* 83 (2006): 101–106.

9. S. J. Rascoff, "Establishing Official Islam? The Law and Strategy of Counterradicalization," *Stanford Law Review* 64 (2012): 125–190; Y. Y. Haddad and T. Golson, "Overhauling Islam: Representation, Construction, and Cooption of 'Moderate Islam' in Western Europe," *Journal of Church and State* 49, no. 3 (2007): 487–515; M. Mamdani, *Good Muslim, Bad Muslim: America, the Cold War and the Roots of Terror* (New York: Three Leaves, 2005); D. J. Stewart, "The Greater Middle East and Reform in the Bush Administration's Ideological Imagination," *Geographical Review* 95, no. 3 (2005): 400–424; D. Motadel, "Uneasy Engagement," *World Today* 67, no. 1 (2011): 27–29; M. Browers, "Official Islam and the Limits of Communicative Action: The Paradox of the Amman Message," *Third World Quarterly* 32, no. 5 (2011): 943–958; S. Gutkowski, "We Are the Very Model of a Moderate Muslim State: The Amman Messages and Jordan's Foreign Policy," *International Relations* 30, no. 2 (2016).

10. F. Gerges, *The Far Enemy: Why Jihad Went Global* (New York: Cambridge University Press, 2005).

11. P. S. Henne, "Assessing the Impact of the Global War on Terrorism on Terrorism Threats in Muslim Countries," *Terrorism and Political Violence* 33, no. 7 (2021): 1511–1529.

12. Prodromou, "U.S. Foreign Policy."

13. Kagan, *Dangerous Nation*, 12.

14. Albright, *Mighty and the Almighty*, 18.

160    **NOTES TO PAGES 65–67**

15. A. T. Kuru, *Secularism and State Policies towards Religion: The United States, France and Turkey* (New York: Cambridge University Press, 2009).

16. Kuru, *Secularism*, 43.

17. R. N. Bellah, "Civil Religion in America," *Daedalus* 96 (1967): 1–21. Quoted in Prodromou, "U.S. Foreign Policy"; Casanova, *Public Religions*; P. Gorski, *American Covenant: A History of Civil Religion from the Puritans to the Present* (Princeton, NJ: Princeton University Press, 2017).

18. Mead, "God's Country?" 256.

19. S. R. Rock, *Faith and Foreign Policy* (New York: Continuum, 2011).

20. Mead, "God's Country?" 247.

21. L. Canipe, "Under God and Anti-Communist: How the Pledge of Allegiance Got Religion in Cold War America," *Journal of Church and State* 45, no. 2 (2003): 305–323.

22. Prodromou, "U.S. Foreign Policy."

23. Rock, *Faith and Foreign Policy*.

24. Albright, *Mighty and the Almighty*, 23.

25. A. D. Hertzke, *Freeing God's Children: The Unlikely Alliance for Global Human Rights* (Lanham, MD: Rowman and Littlefield, 2004); Rock, *Faith and Foreign Policy*; L. F. Turek, *To Bring the Good News to All Nations: Evangelical Influence on Human Rights and U.S. Foreign Relations* (Ithaca, NY: Cornell University Press, 2020).

26. E. Brumiller, "Evangelicals Sway White House on Human Rights Issues Abroad," *New York Times*, 26 October 2003.

27. These discussions of US use of religion as a tool in Cold War and post-Cold War foreign policy come from Henne and Bettiza, "Geopolitical Grand Narratives."

28. D. Kirby, "Harry Truman's Religious Legacy: The Holy Alliance, Containment and the Cold War," *Religion and the Cold War* (New York: Palgrave Macmillan, 2003), 77–103.

29. Inboden, *Religion*, 112.

30. Inboden, *Religion*; Preston, *Sword of the Spirit*.

31. Bronson, *Thicker Than Oil*; M. Doran, *Ike's Gamble: America's Rise to Dominance in the Middle East* (New York: Free Press, 2016).

32. K. Yin and A. Haga, "Rising to the Occasion: The Role of American Missionaries and Korean Pastors in Resisting Communism throughout the Korea War," in *Religion and the Cold War: A Global Perspective*, ed. P. E. Muehlenbeck (Nashville, TN: Vanderbilt University Press, 2012), 88–113.

33. J. M. Chapman, "Religion, Power and Legitimacy in Ngo Dinh Diem's Republic of Vietnam," in Muehlenbeck, *Religion and the Cold War*, 206–229.

34. Bettiza, *Finding Faith*, 2.

35. Prodromou, "U.S. Foreign Policy."

36. Bettiza, *Finding Faith*, 3.

37. Prodromou, "U.S. Foreign Policy."

38. A. Rabasa, "Where Are We in the 'War of Ideas?'" in *The Long Shadow of 9/11: America's Response to Terrorism*, ed. B. M. Jenkins and J. P. Godges (Washington, DC: RAND, 2011), 61–70.

39. M. J. Gerson, *Heroic Conservatism: Why Republicans Need to Embrace America's Ideals (and Why They Deserve to Fail If They Don't)* (New York: HarperOne, 2007), 21–22.

NOTES TO PAGES 67–72     161

40. F. Pandith, *How We Win: How Cutting-Edge Entrepreneurs, Political Visionaries, Enlightened Business Leaders, and Social Media Mavens Can Defeat the Extremist Threat* (New York: HarperCollins, 2019), 52.

41. Al-Rasheed, *Contesting the Saudi State*.

42. "Obama 'Talks to the Enemy,'" *Sahara Reporter*, 26 February 2009; J. K. Glassman, "Finally, Obama's Taking Radical Islam Seriously," *Politico*, 19 February 2015.

43. "ISIL Strategy: The US Strategy to Combat ISIL and Defeat the Terrorist Threat," The White House, accessed 29 December 2022, https://obamawhitehouse.archives.gov/isil-strategy; A. M. Fernandez, "Here to Stay and Growing: Combating ISIS Propaganda Networks," *U.S.–Islamic World Forum Papers* (Washington, DC: Brookings Institution, 2015).

44. For more on this, see Henne, *Islamic Politics*.

45. "The National Security Strategy of the United States of America," The White House, Washington, DC, September 2002.

46. "The National Security Strategy," The White House, Washington, DC, 2006.

47. Prodromou, "U.S. Foreign Policy," 30.

48. Gerson, *Heroic Conservatism*, 74.

49. Gerson, *Heroic Conservatism*, 77.

50. M. Latimer, *Speech-Less: Tales of a White House Survivor* (Danvers, MA: Crown, 2010), 218–219.

51. Farah Pandith (counterterrorism official), interview by author, Washington, DC, October 2019.

52. T. C. Wittes, *The New U.S. Proposal for a Greater Middle East Initiative: An Evaluation* (Washington, DC: Brookings Institute, 2004).

53. Pandith, *How We Win*, 52.

54. Eric Rosand (counterterrorism expert), interview by author, Washington, DC, October 2019.

55. Connie LaRossa (counterterrorism expert), interview by author, Washington, DC, October 2019.

56. LaRossa, interview.

57. James Patton (counterterrorism expert), interview by author, Washington, DC, October 2019.

58. Pandith, interview.

59. Interview with counterterrorism expert, Washington, DC, October 2019.

60. Interview with Eric Rosand, Wasington, DC, October 2019.

61. Gerson, *Heroic Conservatism*, 79.

62. Prodromou, "U.S. Foreign Policy," 307.

63. Prodromou, "U.S. Foreign Policy," 308.

64. Bettiza, *Finding Faith*

65. Pandith, interview.

66. Interview with religious engagement expert, Washington, DC, October 2019.

67. "National Security Strategy," The White House, Washington, DC, May 2010.

68. Bettiza, *Finding Faith*, 147.

69. Bettiza, *Finding Faith*, 146.

70. Interview with Obama-era official, Washington, DC, October 2019.

71. Patton, interview.

72. Interview with counterterrorism expert, Washington, DC, October 2019.

73. Interview with counterextremism expert, Washington, DC, October 2019.

74. LaRossa, interview.

75. Peter Mandaville (counterterrorism expert), interview by author, Washington, DC, October 2019.

76. "Obama's Egypt Speech: What He Said to the Muslim World," Brookings Institute, Washington, DC, 4 June 2009.

77. Rosand, interview.

78. Seamus Hughes (counterterrorism expert), interview by author, Washington, DC, October 2019.

79. Interview with former counterterrorism official, Washington, DC, October 2019.

80. Interview with former counterterrorism official, Washington, DC, October 2019.

81. Interview with counterterrorism expert, Washington, DC, October 2019.

82. Interview with former counterterrorism official, Washington, DC, October 2019.

83. Mandaville, interview.

84. Rosand, interview.

85. E. J. Dionne Jr. and M. Rogers, *A Time to Heal, a Time to Build* (Washington, DC: Brookings Institution, 2020).

86. Kerry, "We Ignore the Global."

87. Interview with counterterrorism experts, Washington, DC, October 2019.

88. Interview with counterterrorism experts, Washington, DC, October 2019.

89. Mandaville, interview.

90. Rosand, interview.

91. R. O. Keohane and P. J. Katzenstein, *Anti-Americanisms in World Politics* (Ithaca, NY: Cornell University Press, 2007).

92. Bronson, *Thicker Than Oil*.

93. Coll, *Ghost Wars*.

94. Henne, *Islamic Politics*.

95. A. M. Wainscott, *Bureaucratizing Islam: Morocco and the War on Terror* (New York: Cambridge University Press, 2017).

96. L. King, Interview with His Majesty King Abdullah II of Jordan, *Larry King Live*, CNN, 18 March 2002.

97. Interview with counterterrorism expert, Washington, DC, October 2019.

98. S. Baer and D. L. Greene, "'Face of Terror Not True Faith of Islam,' Bush Declares," *Baltimore Sun*, 18 September 2001.

99. Pandith, *How We Win*, 283.

100. Pandith, *How We Win*, 287.

101. Interview with counterterrorism expert, Washington, DC, October 2019.

102. Patton, interview.

103. Pandith, interview.

104. S. Kull, *Feeling Betrayed: The Roots of Muslim Anger at America* (Washington, DC: Brookings Institution, 2011).

105. LaRossa, interview.

106. Pandith, *How We Win*, 276.

107. "Manipulating the Minarets," *Economist*, 2 August 2014.

108. Interview with counterterrorism expert, Washington, DC, October 2019.

109. Rosand, interview.

110. Rosand, interview.

111. Interview with counterterrorism expert, Washington, DC, October 2019.

112. Interview with counterterrorism expert, Washington, DC, October 2019.

113. Interview with counterterrorism expert, Washington, DC, October 2019.

114. Interview with former religion policymaker, Washington, DC, October 2019.

115. Hughes, interview.

116. Interview with counterterrorism expert, Washington, DC, October 2019.

117. Interview with former counterterrorism expert, Washington, DC, October 2019.

118. Hughes, interview.

119. Rosand, interview.

120. Interview with Obama-era CVE official, Washington, DC, October 2019.

121. Patton, interview.

122. Patton, interview.

123. Interview with counterterrorism expert, Washington, DC, October 2019.

124. Hughes, interview.

125. Interview with counterterrorism expert, Washington, DC, October 2019.

126. Rosand, interview.

127. Interview with former official, Washington, DC, October 2019.

128. Interview with counterterrorism expert, Washington, DC, October 2019.

129. Patton, interview.

130. LaRossa, interview.

131. Hughes, interview.

132. Interview with counterterrorism expert, Washington, DC, October 2019.

133. Patton, interview.

134. Hughes, interview.

135. Hughes, interview.

136. Patton, interview.

137. Interview with counterterrorism expert, Washington, DC, October 2019.

138. Interview with counterterrorism experts, Washington, DC, October 2019.

139. Interview with author, former Obama CVE expert, Washington, DC, October 2019.

140. Interview with counterterrorism expert, Washington, DC, October 2019.

## 4. Russia

1. I. Tharoor, "Why Putin Says Crimea Is Russia's 'Temple Mount,'" *Washington Post*, 4 December 2014.

2. D. Adamsky, "Nuclear Incoherence: Deterrence Theory and Non-Strategic Nuclear Weapons in Russia," *Journal of Strategic Studies* 37, no. 1 (2014): 91–134; R. Gottemoeller, "Russia Is Updating Their Nuclear Weapons: What Does That Mean for the Rest of Us?" (Carnegie Endowment for International Peace, Washington, DC, 29 January 2020).

3. N. Edwards, *Coup-Proofing: Russia's Military Blueprint to Securing Resources in Africa* (Washington, DC: Council on Foreign Relations, 2021); J. K. Choksy and C. E. B.

## 164   NOTES TO PAGES 88-89

Choksy, "China and Russia Have Iran's Back: Tehran May Be Less Open Than Ever to Threats or Persuasion," *Foreign Affairs*, 17 November 2020.

4. R. K. Knake, *Why the Solarwinds Hack Is a Wake-Up Call: The Sweeping Cyber Espionage Campaign Shows How Sophisticated Adversaries Can Bypass Even Well-Defended Targets* (Washington, DC: Council on Foreign Relations, 2021).

5. K. A. Lieber and G. Alexander, "Waiting for Balancing: Why the World Is Not Pushing Back," *International Security* 30, no. 1 (2005): 109–139.

6. A. A. Velikaya and G. Simons, "Introduction," in *Russia's Public Diplomacy: Evolution and Practice*, ed. A. A. Velikaya and G. Simons (Cham, Switzerland: Palgrave Macmillan, 2020), 1–26; K. Kirillova, *Soft Power and "Positive Propaganda": How Russia Uses Cultural and Historical Stereotypes to Increase Political Influence* (Estonia: International Centre for Defence and Security, 2020); M. Hooper, "Russia's 'Traditional Values' Leadership" (Human Rights First, 24 May 2016); W. Laqueur, "After the Fall: Russia in Search of a New Ideology," *World Affairs*, March/April 2014; M. H. Van Herpen, *Putin's Wars: The Rise of Russia's New Imperialism* (Lanham, MD: Rowman and Littlefield, 2015); M. Galeotti and A. S. Bowen, "Putin's Empire of the Mind: How Russia's President Morphed from Realist to Ideologue—And What He'll Do Next," *Foreign Policy*, 21 April 2014; M. Popkhadze, *Standing Up to Russia's Sharp Power* (Philadelphia, PA: Foreign Policy Research Institute, 2018); J. S. Nye Jr., "How Sharp Power Threatens Soft Power: The Right and Wrong Ways to Respond to Authoritarian Influence," *Foreign Affairs*, 24 January 2018; C. Walker and J. Ludwig, "The Meaning of Sharp Power: How Authoritarian States Project Influence," *Foreign Affairs*, 16 November 2017. For more on the issues surrounding this terminology, see Henne, "What We Talk."

7. A. J. Rieber, "How Persistent Are Persistent Factors?" in *Russian Foreign Policy in the Twenty-First Century and the Shadow of the Past*, ed. R. Levgold (New York: Columbia University Press, 2007), 205–279; L. Caldwell, "Russian Concepts of National Security," in Levgold, *Russian Foreign Policy*, 279–343; N. Malcolm et al., eds., *Internal Factors in Russian Foreign Policy* (London: Oxford University Press, 1996).

8. J. Anderson, *Religion, State and Politics in the Soviet Union and Successor States* (New York: Cambridge University Press, 1994); K. Stoeckl, "Double Bind at the UN: Western Actors, Russia and the Traditionalist Agenda," *Global Constitutionalism* 7, no. 3 (2018): 383–421; R. C. Blitt, "Russia's 'Orthodox' Foreign Policy: The Growing Influence of the Russian Orthodox Church in Shaping Russia's Policies Abroad," *University of Pennsylvania Journal of International Law* 33, no. 2 (2011): 363–460.

9. G. Soroka, "Putin's Patriarch: Does the Kremlin Control the Church?" *Foreign Affairs*, 11 February 2016; G. Shakhanova and P. Kratochvil, "The Patriotic Turn in Russia: Political Convergence of the Russian Orthodox Church and the State?" *Politics and Religion* 15, no. 1 (2022), 114–141.

10. A. Curanovic, *The Religious Factor in Russia's Foreign Policy* (London: Routledge, 2014); E. Stetsko, "The Role of Civil Society in Russian Public Diplomacy," in Velikaya and Simons, *Russia's Public Diplomacy*, 147–157; D. Adamsky, *Russian Nuclear Orthodoxy: Religion, Politics, and Strategy* (Palo Alto, CA: Stanford University Press, 2019); S. Griffin, "Putin's Medieval Weapons in the War against Ukraine," *Studies in Medievalism* 29 (2020): 13–21; D. W. Larson and A. Shevchenko, *Quest for Status: Chinese and Russian Foreign Policy* (New Haven, CT: Yale University Press, 2019); Henne, *Geopolitics of Faith*; N. Lomagin, "Interest Groups in Russian Foreign Policy: The Invisible Hand of the Russian Orthodox Church," *International Politics* 49, no. 4 (2012): 498–516.

NOTES TO PAGES 89–91    165

11. I should note that many of the scholars who discuss religion in Russian foreign policy believe it is partly a strategic calculation by Putin, so they are more in line with my argument. Most of this attention has been on the presence of religion in Russian politics, rather than its impact on international power politics, though.

12. Pouliot, *International Security*.

13. A. A. Pikayev, "Rise and Fall of Start II: The Russian Perspective" (Carnegie Endowment for International Peace, Washington, DC, 1999); M. Gessen, "The Undoing of Bill Clinton and Boris Yeltsin's Friendship, and How It Changed Both of Their Countries," *New Yorker*, 5 September 2018.

14. P. Black, "Russia Protesters Demand Putin's Resignation," *CNN*, 12 June 2012.

15. J. Acosta, "US, Other Powers Kick Russia Out of G8," *CNN*, 24 March 2014.

16. E. H. Christie, "Sanctions after Crimea: Have They Worked?" *NATO Review*, 13 July 2015.

17. J. Anderson, *Conservative Christian Politics in Russia and the United States* (London: Routledge, 2015).

18. Van Herpen, *Putin's Wars*; Larson and Shevchenko, *Quest for Status*.

19. Anderson, *Conservative Christian Politics*, 24.

20. Anderson, *Conservative Christian Politics*, 23.

21. Anderson, *Religion, State and Politics*.

22. M. Bourdeaux, "Introduction," in *The Politics of Religion in Russia and the New States of Eurasia*, ed. Michael Bourdeaux (Armonk, NY: M. E. Sharpe, 1997), 1–12.

23. Anderson, *Religion, State and Politics*.

24. D. V. Pospielovsky, "The Russian Orthodox Church in the Postcommunist CIS," in Bourdeaux *Politics of Religion*, 41–78.

25. J. Anderson, "Putin and the Russian Orthodox Church: Asymmetric Symphonia?" *Journal of International Affairs* 61, no. 1 (2007):185–201; Anderson, *Conservative Christian Politics*.

26. Pospielovsky, "Russian Orthodox Church," 45.

27. Anderson, *Religion, State and Politics*.

28. D. Uzlaner and K. Stoeckl, "The Legacy of Pitirim Sorokin in the Transnational Alliances of Moral Conservatives," *Journal of Classical Sociology* 18, no. 2 (2018): 133–153.

29. J. B. Dunlop, "The Russian Orthodox Church as an Empire-Saving Institution," in Bourdeaux, *Politics of Religion*, 15–40.

30. A. Curanovic, "Guarding the Motherland's Frontiers: The Russian Orthodox Church in the North Caucasus," *Problems of Post-Communism* 67, no. 6 (2020): 446–454; K. Stoeckl, "European Integration and Russian Orthodoxy: Two Multiple Modernities Perspectives," *European Journal of Social Theory* 14, no. 2 (2011): 217–233.

31. Anderson, *Conservative Christian Politics*; J. W. Lamoreaux and L. Flake, "The Russian Orthodox Church, the Kremlin, and Religious (Il)liberalism in Russia," *Palgrave Communications* 4, no. 115 (2018).

32. Anderson, *Religion, State and Politics*.

33. Larson and Shevchenko, *Quest for Status*, 10.

34. Anderson, *Religion, State and Politics*.

35. A. Pravda, "The Public Politics of Foreign Policy," in *Internal Factors in Russian Foreign Policy*, ed. Neil Malcolm et al. (London: Oxford University Press, 1996), 169–230; Dunlop, "Russian Orthodox Church."

166    **NOTES TO PAGES 92–93**

36. J. Anderson, "Dreaming of Christian Nations in the USA and Russia: The Importnace of History," *Journal of Transatlantic Studies* 10, no. 3 (2012): 201–221; J. Anderson, "Religion, State and 'Sovereign Democracy' in Putin's Russia," *Journal of Religious and Political Practice* 2, no. 2 (2016): 249–266.

37. A. Curanovic, "Russia's Contemporary Exceptionalism and Geopolitical Conservatism," in *Contemporary Russian Conservatism: Problems, Paradoxes, and Perspectives*, ed. M. Suslov and D. Uzlaner (Leiden: Brill, 2019), 207–233; R. Levgold, "Russian Foreign Policy during Periods of Great State Transformation," in Levgold, *Russian Foreign Policy*, 77–145.

38. Anderson, *Conservative Christian Politics*; John Anderson, "Rocks, Art, and Sex: The 'Culture Wars' Come to Russia," *Journal of Church and State* 55, no. 2 (2012): 307–334; D. Uzlaner and K. Stoeckl, "From Pussy Riot's 'Punk Prayer' to *Matilda*: Orthodox Believers, Critique and Religious Freedom in Russia," *Journal of Contemporary Religion* 34, no. 3 (2019): 427–445.

39. Anderson, *Religion, State and Politics*, 195.

40. Anderson, *Religion, State and Politics*, 195.

41. Pospielovsky, "Russian Orthodox Church."

42. Anderson, *Conservative Christian Politics*.

43. Anderson, *Conservative Christian Politics*.

44. Anderson, "Dreaming of Christian Nations"; A. P. Tsygankov, *Russia's Foreign Policy: Change and Continuity in National Identity* (Lanham, MD: Rowman and Littlefield, 2016), 207.

45. Anderson, "Putin."

46. Curanovic, "Russia's Contemporary Exceptionalism"; Anderson, "Religion, State"; Larson and Shevchenko, *Quest for Status*.

47. M. Kaylan, "Kremlin Values: Putin's Strategic Conservatism," *World Affairs* 177, no. 1 (2014): 9–17.

48. M. Sivertsev, "Civil Society and Religion in Traditional Political Culture: The Case of Russia," in Bourdeaux, *Politics of Religion*, 91.

49. Dunlop, "Russian Orthodox Church," 22.

50. Dunlop, "Russian Orthodox Church," 22.

51. Stetsko, "Role of Civil Society."

52. Van Herpen, *Putin's Wars*, 240.

53. A. Curanovic, "Russia's Mission in the World: The Perspective of the Russian Orthodox Church," *Problems of Post-Communism* 66, no. 4 (2019): 253–267.

54. Curanovic, "Russia's Mission."

55. D. P. Payne, "Spiritual Security, the Russian Orthodox Church, and the Russian Foreign Ministry: Collaboration or Cooptation?" *Journal of Church and State* 52, no. 4 (2010), 719.

56. Tsygankov, *Russia's Foreign Policy*, 251.

57. A. Curanovic, "The Attitude of the Moscow Patriarchate towards Other Orthodox Churches," *Religion, State and Society* 35, no. 4 (2007): 301–318.

58. Larson and Shevchenko, *Quest for Status*, 230.

59. M. Light, "Foreign Policy Thinking," in Malcolm et al., *Internal Factors*, 33–100.

60. Curanovic, "Russia's Contemporary Exceptionalism."

61. Larson and Shevchenko, *Quest for Status*, 245.

62. Curanovic, "Attitude."

NOTES TO PAGES 93–95    167

63. Light, "Foreign Policy Thinking."

64. Pravda, "Public Politics."

65. N. N. Petro, "Russia's Orthodox Soft Power: U.S. Global Engagement Initiative" (Carnegie Council for Ethics in International Affairs, Washington, DC, 23 March 2015).

66. L. Malksoo, "The History of International Legal Theory in Russia: A Civilizational Dialogue with Europe," *European Journal of International Law* 19, no. 1 (2008).

67. Anderson, "Religion, State."

68. K. Stoeckl, *The Russian Orthodox Church and Human Rights* (New York: Routledge, 2014).

69. Stoeckl, "Double Bind," 396.

70. Van Herpen, *Putin's Wars*, 133–134, 145.

71. Curanovic, "Guarding the Motherland's Frontiers," 449.

72. Payne, "Spiritual Security."

73. Anderson, *Conservative Christian Politics*.

74. K. Roberts, "Understanding Putin: The Politics of Identity and Geopolitics in Russian Foreign Policy Discourse," *International Journal* 72, no. 1 (2017): 28–55.

75. Tsygankov, *Russia's Foreign Policy*.

76. R. Levgold, "Introduction," in Levgold, *Russian Foreign Policy*, 10.

77. Larson and Shevchenko, *Quest for Status*; Van Herpen, *Putin's Wars*.

78. Light, "Foreign Policy Thinking."

79. Uzlaner and Stoeckl, "Legacy of Pitirim Sorokin," 145.

80. Curanovic, "Russia's Contemporary Exceptionalism"; Anderson, *Conservative Christian Politics*; Stoeckl, *Russian Orthodox Church*; L. Malksoo, "The Human Rights Concept of the Russian Orthodox Church and Its Patriarch Kirill I: A Critical Appraisal," *European Yearbook on Human Rights* (2013): 403–416.

81. Curanovic, "Russia's Mission," 257.

82. Tsygankov, *Russia's Foreign Policy*; B. Lo, *Vladimir Putin and the Evolution of Russian Foreign Policy* (London: Chatham House Papers, 2003).

83. Caldwell, "Russian Concepts"; R. Lissner and M. Rapp-Hooper, *An Open World: How America Can Win the Contest for Twenty-First-Century Order* (New Haven, CT: Yale University Press, 2020).

84. V. Huseynov, *Geopolitical Rivalries in the "Common Neighborhood": Russia's Conflict with the West, Soft Power and Neoclassical Realism* (Verlag, Stuttgart: ibidem, 2019).

85. Curanovic, "Russia's Contemporary Exceptionalism," 215.

86. Curanovic, "Russia's Mission."

87. Tsygankov, *Russia's Foreign Policy*.

88. Tsygankov, *Russia's Foreign Policy*, 247.

89. G. Simons, "Aspects of Putin's Appeal to International Publics," *Global Affairs* 1, no. 2 (2015): 205–208.

90. J. M. Permoser and K. Stoeckl, "Reframing Human Rights: The Global Network of Moral Conservative Homeschooling Activists," *Global Networks* 21, no. 4 (2020): 681–702; K. Stoeckl, "The Rise of the Russian Christian Right: The Case of the World Congress of Families," *Religion, State and Society* 48, no. 4 (2020): 223–238.

91. S. A. Semedov and A. G. Kurbatova, "Russian Public Diplomacy and Nation Branding," in Velikaya and Simons, *Russia's Public Diplomacy*, 45–61.

92. N. Bubnova, "Russia's Policy and International Cooperation: The Challenges and Opportunities of Soft Power," in Velikaya and Simons, *Russia's Public Diplomacy*, 79–103.

93. Stoeckl, *Russian Orthodox Church*, 118.

94. K. Stoeckl and K. Medvedeva, "Double Bind at the UN: Western Actors, Russia, and the Traditionalist Agenda," *Global Constitutionalism* 7, no. 3 (2018): 383–421.

95. "Russia's Information Policy Abroad Aims to Defend Traditional Values," *BBC Monitoring Former Soviet Union—Political*, 30 January 2014, accessed via Nexis-Uni. (This section relied on primary sources accessed through Nexis-Uni. All sources from Nexis-Uni are indicated.)

96. V. Isachenkov and N. Vasilyeva, "Putin Defends Russia's Conservative Values, Chides West for Treating Good and Evil Equally," *Record*, 12 December 2013, accessed via Nexis-Uni.

97. D. McElroy, "Putin Asserts Russia's Moral Superiority in the Values War," *Telegraph*, 12 December 2013, accessed via Nexis-Uni.

98. D. McElroy, "Putin Casts Russia as a Force for Moral Good," *Gazette (Montreal)*, 12 December 2013, accessed via Nexis-Uni.

99. D. McElroy, "Russian Prez Defends 'Traditional Values': State of the Nation Address: Putin Denounces Interference from U.S., Other Nations," *Vancouver Province (British Columbia)*, 13 December 2013, accessed via Nexis-Uni.

100. "Putin Interviewed at Length in Russian TV Film 'World Order,'" *BBC Monitoring Former Soviet Union—Political*, 21 December 2015, accessed via Nexis-Uni.

101. "Putin Interviewed at Length."

102. "World: Vladimir Putin Interview," *Thai News Service*, 1 July 2019, accessed via Nexis-Uni.

103. "World: Vladimir Putin Interview."

104. "Putin Highlights Challenges to Traditional Values," *ITAR-TASS*, 4 November 2020, accessed via Nexis-Uni.

105. "Putin Highlights Challenges."

106. "Russia's Vladimir Putin Visits Syria to Meet Bashar Assad, a Key Iran Ally," *Hamilton Spectator*, 7 January 2020, accessed via Nexis-Uni.

107. "Tehran, Moscow on Frontline of Battling Terrorism," *Iran Daily*, 5 December 2017, accessed via Nexis-Uni.

108. "Fred Weir, Russia in Syria: Ghosts of Afghanistan May Limit Kremlin's Options Now," *Christian Science Monitor*, 11 September 2015, accessed via Nexis-Uni.

109. T. Gjelten, "US Evangelicals Push Back against Trump's Syria Pullout Plan," *NPR All Things Considered*, 16 January 2019, accessed via Nexis-Uni.

110. A. Ben Solomon, "Egypt's Coptic Pope: Things Will Get Better. Christians Continue to Be Threatened and Attacked in Arab World," *Jerusalem Post*, 13 September 2013, accessed via Nexis-Uni.

111. "'Regular Guy' or 'Lady with Her Own Opinion': Putin about US Presidential Hopefuls," *RusData Dialine*, 9 November 2016, accessed via Nexis-Uni.

112. "Most Americans Have Ideas about World, Which Are Similar to Russian Traditional Values: Putin," *ITAR-TASS*, 23 December 2016, accessed via Nexis-Uni.

113. L. Kim, "Putin Attacks Obama in Annual Moscow Press Conference," *NPR All Things Considered*, 23 December 2016, accessed via Nexis-Uni.

114. McElroy, "Putin Casts Russia."

115. McElroy, "Russian Prez Defends."

116. "Putin Embodies Defender of Traditional Values in Eyes of Europeans, Americans: Expert," *ITAR-TASS*, 4 October 2017, accessed via Nexis-Uni.

NOTES TO PAGES 97–100    169

117. J. Edgar, "Putin Attacks Eurovision Drag Artist Conchita for Putting Her Lifestyle 'Up for Show,'" *Telegraph*, 26 May 2014, accessed via Nexis-Uni.

118. "Putin Rebukes European Media for Manipulating Public Opinion, Lauds La Stampa for Maintaining Journalism's Traditional Values," *Russia & CIS General Newswire*, 9 February 2017, accessed via Nexis-Uni.

119. "Foreign Minister Sergey Lavrov's Interview Given to Channel One's Bolshaya Igra (Gream Game) Talk Show," *States News Service*, 1 April 2021, accessed via Nexis-Uni.

120. A. Higgins, "In Expanding Russian Influence, Faith Combines with Firepower," *New York Times*, 13 September 2016, accessed via Nexis-Uni.

121. B. Waterfield, "Austrian Far Right Allies with Putin," *Times*, 21 December 2016, accessed via Nexis-Uni.

122. R. Boyes, "The New Mussolini and His Axis of the Macho," *Times*, 7 May 2014, accessed via Nexis-Uni.

123. O. Carroll, "Britain First: Far-Right British Group Invited to Speak at Russian Parliament," *Independent*, 2 July 2019, accessed via Nexis-Uni.

124. V. Dergachev, "Russian, European Far-Right Parties Converge in St. Petersburg," *RusData Dialine*, 23 March 2015, accessed via Nexis-Uni.

125. H. LaFranchi, "Why Putin Is Suddenly Gaining Popularity among Conservatives," *Christian Science Monitor*, 16 December 2016, accessed via Nexis-Uni.

126. LaFranchi, "Why Putin."

127. LaFranchi, "Why Putin."

128. LaFranchi, "Why Putin."

129. "Russia and the Republicans: How Vladimir Putin Got an American Subsidiary," *Salon.com*, 14 December 2019, accessed via Nexis-Uni.

130. "Russia and the Republicans."

131. "How Russia Became the Leader of the Global Christian Right," *Politico*, 9 February 2017, accessed via Nexis-Uni.

132. R. Brownstein, "Putin and the Populists," *Atlantic*, 6 January 2017, accessed via Nexis-Uni.

133. J. W. Peters, "A Reverence for Putin on the Right Provides Cover for the President," *New York Times*, 15 July 2017, accessed via Nexis-Uni.

134. Peters, "Reverence for Putin."

135. N. Bertrand, "A Model for Civilization," *Business Insider*, 10 December 2016, accessed via Nexis-Uni.

136. Bertrand, "Model for Civilization."

137. "Tycoon Emerges as Link between Russia and Rebels: Kiev Investigation," *Financial Times*, 25 July 2014, accessed via Nexis-Uni.

138. "European Far-Right Groups Back Putin at Russia Forum," *Agence France Presse*, 22 March 2015, accessed via Nexis-Uni.

139. "Putin Embodies Defender."

140. Brownstein, "Putin and the Populists."

141. G. Tetraut-Farber, "Far-Right Europe Has a Crush on Moscow," *Moscow Times*, 25 November 2014, accessed via Nexis-Uni.

142. Bertrand, "Model for Civilization."

143. Bertrand, "Model for Civilization."

144. "Putin Is Down with Polygamy," *Weekly Cutting Edge*, 8 August 2015, accessed via Nexis-Uni.

145. "Putin Is Down."

146. A. Feuer and A. Higgins, "Extremists Turn to a Leader to Protect Western Values: Vladimir Putin," *New York Times*, 3 November 2016, accessed via Nexis-Uni.

147. Higgins, "In Expanding Russian Influence."

148. Higgins, "In Expanding Russian Influence."

149. Bertrand, "Model for Civilization."

150. N. MacFarquhar, "On the Air in Kansas City: Russian Propaganda," *New York Times*, 14 February 2020, accessed via Nexis-Uni.

151. MacFarquhar, "On the Air."

152. "How Russia Became."

153. S. Patrick, "How U.S. Allies Are Adapting to 'America First,'" *Foreign Affairs*, 23 January 2018.

154. "How Russia Became."

155. Brownstein, "Putin and the Populists."

156. C. Woodhouse, "Vladdy Idiot; Farage Hands Putin Propaganda Coup on EU," *Sun*, 30 March 2014, accessed via Nexis-Uni.

157. "Russia Promises to Improve Lifestyles in Crimea," *Western Daily Press*, 5 April 2014, accessed via Nexis-Uni.

158. T. N. Dunn, "Nige Wins on Points," *Sun*, 3 April 2014, accessed via Nexis-Uni.

159. "Nationalists Defy EU Condemnation of Russia Abuses," *BBC News*, 10 June 2015, accessed via Nexis-Uni.

160. A. Osborn and W. James, "UK's Anti-EU Leader Accused of Being Apologist for Russia Before Vote," Reuters, 27 March 2014, accessed via Nexis-Uni.

161. T. Karasik, "Putin's Rome Trip Highlights Italy's Importance to Russia," *Arab News*, 7 July 2019, accessed via Nexis-Uni.

162. "France's Front National Hails Greek Syriza," *New Europe*, 30 December 2014, accessed via Nexis-Uni.

163. "Italian Party Leader Visits Russia, Crimea, Slams Western Sanctions," *BBC Monitoring Europe—Political*, 13 October 2014, accessed via Nexis-Uni.

164. "Italy's Northern League Pledges to Start Campaign against Anti-Russian Sanctions," *Russia and CIS Military Newswire*, 15 October 2014, accessed via Nexis-Uni.

165. "Opposition Leader: Italy's Support for EU Sanctions on Russia Harming National Interests," *FARS News Agency*, 24 September 2014, accessed via Nexis-Uni.

166. "French National Front Adviser Praises Crimea Referendum," *Russia and CIS Military Newswire*, 18 March 2014, accessed via Nexis-Uni.

167. Tetraut-Farber, "Far Right Europe."

168. "France's Front National."

169. "Europarl Deputy: Russia–Crimea Reunion is Forced Response to Aggressive West," *Russia and CIS Diplomatic Panorama*, 26 December 2014, accessed via Nexis-Uni.

170. A. Higgins, "Far Right Fever for a Europe Tied to Russia," *New York Times*, 21 May 2014, accessed via Nexis-Uni.

171. "The Problems between Our Countries Are between Politicians, Not Christians," *US Official News*, 20 November 2014, accessed via Nexis-Uni.

172. "Problems between Our Countries."

173. J. Merritt, "Can Evangelicals Help Trump Thaw Relations with Russia?" *Atlantic*, 14 January 2017, accessed via Nexis-Uni.

# NOTES TO PAGES 103–105   171

174. N. Mackay, "America: In the Shadow of Putin," *Sunday Herald (Glasgow)*, 26 March 2017, accessed via Nexis-Uni.

175. L. Hadar, "US Should Not Oppose Russian Intervention in Syria," *Business Times Singapore*, 2 October 2015, accessed via Nexis-Uni.

176. E.-I. Dovere, "Politics of Blaming Obama on Ukraine," *Politico*, 5 March 2014.

177. K. Demirjian, "Trump Praises Putin's Response to Sanctions, Calls Russian Leader 'Very Smart,'" *Washington Post*, 30 December 2016, accessed via Nexis-Uni.

178. A. Nardelli and J. Ioffe, "Trump Told G7 Leaders That Crimea Is Russian Because Everyone Speaks Russian in Crimea," *BuzzFeed*, 14 June 2018, accessed via Nexis-Uni.

179. A. Gearan, J. Wagner, and J. Dawsey, "Trump Says Investigation of 2016 Election Interference Is Now Interfering with 2018 Elections," *Washington Post*, 29 May 2018, accessed via Nexis-Uni.

180. C. Weaver and M. Seddon, "US Conservatives Keep Faith with Putin Despite Trump Travails," *Financial Times*, 18 April 2017, accessed via Nexis-Uni.

181. J. Husser, "Why Trump Is Reliant on White Evangelicals," Fixgov (Washington, DC: Brookings Institution, 2020), accessed via Nexis-Uni.

182. S. L. Perry, "How Trump Stole Christmas: And Why Evangelicals Rally to Their Savior," *Time*, 20 December 2021, accessed via Nexis-Uni.

183. Green, "Protecting Religious Freedom."

184. Y. Torbati, "How Mike Pence's Office Meddled in Foreign Aid to Reroute Money to Favored Christian Groups," *Propublica*, 6 November 2019; Henne, *Economic Integration*.

185. J. Spike, "Populist Leaders Meet, Seek 'European Renaissance,'" *Canadian Press*, 1 April 2021, accessed via Nexis-Uni.

186. D. Kennedy, "Russia's Role in Fostering Extremism Under Scrutiny," *Times*, 6 February 2017, accessed via Nexis-Uni.

187. M. Bennett and O. Moody, "President Putin to Strengthen Austrian Ties by Attending Foreign Minister Karin Kneissl's Wedding," *Times*, 17 August 2018, accessed via Nexis-Uni.

188. Bennett and Moody, "President Putin to Strengthen."

189. S. Walker, "Europe's Far-Right Divided Over Russia as Salvini Stages Pre-Election Rally in Milan," *Guardian*, 17 May 2019.

190. D. Chinni, "Democrats, GOP Move in Opposite Directions on Russia Views," *NBC News*, 8 December 2019; J. Herb, "Democrats Urge Trump Administration to Impose Sanctions on Russians Meddling in 2020 Election," *CNN*, 3 September 2020.

191. J. Kirchik, "How the GOP Became the Party of Putin," *Politico*, 18 July 2017.

192. This can be seen by the Biden administration's policies on Russia, as I discuss in the concluding chapter.

193. W. Szary and T. Grove, "U.K. Allies Blame Russia for Poisoning in Unified Statement," *Wall Street Journal*, 15 March 2018, accessed via Nexis-Uni.

194. D. Khrennikova and A. Shiryaevskaya, "Why the World Worries about Russia's Nord Stream 2 Pipeline," *Washington Post*, 21 May 2021; "Parliament Demands Significantly Tighter EU Sanctions against Russia," press release News European Parliament, 21 January 2021.

195. Huseynov, *Geopolitical Rivalries*, 160.

## 172 NOTES TO PAGES 105-113

196. Henne, "What We Talk."

197. "Latvian Media: Ex-Spy Poisoning, Vote on Orthodox Christmas," *BBC Monitoring Europe—Political*, 9 April 2018, accessed via Nexis-Uni.

198. "Estonia Expert Sees Putin History Article as 'Coded Message,'" *BBC Monitoring Europe—Political*, 10 July 2020, accessed via Nexis-Uni.

199. Curanovic, "Russia's Mission."

200. Anderson, "Putin and the Russian"; Larson and Shevchenko, *Quest for Status.*

201. "Putin's Moment in the Middle East," *Gulf Times*, 25 October 2015, accessed via Nexis-Uni; Tetraut-Farber, "Far-Right Europe."

202. Anderson, "Religion, State"; Tsygankov, *Russia's Foreign Policy*; A. Pankin, "A Boost for the Kremlin's Soft Power," *Moscow Times*, 23 December 2013.

203. Boyes, "New Mussolini."

204. S. Mufson, "Bush Saw Putin's 'Soul': Obama Wants to Appeal to His Brain," *Washington Post*, 1 December 2015.

205. A. Cheng, "Merkel Defends Ukraine Policy, Does Not Regret Engaging Russia," *Washington Post*, 8 June 2022.

206. L. A. Way, "The Rebirth of the Liberal World Order?" *Journal of Democracy* 33, no. 2 (2022): 5–17.

## 5. Expanding the Analysis

1. For more on this, see George and Bennett's discussion of typological theories. George and Bennett, *Case Studies.*

2. Sources for this case study come from the same analysis conducted for the Saudi Arabia chapter at the LBJ Presidential Library, Austin, Texas. I refer to the documents in a similar manner as in that chapter: box, envelope, and document.

3. 136/4/183.

4. 155/5/5.

5. 155/5/7.

6. 136/1/24.

7. P. Norris and R. Inglehart, *Sacred and Secular: Religion and Politics Worldwide* (New York: Cambridge University Press, 2004); "Being Christian in Western Europe" (Pew Research Center, Washington, DC, 29 May 2018).

8. Grzymala-Busse, *Nations Under God*, 364–365.

9. D. T. Buckley, "Citizenship, Multiculturalism and Cross-National Muslim Minority Public Opinion," *West European Politics* 36, no. 1 (January 2013): 150–175; A. Barras, "A Rights-Based Discourse to Contest the Boundaries of State Secularism? The Case of the Headscarf Bans in France and Turkey," *Democratization* 16, no. 6 (2009): 1237–1260.

10. S. Lyons-Padilla et al., "Belonging Nowhere: Marginalization & Radicalization Risk among Muslim Immigrants," *Behavioral Science and Policy* 1, no. 2 (2015): 1–12; A. Rabasa, *Eurojihad: Patterns of Islamist Radicalization and Terrorism in Europe* (New York: Cambridge University Press, 2015).

11. J. Cesari, "The Securitisation of Islam in Europe" (Research Paper No. 15, Sixth EU Framework Programme, April 2009).

12. R. Jackson, "An Analysis of EU Counterterrorism Discourse Post-September 11," *Cambridge Review of International Affairs* 20, no. 2 (2007): 233–247.

NOTES TO PAGES 114–119     173

13. F. Foret and M. Markoviti, "The EU Counter-Radicalisation Strategy as 'Business as Usual?' How European Political Routine Resists Radical Religion," *Journal of European Integration* 42, no. 4 (2020): 547–563.

14. "A Counter-Terrorism Agenda for the EU: Anticipate, Prevent, Protect, Respond," (COM(2020)795 final, European Commission, Brussels, Belgium, 9 December 2020).

15. "Informal Meeting of the Heads of State or Government, 12 February 2015" (European Council, 12 February 2015).

16. Interview with counterterrorism expert, Washington, DC, October 2019.

17. Interview with counterterrorism expert, Washington, DC, October 2019.

18. Interview with counterterrorism expert, Washington, DC, October 2019.

19. Ozturk, *Religion, Identity and Power.*

20. Interview with counterterrorism expert, Washington, DC, October 2019.

21. Interview with counterterrorism expert, Washington, DC, October 2019.

22. Bronson, *Thicker Than Oil*, 193.

23. J. Miller, "War in the Gulf: Muslims; Saudis Decree Holy War on Hussein," *New York Times*, 20 January 1991.

24. Miller, "War in the Gulf."

25. "Saddam Hussein Is No Saladin," *New York Times*, 26 January 1991.

26. P. Smucker, "Iraq Builds 'Mother of All Battles' Mosque in Praise of Saddam," *Guardian*, 29 July 2001.

27. P. Mattar, "The PLO and the Gulf Crisis," *Middle East Journal* 48, no. 1 (1994): 31–46.

28. S. Reed, "Jordan and the Gulf Crisis," *Foreign Affairs* (Winter 1990/1991).

29. E. A. Torriero, "Hussein Dots Iraq Landscape with Mosques," *Chicago Tribune*, 10 October 2002.

30. Bronson, *Thicker Than Oil*, 195.

31. Bronson, *Thicker Than Oil*, 220–221.

32. This dispute has not received a great amount of attention in international relations but for background and details see A. Zellman and D. Brown, "Uneasy Lies the Crown: External Threats to Religious Legitimacy and Interstate Dispute Militarization," *Security Studies* 31, no. 1 (2022): 152–182; P. Sothirak, "Cambodia's Border Conflict with Thailand," *Southeast Asian Affairs* (2013): 87–100; J. Della-Giacoma, "Marking Time on the Thai–Cambodian Border Conflict" (International Crisis Group, 26 July 2012); D. Breitenbücher, "Cambodia/Thailand, Border Conflict Around the Temple of Preah Vihear" (International Committee of the Red Cross, 2013); "Preah Vihear Temple: Disputed Land Cambodian, Court Rules," *BBC News*, 11 November 2013; K. Ngoun, "Thai–Cambodian Conflict Rooted in History" (East Asia Forum, 27 January 2012).

33. Sothirak, "Cambodia's Border Conflict."

34. Zellman and Brown, "Uneasy Lies the Crown."

35. "Waging Peace: ASEAN and the Thai–Cambodian Border Conflict" (International Crisis Group, 6 December 2011).

36. P. Golingai, "Peace Vigil, Black Magic and Sabre-Rattling Over a Temple," *Star Online*, 9 August 2008.

37. "Waging Peace."

38. Sothirak, "Cambodia's Border Conflict."

39. Della-Giacoma, "Marking Time."

40. R. Christian, "Pope Francis' One Big Mistake: Syria," *Time*, 12 March 2014.

## NOTES TO PAGES 119–122

41. L. Davies, "G20 Summit: Vatican—Pope Francis Urges Leaders, Abandon Military Solution," *Guardian*, 6 September 2013.

42. J. L. Allen Jr., "Vatican on Syria: 'Don't Go In If You Can't Get Out,'" *Boston Globe*, 11 February 2014.

43. O. Bennett, "Pope Francis Uses Christmas Address to Call for Peace in the Middle East," *Express Online*, 25 December 2013; "Pope Francis Leads Global Fasting, Prayer Day for Syria Peace," *Al-Arabiya*, 7 September 2013; "Pope Francis Holds Largest Rally against US-Led Military Action on Syria, 100,000 Attend Peace Vigil in Rome, Others around the World," *International Business Times* (Australia), 9 September 2013; "Catholics Gather at Vatican to Oppose Syria Intervention," *France24*, 9 August 2013.

44. L. Goodstein, "Pope Francis' Once-Soaring Popularity Has Dropped Dramatically, New Poll Says," *New York Times*, 2 October 2018.

45. "Public Opinion Runs against Syrian Airstrikes" (Pew Research Center, Washington, DC, 3 September 2013); S. Westall and J. Irish, "Four Years On, Some in Europe Support Talking to Assad," *Reuters*, 18 February 2015.

46. Goddard and Nexon, "Dynamics of Global Power."

47. O. Roy, *The Failure of Political Islam*, trans. Carol Volk (Cambridge, MA: Harvard University Press, 1994), 184–185.

48. Nasr, *The Shia Revival*, 61.

49. Roy, *Failure of Political Islam*.

50. I. Levy, "How Iran Fuels Hamas Terrorism" (Washington Institute for Near East Policy, Washington, DC, 1 June 2021).

51. Roy, *Failure of Political Islam*; Tabaar, *Religious Statecraft*, 191.

52. Nasr, *The Shia Revival*.

53. Nasr, *The Shia Revival*, 131–133.

54. Roy, *Failure of Political Islam*, 190, 184.

55. A. Chatzky and J. McBride, "China's Massive Belt and Road Initiative" (Council on Foreign Relations, Washington, DC, 28 January 2020).

56. "China Releases Analects of Confucius Versions for Belt and Road Countries," *Xinhua*, 16 May 2021.

57. M. Sahlins, "Confucius Institutes: Academic Malware," *Asia-Pacific Journal* 12, no. 46 (November 2014); D. Torres, "China's Soft Power Offensive," *Politico*, 26 December 2017.

58. H. Wang et al., "Confucius Institute, Belt and Road Initiative, and Internationalization," *International Review of Economics and Finance* 71 (2021): 237–256; S. Marwah and R. Ervina, "The China Soft Power: Confucius Institute in Build Up One Belt One Road Initiative in Indonesia," *Wenchuang Journal of Foreign Language Studies, Linguistics, Education, Literatures and Cultures* 1, no. 1 (2021).

59. "Confucius Institutes Lauded in Promoting 'Belt and Road' Initiative," *Xinhua*, 12 December 2016.

60. E. J. Graham, "Confucius Institutes Threaten Academic Freedom" (American Association of University Professors, Washington, DC, September–October 2014).

61. J. P. Horsley, "It's Time for a New Policy on Confucius Institutes" (Brookings, Washington, DC, 1 April 2021).

62. "Australian Universities Are Accused of Trading Free Speech for Cash," *Economist*, 19 September 2019.

63. M. O'Neill, "Europe Closes Confucius Institutes," *EJ Insight*, 16 July 2021.

## Conclusion

1. A. M. Banks, "Trump White House Faith Outreach a Picture of Selective Access," *Religion News Service*, 5 October 2018; D. Chandler, "Trump White House Faith Outreach a Picture of Selective Access," *Baptist Press*, 18 May 2018; Green, "Protecting Religious Freedom."

2. A. M. Banks, "State Department Religious Freedom Summit Ends with Commitments, Critiques," *Religion News Service*, 27 July 2018.

3. K. Shellnutt, "Still No Churches in Saudi Arabia, But Small Steps toward Religious Freedom," *Religion News Service*, 5 October 2018; C. Mitchell, "Egyptian President Meeting with US Evangelicals 'Prophetic' and 'Historic,'" *Christian Broadcasting Network*, 3 November 2017.

4. Henne, *Economic Integration*.

5. P. Mandaville, K. Thames, and E. Scolaro, "Finding Common Ground on U.S. International Religious Freedom Policy: Overcoming Partisan Mistrust through a Focus on Bipartisan Priorities" (United States Institute of Peace, Washington, DC, 20 May 2021).

6. "Saudi Arabia Arrests More Women's Rights Activists," *Reuters*, 20 June 2018; D. D. Kirkpatrick and B. Hubbard, "Saudi Prince Detains Senior Members of Royal Family," *New York Times*, 6 March 2020.

7. K. Fahim and D. D. Kirkpatrick, "Saudi Arabia Seeks Union of Monarchies in Region," *New York Times*, 14 May 2012; S. Hamdan, "Gulf Council Reaches Out to Morocco and Jordan," *New York Times*, 25 May 2011.

8. Some sources for this paragraph come from an interview conducted with Sean Flynn via telephone, 22 March 2022, and George Soroka, 2 June 2022.

9. P. Kirby, "Why Has Russia Invaded Ukraine and What Does Putin Want?" *BBC News*, 9 May 2022.

10. P. Mandaville, "How Putin Turned Religion's 'Sharp Power' against Ukraine: Moscow's Stance on the Orthodox Church Is Indicative of How Aspiring Powers Use Religion to Either Build Solidarity Or Sow Seeds of Conflict" (United States Institute of Peace, Washington, DC, 9 February 2022).

11. "Ukraine War: The Role of Russia's Patriarch Kirill," *Deutsche Welle*, 16 May 2022.

12. J. Stone, "Nigel Farage Says Ukraine Invasion Is Result of EU and NATO Provoking Putin," *Independent*, 24 February 2022; M. Johnston, "Why Tucker Carlson Hates Ukraine So Much," *Haaretz*, 18 April 2022.

13. "Moscow-Led Ukrainian Orthodox Church Breaks Ties with Russia," *Reuters*, 28 May 2022; P. Pullella, "Analysis: Ukraine Invasion Splits Orthodox Church, Isolates Russian Patriarch," *Reuters*, 14 March 2022.

14. D. Johnston and C. Sampson, eds., *Religion, the Missing Dimension of Statecraft* (New York: Oxford University Press, 1994); P. Hatzopoulos and F. Petito, "The Return from Exile: An Introduction," in *Religion in International Relations: The Return from Exile*, ed. Pavlos Hatzopoulos and Fabio Petito (New York: Palgrave Macmillan, 2003), 1–21; Dark, "Large-Scale Religious Change"; Shah, Stepan, and Toft, *Rethinking Religion*; Snyder, *Religion and International Relations*; Fox and Sandler, *Bringing Religion*; Appleby, *Ambivalence of the Sacred*.

15. J. Fox, "The Rise of Religious Nationalism and Conflict: Ethnic Conflict and Revolutionary Wars, 1945–2001," *Journal of Peace Research* 41, no. 6 (2004): 715–731; Fox, *World Survey of Religion*; B. J. Grim and R. Finke, *Price of Freedom Denied*; Y. Akbaba and

Z. Taydas, "Does Religious Discrimination Promote Dissent? A Quantitative Analysis," *Ethnopolitics* 10, no. 3–4 (September 2011): 271–295; Toft, "Getting Religion?"; Hassner, *War on Sacred Grounds*; Basedau, Pfieffer, and Vullers, "Bad Religion?"

16. Banchoff, *Embryo Politics*; J. Haynes, *Faith-Based Organizations at the United Nations* (New York: Palgrave Macmillan, 2014); Svensson, "Fighting with Faith"; N. A. Sandal, *Religious Leaders and Conflict Transformation: Northern Ireland and Beyond* (New York: Cambridge University Press, 2017).

17. Bettiza, *Finding Faith*; D. T. Buckley, *Faithful to Secularism: The Religious Politics of Democracy in Ireland, Senegal, and the Philippines* (New York: Columbia University Press, 2017); J. C. Agensky, "Recognizing Religion: Politics, History, and the 'Long 19th Century,'" *European Journal of International Relations* 23, no. 4 (December 2017): 729–775; J. Cesari, *The Awakening of Muslim Democracy: Religion, Modernity and the State* (New York: Cambridge University Press, 2013); Cesari, "Securitisation of Islam."

18. Henne, "Ancient Fire"; Henne, "Two Swords."

19. Hassner, *Religion on the Battlefield*; Henne, "Two Swords."

20. D. H. Nexon, "Religion and International Relations: No Leap of Faith Required," in *Religion and International Relations Theory*, ed. Jack Snyder (New York: Columbia University Press, 2011): 141–168.

21. Hassner, *Religion on the Battlefield*; Thomas, *Global Resurgence*; A. Hasenclever and V. Rittberger, "Does Religion Make a Difference? Theoretical Approaches to the Impact of Faith on Political Conflict," in Hatzopoulos and Petito, *Religion in International Relations*, 107–147.

22. Stamatov, *Origins of Global Humanitarianism*, 4.

23. R. A. Nielsen, *Deadly Clerics: Blocked Ambition and the Paths to Jihad* (New York: Cambridge University Press, 2018).

24. Mandaville, *Geopolitics*; G. Bettiza and P. S. Henne, "Religious Soft Power: Promises, Limits and Ways Forward," in Mandaville, *Geopolitics*.

25. Nexon, "Religion and International Relations"; Goddard, S. E., and D. H. Nexon. "The Dynamics of Global Power Politics." *Journal of Global Security Studies* 1, no. 1 (February 2016): 4–18.

26. P. T. Jackson and D. H. Nexon, "Reclaiming the Social: Relationalism in Anglophone International Studies," *Cambridge Review of International Affairs* 32, no. 5 (2019): 582–600.

27. Te Brake, *Religious War*.

28. For an overview, see E. M. Hafner-Burton, M. Kahler, and A. H. Montgomery, "Network Analysis for International Relations," *International Organization* 63 (Summer 2009): 559–592.

29. V. Asal and R. K. Rethemeyer, "The Nature of the Beast: Organizational Structures and the Lethality of Terrorist Attacks," *Journal of Politics* 70, no. 2 (April 2008): 437–449; S. D. Everton, *Networks and Religion: Ties That Bind, Loose, Build-Up and Tear Down* (New York: Cambridge University Press, 2018); P. S. Henne, "Issues in Quantitative Analysis and Security Studies Involving Muslims," *International Journal of Religion* 2, no. 1 (2021): 23–32.

30. Renshon, *Fighting for Status*; M. G. Duque, "Recognizing International Status: A Relational Approach," *International Studies Quarterly* 62 (2018): 577–592; D. H. Nexon and T. Wright, "What's at Stake in the American Empire Debate?" *American Political Science Review* 101, no. 2 (May 2007): 253–271.

# NOTES TO PAGES 135–144

31. P. S. Henne, "The Role of Islam in Post-Arab Spring International Relations: A Social Network Analysis" (International Studies Association, Toronto, Canada, March 2019).

32. P. S. Henne and D. H. Nexon, "One Cheer for Classical Realism, Or towards a Power Politics of Religion," in *Religion and the Realist Tradition: From Political Theology to International Relations Theory and Back*, ed. J. Troy (London: Routledge, 2013), 164–175.

33. J. S. Barkin, *Realist Constructivism: Rethinking International Relations Theory* (New York: Cambridge University Press, 2010).

34. R. Niebuhr, *The Irony of American History* (Chicago: University of Chicago Press, 1952), xxiv.

35. Niebuhr, *Irony of American History*, 2.

36. Niebuhr, *Irony of American History*, 7.

37. E. Van Rythoven, "Walter Lippmann, Emotion, and the History of International Theory," *International Theory* 14, no. 3 (2022): 526–550; E. Van Rythoven, "The Securitization Dilemma," *Journal of Global Security Studies* 5, no. 3 (July 2020): 478–493.

38. T. Masuzawa, *The Invention of World Religions: Or, How European Universalism Was Preserved in an Age of Pluralism* (Chicago: University of Chicago Press, 2005); M. E. Marty and R. S. Appleby, eds., *Fundamentalisms Comprehended* (Chicago: University of Chicago Press, 2004).

39. Lieber and Alexander, "Waiting for Balancing."

40. S. E. Goddard, P. K. MacDonald, and D. H. Nexon, "Repertoires of Statecraft: Instruments and Logics of Power Politics," *International Relations* 33, no. 2 (2019).

41. J. Lepgold and M. Nincic, *Beyond the Ivory Tower: International Relations Theory and the Problem of Policy Relevance* (New York: Columbia University Press, 2001), 35.

42. Nye, "Soft Power"; J. S. Nye Jr., "Soft Power and American Foreign Policy," *Political Science Quarterly* 119, no. 2 (2004): 255–270; J. S. Nye Jr., "Public Diplomacy and Soft Power," *ANNALS of the American Academy of Political and Social Science* 616 (March 2008): 94–109.

43. Mandaville and Hamid, *Islam as Statecraft*.

44. Henne, *Geopolitics of Faith*.

45. Henne, "What We Talk."

46. S. Casey, "How the State Department Has Sidelined Religion's Role in Diplomacy" (John C. Danforth Center on Religion and Politics, Washington University in St. Louis, MI, 5 September 2017).

47. P. Mandaville and K. Thames, "A Ripe Moment for Building Peace by Promoting International Religious Freedom" (United States Institute of Peace, Washington, DC, 27 June 2022); Dionne and Rogers, *A Time to Heal*.

48. Niebuhr, *Irony of American History*, 168.

49. G. J. Moore, *Niebuhrian International Relations: The Ethics of Foreign Policymaking* (New York: Oxford University Press, 2020), 38.

50. Niebuhr, *Irony of American History*, 169.

51. Niebuhr, *Irony of American History*, 169.

# BIBLIOGRAPHY

Aburish, Said K. *Nasser: The Last Arab*. New York: St. Martin's Press, 2004.

Acharya, Amitav. "How Ideas Spread: Whose Norms Matter? Norm Localization and Institutional Change in Asian Regionalism." *International Organization* 58, no. 2 (2004): 239–275.

Acosta, Jim. "US, Other Powers Kick Russia out of G8." *CNN*, 24 March 2014.

Adamsky, Dmitry. "Nuclear Incoherence: Deterrence Theory and Non-Strategic Nuclear Weapons in Russia." *Journal of Strategic Studies* 37, no. 1 (2014): 91–134.

———. *Russian Nuclear Orthodoxy: Religion, Politics, and Strategy*. Palo Alto, CA: Stanford University Press, 2019.

Adamson, Fiona B. "Global Liberalism versus Political Islam: Competing Ideological Frameworks in International Politics." *International Studies Review* 7 (2005): 547–569.

Agensky, Jonathan C. "Dr Livingstone, I Presume? Evangelicals, Africa and Faith-Based Humanitarianism." *Global Society* 27, no. 4 (2013): 1–21.

———. "Evangelical Globalism and the Internationalization of Sudan's Second Civil War." *Cambridge Review of International Affairs* 33, no. 2 (2019): 274–293.

———. "Recognizing Religion: Politics, History, and the 'Long 19th Century.'" *European Journal of International Relations* 23, no. 4 (December 2017): 729–775.

Akbaba, Yasemin, and Zeynep Taydas. "Does Religious Discrimination Promote Dissent? A Quantitative Analysis." *Ethnopolitics* 10, no. 3–4 (September 2011): 271–295.

Albright, Madeleine. *The Mighty and the Almighty: Reflections on America, God and World Affairs*. New York: Harper, 2006.

Alexander, Kathryn J. "The Impact of Religious Commitment on Patterns of Interstate Conflict." *Journal of Global Security Studies* 4, no. 1 (October 2017): 271–287.

Allen, John L., Jr. "Vatican on Syria: 'Don't Go In If You Can't Get Out.'" *Boston Globe*, 11 February 2014

al Otaiba, Yousef. "A Vision for a Moderate Muslim World." *Foreign Policy*, 2 December 2015.

al-Rasheed, Madawi. *Contesting the Saudi State: Islamic Voices from a New Generation*. New York: Cambridge University Press, 2007.

———. *A History of Saudi Arabia*. 2nd ed. New York: Cambridge University Press, 2010.

Anderson, John. *Conservative Christian Politics in Russia and the United States*. London: Routledge, 2015.

———. "Dreaming of Christian Nations in the USA and Russia: The Importnace of History." *Journal of Transatlantic Studies* 10, no. 3 (September 2012): 201–221.

## 180     BIBLIOGRAPHY

——. "Putin and the Russian Orthodox Church: Asymmetric Symphonia?" *Journal of International Affairs* 61, no. 1 (Fall/Winter 2007): 185–201.

——. *Religion, State and Politics in the Soviet Union and Successor States*. New York: Cambridge University Press, 1994.

——. "Religion, State and 'Sovereign Democracy' in Putin's Russia." *Journal of Religious and Political Practice* 2, no. 2 (2016): 249–266.

——. "Rocks, Art, and Sex: The 'Culture Wars' Come to Russia." *Journal of Church and State* 55, no. 2 (October 2012): 307–334.

Appiah, Kwame Anthony. "Causes of Quarrel: What's Special about Religious Disputes?" In *Religious Pluralism, Globalization, and World Politics*, edited by Thomas Banchoff, 41–65. New York: Oxford University Press, 2008.

Appleby, R. Scott. *The Ambivalence of the Sacred*. Lanham, MD: Rowman and Littlefield, 2000.

——. "Building Sustainable Peace: The Roles of Local and Transnational Religious Actors." In *Religious Pluralism, Globalization and World Politics*, edited by Thomas Banchoff, 125–155. New York: Oxford University Press, 2008.

"Arabs Must Follow Saladin's Example to Capture Jerusalem: Iraq." *Agence France Presse*, 2 October 2000.

Asal, Victor, and R. Karl Rethemeyer. "The Nature of the Beast: Organizational Structures and the Lethality of Terrorist Attacks." *Journal of Politics* 70, no. 2 (April 2008): 437–449.

"Australian Universities Are Accused of Trading Free Speech for Cash." *Economist*, 19 September 2019.

Ayoob, Mohammed, and Etga Ugur, eds. *Assessing the War on Terror*. Boulder, CO: Lynne Rienner, 2013.

Ayubi, Nazih N. *Over-Stating the Arab State: Politics and Society in the Middle East*. London: I. B. Taurus, 1995.

Baer, Susan, and David L. Greene. "'Face of Terror Not True Faith of Islam,' Bush Declares." *Baltimore Sun*, 18 September 2001.

Banchoff, Thomas. *Embryo Politics: Ethics and Policy in Atlantic Democracies*. Ithaca, NY: Cornell University Press, 2011.

——. "Introduction: Religious Pluralism in World Affairs." In *Religious Pluralism, Globalization, and World Politics*, edited by Thomas Banchoff, 3–41. New York: Oxford University Press, 2008.

——. "Religious Pluralism and the Politics of a Global Cloning Ban." In *Religious Pluralism, Globalization and World Politics*, edited by Thomas Banchoff, 275–297. New York: Oxford University Press, 2008.

——, ed. *Religious Pluralism, Globalization and World Politics*. New York: Oxford University Press, 2008.

Banks, Adelle M. "State Department Religious Freedom Summit Ends with Commitments, Critiques." *Religion News Service*, 27 July 2018.

——. "Trump White House Faith Outreach a Picture of Selective Access." *Religion News Service*, 5 October 2018.

Bar-Maoz, Moria. "On Religion and the Politics of Security: How Religion's Involvement in Domestic Politics Affects National Securitymaking." *Review of Faith and International Affairs* 16, no. 2 (2018): 36–49.

# BIBLIOGRAPHY 181

Barbato, Mariano. "A State, a Diplomat, and a Transnational Church: The Multi-Layered Actorness of the Holy See." *Perspectives* 21, no. 2 (2013): 27–48.

Barkin, J. Samuel. *Realist Constructivism: Rethinking International Relations Theory.* New York: Cambridge University Press, 2010.

Barnett, Michael N. *Dialogues in Arab Politics: Negotiations in International Order.* New York: Columbia University Press, 1998.

Barras, Amélie. "A Rights-Based Discourse to Contest the Boundaries of State Secularism? The Case of the Headscarf Bans in France and Turkey." *Democratization* 16, no. 6 (2009): 1237–1260.

Basedau, Matthias, Birte Pfieffer, and Johannes Vullers. "Bad Religion? Religion, Collective Action, and the Onset of Armed Conflict in Developing Countries." *Journal of Conflict Resolution* 60, no. 2 (2016): 226–255.

"Being Christian in Western Europe." Pew Research Center, Washington, DC, 2018.

Bellah, Robert N. "Civil Religion in America." *Daedalus* 96 (1967): 1–21.

Bennett, Andrew. "Process Tracing and Causal Inference." In *Rethinking Social Inquiry: Diverse Tools, Shared Standards*, edited by Henry Brady and David Collier, 207–221. Lanham, MD: Rowman and Littlefield, 2010.

Bennett, Andrew, and Jeffrey Checkel. "Process Tracing: From Philosophical Roots to Best Practices." In *Process Tracing: From Metaphor to Analytic Tool*, edited by Andrew Bennett and Jeffrey Checkel, 3–38. New York: Cambridge University Press, 2014.

Bennett, Owen. "Pope Francis Uses Christmas Address to Call for Peace in the Middle East." *Express Online*, 25 December 2013.

Bergen, Peter. *The Longest War: The Enduring Conflict between Al-Qaeda and America.* New York: Free Press, 2011.

Bettiza, Gregorio. *Finding Faith in Foreign Policy: Religion and American Diplomacy in a Postsecular World.* New York: Oxford University Press, 2019.

Bettiza, Gregorio, and Peter S. Henne. "Religious Soft Power: Promises, Limits and Ways Forward." In *The Geopolitics of Religious Soft Power: How States Use Religion in Foreign Policy*, edited by Peter Mandaville. New York: Oxford University Press, 2023.

Black, Phil. "Russia Protesters Demand Putin's Resignation." *CNN*, 12 June 2012.

Blitt, Rober C. "Russia's 'Orthodox' Foreign Policy: The Growing Influence of the Russian Orthodox Church in Shaping Russia's Policies Abroad." *University of Pennsylvania Journal of International Law* 33, no. 2 (2011): 363–460.

Bob, Clifford. *Rights as Weapons: Instruments of Conflict, Tools of Power.* Princeton, NJ: Princeton University Press, 2019.

Bourdeaux, Michael. "Introduction." In *The Politics of Religion in Russia and the New States of Eurasia*, edited by Michael Bourdeaux, 1–12. Armonk, NY: M. E. Sharpe, 1997.

Breitenbücher, Danielle. "Cambodia/Thailand, Border Conflict Around the Temple of Preah Vihear." International Committee of the Red Cross, 2013.

Bronson, Rachel. *Thicker Than Oil: America's Uneasy Partnership with Saudi Arabia.* New York: Oxford University Press, 2006.

Browers, Michaelle. "Official Islam and the Limits of Communicative Action: The Paradox of the Amman Message." *Third World Quarterly* 32, no. 5 (2011): 943–958.

## 182  BIBLIOGRAPHY

Brumiller, Elisabeth. "Evangelicals Sway White House on Human Rights Issues Abroad." *New York Times*, 26 October 2003.

Bubnova, Natalia. "Russia's Policy and International Cooperation: The Challenges and Opportunities of Soft Power." In *Russia's Public Diplomacy: Evolution and Practice*, edited by Anna A. Velikaya and Greg Simons, 79–103. Cham, Switzerland: Palgrave Macmillan, 2020.

Buckley, David T. "Citizenship, Multiculturalism and Cross-National Muslim Minority Public Opinion." *West European Politics* 36, no. 1 (January 2013): 150–175.

——. *Faithful to Secularism: The Religious Politics of Democracy in Ireland, Senegal, and the Philippines*. New York: Columbia University Press, 2017.

——. "Religious Elite Cues, Internal Division, and the Impact of Pope Francis' Laudato Si'." *Politics and Religion* 15 (2022): 1–33.

Burge, Ryan P., and Paul A. Djupe. "Religious Authority in a Democratic Society: Clergy and Citizen Evidence from a New Measure." *Politics and Religion* 15 (2022): 169–196.

Busby, Joshua W. *Moral Movements and Foreign Policy*. New York: Cambridge University Press, 2010.

Bush, George W. "Remarks Prior to Discussions with King Abdullah II of Jordan and an Exchange with Reporters" news release, 28 September 2001, https://www.presidency.ucsb.edu/documents/remarks-prior-discussions-with-king-abdullah-ii-jordan-and-exchange-with-reporters-2.

Buzan, Barry. *From International to World Society? English School Theory and the Social Structure of Globalisation*. New York: Cambridge University Press, 2004.

Buzan, Barry, and Ole Wæver. *Regions and Powers: The Structure of International Security*. New York: Cambridge University Press, 2003.

Byrnes, Timothy A., and Peter J. Katzenstein, eds. *Religion in an Expanding Europe*. New York: Cambridge University Press, 2006.

Caldwell, Lawrence. "Russian Concepts of National Security." In *Russian Foreign Policy in the Twenty-First Century and the Shadow of the Past*, edited by Robert Levgold, 279–343. New York: Cambridge University Press, 2007.

Canipe, Lee. "Under God and Anti-Communist: How the Pledge of Allegiance Got Religion in Cold War America." *Journal of Church and State* 45, no. 2 (Spring 2003): 305–323.

Casanova, Jose. "Globalizing Catholicism and the Return to a 'Universal' Church." In *Transnational Religion and Fading States*, edited by Susanna Hoeber and James Piscatori Rudolph, 121–143. Boulder, CO: Westview Press, 1996.

——. *Public Religions in the Modern World*. Chicago: University of Chicago Press, 1994.

Casey, Shaun. "How the State Department Has Sidelined Religion's Role in Diplomacy." John C. Danforth Center on Religion and Politics, Washington University in St. Louis, MI, 5 September 2017.

"Catholics Gather at Vatican to Oppose Syria Intervention." *France24*, 9 August 2013.

Cesari, Jocelyne. *The Awakening of Muslim Democracy: Religion, Modernity and the State*. New York: Cambridge University Press, 2013.

——. "The Securitisation of Islam in Europe." Research Paper No. 15, Sixth EU Framework Programme, April 2009.

## BIBLIOGRAPHY 183

Chandler, Diana. "Trump White House Faith Outreach a Picture of Selective Access." *Baptist Press*, 18 May 2018.

Chapman, Jessica M. "Religion, Power and Legitimacy in Ngo Dinh Diem's Republic of Vietnam." In *Religion and the Cold War: A Global Perspective*, edited by Philip E. Muehlenbeck, 206–229. Nashville, TN: Vanderbilt University Press, 2012.

Chatzky, Andrew, and James McBride. "China's Massive Belt and Road Initiative." Council on Foreign Relations, Washington, DC, 28 January 2020.

Cheng, Amy. "Merkel Defends Ukraine Policy, Does Not Regret Engaging Russia." *Washington Post*, 8 June 2022.

"China Releases Analects of Confucius Versions for Belt and Road Countries." *Xinhua*, 16 May 2021.

Chinni, Dante. "Democrats, GOP Move in Opposite Directions on Russia Views." *NBC News*, 8 December 2019.

Chiozza, Giacomo. "Is There a Clash of Civilizations? Evidence from Patterns of International Conflict Involvement, 1946–1997." *Journal of Peace Research 39*, no. 6 (November 2002): 711–734.

Choksy, Jamsheed K., and Carol E. B. Choksy. "China and Russia Have Iran's Back: Tehran May Be Less Open Than Ever to Threats or Persuasion." *Foreign Affairs*, 17 November 2020.

Christian, Robert. "Pope Francis' One Big Mistake: Syria." *Time*, 12 March 2014.

Christie, Edward Hunter. "Sanctions After Crimea: Have They Worked?" *NATO Review*, 13 July 2015.

Coll, Steve. *Ghost Wars: The Secret History of the CIA, Afghanistan and Bin Ladin, from the Soviet Invasion to September 10, 2011*. New York: Penguin Press, 2004.

Collier, David, Henry E. Brady, and Jason Seawright. "Sources of Leverage in Causal Inference: Toward an Alternative View of Methodology." In *Rethinking Social Inquiry: Diverse Tools, Shared Standards*, edited by Henry E. Brady and David Collier, 161–201. Lanham, MD: Rowman and Littlefield, 2010.

"Confucius Institutes Lauded in Promoting 'Belt and Road' Initiative." *Xinhua*, 12 December 2016.

"A Counter-Terrorism Agenda for the EU: Anticipate, Prevent, Protect, Respond." COM(2020)795 final, European Commission, Brussels, Belgium, 9 December 2020.

Crescenzi, Mark J. C., Jacob D. Kathman, Katja B. Kleinberg, and Reed M. Wood. "Reliability, Reputation, and Alliance Formation." *International Studies Quarterly 56*, no. 2 (June 2012): 259–274.

Curanovic, Alicja. "The Attitude of the Moscow Patriarchate towards Other Orthodox Churches." *Religion, State and Society 35*, no. 4 (December 2007): 301–318.

———. "Guarding the Motherland's Frontiers: The Russian Orthodox Church in the North Caucasus." *Problems of Post-Communism 67*, no. 6 (2020): 446–454.

———. *The Religious Factor in Russia's Foreign Policy*. London: Routledge, 2014.

———. "Russia's Contemporary Exceptionalism and Geopolitical Conservatism." In *Contemporary Russian Conservatism: Problems, Paradoxes, and Perspectives*, edited by Mikhail Suslov and Dmitry Uzlaner, 207–233. Leiden: Brill, 2019.

———. "Russia's Mission in the World: The Perspective of the Russian Orthdoox Church." *Problems of Post-Communism 66*, no. 4 (2019): 253–267.

184 **BIBLIOGRAPHY**

Dark, K. R. "Large-Scale Religious Change and World Politics." In *Religion in International Relations*, edited by K. R. Dark, 50–82. New York: St. Martin's Press, 2000.

Darwich, May, and Tamirace Fakhoury. "Casting the Other as an Existential Threat: The Securitisation of Sectarianism in the International Relations of the Syria Crisis." *Global Discourse* 6, no. 4 (2016): 712–732.

Davies, Lizzie. "G20 Summit: Vatican—Pope Francis Urges Leaders, Abandon Military Solution." *Guardian*, 6 September 2013.

Dawisha, Adeed. *Arab Nationalism in the Twentieth Century: From Triumph to Despair*. Princeton, NJ: Princeton University Press, 2016.

Deitelhoff, Nicole, and Lisbeth Zimmerman. "Norms under Challenge: Unpacking the Dynamics of Norm Robustness." *Journal of Global Security Studies* 4, no. 1 (January 2019): 2–17.

Della-Giacoma, Jim. "Marking Time on the Thai-Cambodian Border Conflict." International Crisis Group, 2012.

Dionne, E. J., and Melissa Rogers. *A Time to Heal, a Time to Build*. Washington, DC: Brookings Institution, 2020.

Doran, Michael. *Ike's Gamble: America's Rise to Dominance in the Middle East*. New York, NY: Free Press, 2016.

Dovere, Edward-Isaac. "Politics of Blaming Obama on Ukraine." *Politico*, 5 March 2014.

Dueck, Colin. *Reluctant Crusaders: Power, Culture, and Change in American Grand Strategy*. Princeton, NJ: Princeton University Press, 2006.

Dunlop, John B. "The Russian Orthodox Church as an Empire-Saving Institution." In *The Politics of Religion in Russia and the New States of Eurasia*, edited by Michael Bourdeaux, 15–40. Armonk, NY: M. E. Sharpe, 1997.

Duque, Marina G. "Recognizing International Status: A Relational Approach." *International Studies Quarterly* 62 (2018): 577–592.

Edwards, Neil. *Coup-Proofing: Russia's Military Blueprint to Securing Resources in Africa*. Washington, DC: Council on Foreign Relations, 2021.

Elshtain, Jean Bethke. "Military Intervention and Justice as Equal Regard." In *Religion and Security: The New Nexus in International Relations*, edited by Robert Seiple and Dennis R. Hoover, 115–131. Lanham, MD: Rowman and Littlefield, 2004.

Etzioni, A. "Leveraging Islam." *National Interest* 83 (2006): 101–106.

Everton, Sean D. *Networks and Religion: Ties That Bind, Loose, Build-Up and Tear Down*. New York: Cambridge University Press, 2018.

Fahim, Kareem, and David D. Kirkpatrick. "Saudi Arabia Seeks Union of Monarchies in Region." *New York Times*, 14 May 2012.

Farr, Thomas F. "Diplomacy in an Age of Faith: Religious Freedom and National Security." *Foreign Affairs* 87, no. 2 (March/April 2008): 122–124.

——. *World of Faith and Freedom: Why International Religious Liberty Is Vital to American National Security*. New York: Oxford University Press, 2008.

Feltman, Jeff, Samantha Gross, Martin Indyk, Kemal Kirişci, Suzanne Maloney, Bruce Riedel, Natan Sachs, Amanda Sloat, Angela Stent, and Tamara Cofman Wittes. *The New Geopolitics of the Middle East: America's Role in a Changing Region*, edited by Bruce Jones. Washington, DC: Brookings Institute, 2019.

## BIBLIOGRAPHY 185

Fernandez, Alberto M. "Here to Stay and Growing: Combating ISIS Propaganda Networks." In *U.S.–Islamic World Forum Papers*. Washington, DC: Brookings Institution, 2015.

Finnemore, Martha. "Legitimacy, Hypocrisy, and the Social Structure of Unipolarity: Why Being a Unipole Isn't All It's Cracked Up to Be." *World Politics* 61, no. 1 (January 2009): 58–85.

Foret, François, and Margarita Markoviti. "The EU Counter-Radicalisation Strategy as 'Business as Usual'? How European Political Routine Resists Radical Religion." *Journal of European Integration* 42, no. 4 (2020): 547–563.

Fox, Jonathan. "The Increasing Role of Religion in State Failure: 1960 to 2004." *Terrorism and Political Violence* 19, no. 3 (2007): 395–414.

——. "The Rise of Religious Nationalism and Conflict: Ethnic Conflict and Revolutionary Wars, 1945–2001." *Journal of Peace Research* 41, no. 6 (2004): 715–731.

——. *A World Survey of Religion and the State*. New York: Cambridge University Press, 2008.

Fox, Jonathan, and Nukhet Sandal. "State Religious Exclusivity and International Crises between 1990 and 2002." In *Religion, Identity, and Global Governance: Theory, Evidence, and Practice*, edited by Patrick James, 81–107. Toronto: University of Toronto Press, 2010.

Fox, Jonathan, and Shmuel Sandler. *Bringing Religion into International Relations*. New York: Palgrave Macmillan, 2004.

Fraser, Cary. "In Defense of Allah's Realm: Religion and Statecraft in Saudi Foreign Policy." In *Transnational Religion and Fading States*, edited by Susanna Hoeber Rudolph and James P. Piscatori, 212–243. Boulder, CO: Westview Press, 1997.

Galeotti, Mark, and Andrew S. Bowen. "Putin's Empire of the Mind: How Russia's President Morphed from Realist to Ideologue—And What He'll Do Next." *Foreign Policy*, 21 April 2014.

Gartzke, Erik, and Kristian Skrede Gleditsch. "Identity and Conflict: Ties That Bind and Differences That Divide." *European Journal of International Relations* 12, no. 1 (2006): 53–87.

Gartzke, Erik, and Alex Weisiger. "Fading Friendships: Alliances, Affinities and the Activation of International Identities." *British Journal of Political Science* 43, no. 1 (January 2013): 25–52.

Gause, F. Gregory, III. "Balancing What? Threat Perception and Alliance Choice in the Gulf." *Security Studies* 13, no. 2 (2004): 273–305.

——. *The International Relations of the Persian Gulf*. New York: Cambridge University Press, 2010.

——. *Saudi–Yemen Relations: Domestic Structures and Foreign Influences*. New York: Columbia University Press, 1990.

George, Alexander, and Andrew Bennett. *Case Studies and Theory Development in the Social Sciences*. Cambridge, MA: MIT Press, 2005.

Gerges, Fawaz. *The Far Enemy: Why Jihad Went Global*. New York: Cambridge University Press, 2005.

Gerson, Michael J. *Heroic Conservatism: Why Republicans Need to Embrace America's Ideals (and Why They Deserve to Fail If They Don't)*. New York: HarperOne, 2007.

## 186    BIBLIOGRAPHY

Gessen, Masha. "The Undoing of Bill Clinton and Boris Yeltsin's Friendship, and How It Changed Both of Their Countries." *New Yorker*, 5 September 2018.

Gill, Anthony. *The Political Origins of Religious Liberty*. New York: Cambridge University Press, 2008.

Gilliam, Terry, and Terry Jones. "Monty Python and the Holy Grail." EMI Films, 1975.

Glassman, James K. "Finally, Obama's Taking Radical Islam Seriously." *Politico*, 19 February 2015.

Goddard, Stacie E. *When Right Makes Might: Rising Powers and World Order*. Ithaca, NY: Cornell University Press, 2018.

Goddard, Stacie E., and Ronald R. Krebs. "Rhetoric, Legitimation and Grand Strategy." *Security Studies* 24 (2015): 5–36.

Goddard, Stacie E., Paul K. MacDonald, and Daniel H. Nexon. "Repertoires of Statecraft: Instruments and Logics of Power Politics." *International Relations* 33, no. 2 (2019): 304–312.

Goddard, Stacie E., and Daniel H. Nexon. "The Dynamics of Global Power Politics: A Framework for Analysis." *Journal of Global Security Studies* 1, no. 1 (February 2016): 4–18.

Golingai, Philip. "Peace Vigil, Black Magic and Sabre-Rattling Over a Temple." *Star Online*, 9 August 2008.

Goodstein, Laurie. "Pope Francis' Once-Soaring Popularity Has Dropped Dramatically, New Poll Says." *New York Times*, 2 October 2018.

Gorski, Philip. *American Covenant: A History of Civil Religion from the Puritans to the Present*. Princeton, NJ: Princeton University Press, 2017.

Gottemoeller, Rose. "Russia Is Updating Their Nuclear Weapons: What Does That Mean for the Rest of Us?" Carnegie Endowment for International Peace, Washington, DC, 29 January 2020.

Gradert, Kenyon, and James Strasburg. "Billy Graham, Cold Warrior for God." *New York Times*, 23 February 2018.

Graham, Edward J. "Confucius Institutes Threaten Academic Freedom." American Association of University Professors, Washington, DC, September–October 2014.

Green, Emma. "Protecting Religious Freedom Is a Foreign-Policy Priority of the Trump Administration." *Atlantic*, 12 May 2017.

Griffin, Sean. "Putin's Medieval Weapons in the War against Ukraine." *Studies in Medievalism* 29 (2020): 13–21.

Grim, Brian J., and Roger Finke. *The Price of Freedom Denied: Religious Persecution and Conflict in the Twenty-First Century*. New York: Cambridge University Press, 2011.

Grzymala-Busse, Anna. *Nations under God: How Churches Use Moral Authority to Influence Policy*. Princeton, NJ: Princeton University Press, 2015.

Gutkowski, Stacey. "We Are the Very Model of a Moderate Muslim State: The Amman Messages and Jordan's Foreign Policy." *International Relations* 30, no. 2 (2016): 206–226.

Haddad, Yvonne Yazbeck, and Tyler Golson. "Overhauling Islam: Representation, Construction, and Cooption of 'Moderate Islam' in Western Europe." *Journal of Church and State* 49, no. 3 (2007): 487–515.

## BIBLIOGRAPHY 187

Hafner-Burton, Emilie M., Miles Kahler, and Alexander H. Montgomery. "Network Analysis for International Relations." *International Organization* 63 (Summer 2009): 559–592.

Hall, Rodney Bruce. "Moral Authority as a Power Resource." *International Organization* 51, no. 3 (1997): 591–622.

Hamdan, Sara. "Gulf Council Reaches Out to Morocco and Jordan." *New York Times*, 25 May 2011.

Haris, Ahmad. "The Role of Muslims in the Struggle against Violent Extremist Ideology in Indonesia." *Connections* 5, no. 4 (Winter 2006): 157–166.

Hasenclever, Andreas, and Volker Rittberger. "Does Religion Make a Difference? Theoretical Approaches to the Impact of Faith on Political Conflict." In *Religion in International Relations: The Return from Exile*, edited by Pavlos Hatzopoulos and Fabio Petito, 107–147. New York: Palgrave Macmillan, 2003.

Hassner, Ron E. *Religion on the Battlefield*. Ithaca, NY: Cornell University Press, 2016.

——. "Religious Intelligence." *Terrorism and Political Violence* 23, no. 5 (2011): 684–710.

——. "To Halve and to Hold: Conflicts over Sacred Space and the Problem of Indivisibility." *Security Studies* 12, no. 4 (Summer 2003): 1–33.

——. *War on Sacred Grounds*. Ithaca, NY: Cornell University Press, 2009.

Hatzopoulos, Pavlos, and Fabio Petito. "The Return from Exile: An Introduction." In *Religion in International Relations: The Return from Exile*, edited by Pavlos Hatzopoulos and Fabio Petito, 1–21. New York: Palgrave Macmillan, 2003.

Haynes, Jeffrey. *Faith-Based Organizations at the United Nations*. New York: Palgrave Macmillan, 2014.

——. *Religion, Politics and International Relations: Selected Essays*. New York: Routledge, 2011.

Henderson, Erroll, and Richard Tucker. "Clear and Present Strangers: The Clash of Civilizations and International Conflict." *International Studies Quarterly* 45 (2001): 317–338.

Henke, Marina E. "Buying Allies: Payment Practices in Multilateral Military Coalition-Building." *International Security* 43, no. 4 (Spring 2019): 128–162.

Henne, Peter S. "The Ancient Fire: Religion and Suicide Terrorism." *Terrorism and Political Violence* 24, no. 1 (2012): 38–60.

——. "Assessing the Impact of the Global War on Terrorism on Terrorism Threats in Muslim Countries." *Terrorism and Political Violence* 33, no. 7 (2021): 1511–1529.

——. "The Domestic Politics of International Religious Defamation." *Politics and Religion* 6, no. 3 (2013): 512–537.

——. *Economic Integration and Political Reconciliation in Iraq*. Washington, DC: Center for American Progress, 2018.

——. *The Geopolitics of Faith: Religious Soft Power in Russian and U.S. Foreign Policy*. Brookings Institute / Berkley Center for Religion, Peace and World Affairs, Washington, DC, 6 June 2019.

——. *Islamic Politics, Muslim States and Counterterrorism Tensions*. New York: Cambridge University Press, 2017.

——. "Issues in Quantitative Analysis and Security Studies Involving Muslims." *International Journal of Religion* 2, no. 1 (2021): 23–32.

188 BIBLIOGRAPHY

——. "The Role of Islam in Post-Arab Spring International Relations: A Social Network Analysis." International Studies Association, Toronto, Canada, March 2019.

——. "The Two Swords: Religion–State Connections and Interstate Conflict." *Journal of Peace Research* 49, no. 6 (2012): 753–768.

——. "What We Talk About When We Talk About Soft Power." *International Studies Perspectives* 23, no. 1 (2022): 94–111.

Henne, Peter S., and Gregorio Bettiza. "Geopolitical Grand Narratives, Religious Outreach, and Religious Soft Power in US Foreign Policy." In *The Geopolitics of Religious Soft Power: How States Use Religion in Foreign Policy*, edited by Peter Mandaville. New York: Oxford University Press, 2023.

Henne, Peter S., Sarabrynn Hudgins, and Timothy Shah. *Religious Freedom and Violent Religious Extremism: A Sourcebook*. Washington, DC: Berkley Center for Religion, Peace and World Affair's Religious Freedom Project, 2012.

Henne, Peter S., and Jason Klocek. "Taming the Gods: How Religious Conflict Shapes Religious Repression." *Journal of Conflict Resolution* 63, no. 1 (2019): 112–138.

Henne, Peter S., and Daniel H. Nexon. "One Cheer for Classical Realism, or Towards a Power Politics of Religion." In *Religion and the Realist Tradition: From Political Theology to International Relations Theory and Back*, edited by Jodok Troy, 164–175. London: Routledge, 2013.

Henne, Peter S., Nilay Saiya, and Ashlyn W. Hand. "Weapon of the Strong? Government Support for Religion and Majoritarian Terrorism." International Studies Association, Toronto, Canada, 2019.

Herb, Jeremy. "Democrats Urge Trump Administration to Impose Sanctions on Russians Meddling in 2020 Election." *CNN*, 3 September 2020.

Hersh, Seymour M. "King's Ransom: How Vulnerable Are the Saudi Royals?" *New Yorker*, 14 October 2001.

Hertzke, Alan D. *Freeing God's Children: The Unlikely Alliance for Global Human Rights*. Lanham, MD: Rowman and Littlefield, 2004.

Hitchcock, William I. "The President Who Made Billy Graham 'America's Pastor.'" *Washington Post*, 28 February 2018.

Hooper, Melissa. "Russia's 'Traditional Values' Leadership." Human Rights First, 2016.

Horowitz, Michael. "Long Time Going: Religion and the Duration of Crusading." *International Security* 34, no. 2 (Fall 2009): 162–193.

Horsley, Jamie P. "It's Time for a New Policy on Confucius Institutes." Brookings Institution, Washington, DC, 1 April 2021.

Hudson, Michael C. *Arab Politics: The Search for Legitimacy*. New Haven, CT: Yale University Press, 1977.

Hunter, Robert. *A Box of Rain: Lyrics, 1965–1993*. New York: Viking, 1990.

Huntington, Samuel P. *The Clash of Civilizations and the Remaking of World Order*. New York: Simon and Schuster, 1996.

Hurd, Elizabeth Shakman. "The Political Authority of Secularism in International Relations." *European Journal of International Relations* 10, no. 2 (June 2004): 235–262.

Huseynov, Vasif. *Geopolitical Rivalries in the 'Common Neighborhood': Russia's Conflict with the West, Soft Power and Neoclassical Realism*. Verlag, Stuttgart: ibidem, 2019.

# BIBLIOGRAPHY 189

Inboden, William. *Religion and American Foreign Policy, 1945–1960: The Soul of Containment*. New York: Cambridge University Press, 2008.

"Informal Meeting of the Heads of State or Government, 12 February 2015." European Council, 12 February 2015.

"ISIL Strategy: The US Strategy to Combat ISIL and Defeat the Terrorist Threat," The White House, accessed 29 December 2022, https://obamawhitehouse.archives.gov/isil-strategy.

Jackson, Galen. "The Showdown That Wasn't: U.S.–Israeli Relations and American Domestic Politics, 1973–75." *International Security* 39, no. 4 (Spring 2015): 130–169.

Jackson, Patrick Thaddeus. *Civilizing the Enemy: German Reconstruction and the Invention of the West*. Ann Arbor: University of Michigan Press, 2006.

Jackson, Patrick Thaddeus, and Daniel H. Nexon. "Reclaiming the Social: Relationalism in Anglophone International Studies." *Cambridge Review of International Affairs* 32, no. 5 (2019): 582–600.

Jackson, Richard. "An Analysis of EU Counterterrorism Discourse Post-September 11." *Cambridge Review of International Affairs* 20, no. 2 (2007): 233–247.

Jelen, Ted G., and Clyde Wilcox. "Religion: The One, the Few and the Many." In *Religion and Politics in Comparative Perspective: The One, the Few and the Many*, edited by Ted G. Jelen and Clyde Wilcox, 1–27. New York: Cambridge University Press, 2002.

Johnston, Douglas, and Cynthia Sampson, eds. *Religion, the Missing Dimension of Statecraft*. New York: Oxford University Press, 1994.

——. "Introduction: Beyond Power Politics." In *Religion, the Missing Dimension of Statecraft*, edited by Douglas Johnston and Cynthia Sampson, 8–34. New York: Oxford University Press, 1994.

Johnston, Matt. "Why Tucker Carlson Hates Ukraine So Much." *Haaretz*, 18 April 2022.

Juergensmeyer, Mark. *Terror in the Mind of God: The Global Rise of Religious Violence*. Berkeley: University of California Press, 2003.

Kagan, Robert. *Dangerous Nation: America's Foreign Policy from Its Earliest Days to the Dawn of the Twentieth Century*. New York, NY: Vintage, 2007.

Kaya, Ahyan, and Ayse Tecmen. "Europe versus Islam? Right-Wing Populist Discourse and the Construction of a Civilized Identity." *Review of Faith and International Affairs* 17, no. 1 (2019): 49–64.

Kayaoglu, Turan. *The Organization of Islamic Cooperation: Politics, Problems, and Potential*. New York: Routledge, 2017.

Kaylan, Melik "Kremlin Values: Putin's Strategic Conservatism." *World Affairs* 177, no. 1 (2014): 9–17.

Kechichian, Joseph A. *Faysal: Saudi Arabia's King for All Seasons*. Gainesville, FL: University of Florida Press, 2008.

Keck, Margaret E., and Kathryn Sikkink. *Activists Beyond Borders: Advocacy Networks in International Politics*. Ithaca, NY: Cornell University Press, 1998.

Keohane, Robert O., and Peter J. Katzenstein. *Anti-Americanisms in World Politics*. Ithaca, NY: Cornell University Press, 2007.

Kerry, John. "We Ignore the Global Impact of Religion at Our Peril." *America*, 2 September 2015.

190 **BIBLIOGRAPHY**

Kettell, Steven, and Paul A. Djupe. "Do Religious Justifications Distort Policy Debates? Some Empirics on the Case for Public Reason." *Politics and Religion* 13, no. 3 (2020): 517–543.

Khrennikova, Dina, and Anna Shiryaevskaya. "Why the World Worries about Russia's Nord Stream 2 Pipeline." *Washington Post*, 21 May 2021.

King, Larry. "Interview with His Majesty King Abdullah II of Jordan." *Larry King Live*, CNN, 18 March 2002.

Kirby, Dianne. "Harry Truman's Religious Legacy: The Holy Alliance, Containment and the Cold War." In *Religion and the Cold War*, edited by Dianne Kirby, 77–103. New York: Palgrave Macmillan, 2003.

——. "Religion and the Cold War: An Introduction." In *Religion and the Cold War*, edited by Dianne Kirby, 1–23. New York: Palgrave Macmillan, 2003.

Kirby, Paul. "Why Has Russia Invaded Ukraine and What Does Putin Want?" *BBC News*, 9 May 2022.

Kirchik, James. "How the GOP Became the Party of Putin." *Politico*, 18 July 2017.

Kirillova, Kseniya. *Soft Power and "Positive Propaganda": How Russia Uses Cultural and Historical Stereotypes to Increase Political Influence.* Estonia: International Center for Defence and Security, 2020.

Kirkpatrick, David D., and Ben Hubbard. "Saudi Prince Detains Senior Members of Royal Family." *New York Times*, 6 March 2020.

Knake, Robert K. *Why the Solarwinds Hack Is a Wake-Up Call: The Sweeping Cyber Espionage Campaign Shows How Sophisticated Adversaries Can Bypass Even Well-Defended Targets.* Washington, DC: Council on Foreign Relations, 2021.

Kratochvil, Petr. "Religion as a Weapon: Invoking Religion in Secularized Societies." *Review of Faith and International Affairs* 17, no. 1 (2019): 78–88.

Krebs, Ronald R., and Patrick Thaddeus Jackson. "Twisting Tongues and Twisting Arms: The Power of Political Rhetoric." *European Journal of International Relations* 13, no. 1 (2007): 35–66.

Krebs, Ronald R., and Jennifer K. Lobasz. "Fixing the Meaning of 9/11: Hegemony, Coercion, and the Road to War in Iraq." *Security Studies* 16, no. 3 (August 2007): 409–451.

Kull, Steven. *Feeling Betrayed: The Roots of Muslim Anger at America.* Washington, DC: Brookings Institution, 2011.

Kupchan, C. A. *The End of the American Era: U.S. Foreign Policy and the Geopolitics of the Twentieth Century.* New York: Random House, 2002.

Kuru, Ahmet T. *Secularism and State Policies towards Religion: The United States, France and Turkey.* New York: Cambridge University Press, 2009.

Lamoreaux, Jeremy W., and Lincoln Flake. "The Russian Orthodox Church, the Kremlin, and Religious (Il)liberalism in Russia." *Palgrave Communications* 4, no. 115 (2018): online.

Laqueur, Walter. "After the Fall: Russia in Search of a New Ideology." *World Affairs*, March/April 2014.

Larson, Deborah Welch, and Alexei Shevchenko. *Quest for Status: Chinese and Russian Foreign Policy.* New Haven, CT: Yale University Press, 2019.

"Latest Trends in Religious Restrictions and Hostilities: Overall Decline in Social Hostilities in 2013, Though Harassment of Jews Worldwide Reached a Seven-Year High." Pew Research Center, Washington, DC, 26 February 2015.

Latimer, Matthew. *Speech-Less: Tales of a White House Survivor*. Danvers, MA: Crown, 2010.

Leeds, Brett Ashley. "Alliance Reliability in Times of War: Explaining State Decisions to Violate Treaties." *International Organization* 57, no. 4 (Fall 2003): 801–827.

Leeds, Brett Ashley, and Burcu Savun. "Terminating Alliances: Why Do States Abrogate Agreements?" *Journal of Politics* 69, no. 4 (2007): 1118–1132.

Lepgold, Joseph, and Miroslav Nincic. *Beyond the Ivory Tower: International Relations Theory and the Problem of Policy Relevance*. New York: Columbia University Press, 2001.

Levgold, Robert. "Introduction." In *Russian Foreign Policy in the Twenty-First Century and the Shadow of the Past*, edited by Robert Levgold, 3–35. New York: Columbia University Press, 2007.

——. "Russian Foreign Policy During Periods of Great State Transformation." In *Russian Foreign Policy in the Twenty-First Century and the Shadow of the Past*, edited by Robert Levgold, 77–145. New York: Columbia University Press, 2007.

Levy, Ido. "How Iran Fuels Hamas Terrorism." Washington Institute for Near East Policy, Washington, DC, 1 June 2021.

Lieber, Kier A., and Gerard Alexander. "Waiting for Balancing: Why the World Is Not Pushing Back." *International Security* 30 no. 1 (Summer 2005): 109–139.

Lieber, Robert J. *The American Era: Power and Strategy for the 21st Century*. New York: Cambridge University Press, 2007.

Lieberman, Joseph. "The Theological Iron Curtain: A Foreign Policy Strategy for Engaging the Muslim World." *National Interest* 73 (Fall 2003): 5–9.

Light, Margot. "Foreign Policy Thinking." In *Internal Factors in Russian Foreign Policy*, edited by Neil Malcolm, Alex Pravda, Roy Allison, and Margot Light, 33–100. London: Oxford University Press, 1996.

Lissner, Rebecca, and Mira Rapp-Hooper. *An Open World: How America Can Win the Contest for Twenty-First-Century Order*. New Haven, CT: Yale University Press, 2020.

Lo, Bobo. *Vladimir Putin and the Evolution of Russian Foreign Policy*. London: Chatham House Papers, 2003.

Lomagin, Nikita. "Interest Groups in Russian Foreign Policy: The Invisible Hand of the Russian Orthodox Church." *International Politics* 49, no. 4 (2012): 498–516.

Long, David E. "King Faisal's World View." In *King Faisal and the Modernisation of Saudi Arabia*, edited by Willard A. Beling, 173–184. London: Croom Helm, 1980.

Lustick, Ian S. "History, Historiography, and Political Science: Multiple Historical Records and the Problem of Selection Bias." *American Political Science Review* 90, no. 3 (1996): 605–617.

Lyons-Padilla, S., M. J. Gelfand, H. Mirahmadi, M. Farooq, and M. van Egmond. "Belonging Nowhere: Marginalization & Radicalization Risk among Muslim Immigrants." *Behavioral Science and Policy* 1, no. 2 (2015): 1–12.

Mabon, Simon. *Saudi Arabia and Iran: The Struggle to Shape the Middle East*. London: Foreign Policy Center, 2018.

Malcolm, Neil, Alex Pravda, Roy Allison, and Margot Light, eds. *Internal Factors in Russian Foreign Policy*. London: Oxford University Press, 1996.

Malksoo, Lauri. "The History of International Legal Theory in Russia: A Civilizational Dialogue with Europe." *European Journal of International Law* 19, no. 1 (2008): 211–232.

## 192 BIBLIOGRAPHY

———. "The Human Rights Concept of the Russian Orthodox Church and Its Patriarch Kirill I: A Critical Appraisal." *European Yearbook on Human Rights* (2013): 403–416.

Mamdani, Mahmoud. *Good Muslim, Bad Muslim: America, the Cold War and the Roots of Terror.* New York: Three Leaves, 2005.

Mandaville, Peter, ed. *The Geopolitics of Religious Soft Power: How States Use Religion in Foreign Policy.* New York: Oxford University Press, 2022.

———. "How Putin Turned Religion's 'Sharp Power' against Ukraine: Moscow's Stance on the Orthodox Church Is Indicative of How Aspiring Powers Use Religion to Either Build Solidarity or Sow Seeds of Conflict." United States Institute of Peace, Washington, DC, 9 February 2022.

Mandaville, Peter, and Shadi Hamid. *Islam as Statecraft: How Governments Use Religion in Foreign Policy.* Washington, DC: Brookings Institute, 2018.

Mandaville, Peter, and Knox Thames. "A Ripe Moment for Building Peace by Promoting International Religious Freedom." United States Institute of Peace, Washington, DC, 27 June 2022.

Mandaville, Peter, Knox Thames, and Emily Scolaro. "Finding Common Ground on U.S. International Religious Freedom Policy: Overcoming Partisan Mistrust through a Focus on Bipartisan Priorities." United States Institute of Peace, Washington, DC, 20 May 2021.

"Manipulating the Minarets." *Economist*, 2 August 2014.

Marty, Martin E., and R. Scott Appleby, eds. *Fundamentalisms Comprehended.* Chicago: University of Chicago Press, 2004.

Marwah, Sitti, and Ratna Ervina. "The China Soft Power: Confucius Institute in Build Up One Belt One Road Initiative in Indonesia." *Wenchuang Journal of Foreign Language Studies, Linguistics, Education, Literatures and Cultures* 1, no. 1 (2021): 22–38.

Masuzawa, Tomoko. *The Invention of World Religions: Or, How European Universalism Was Preserved in an Age of Pluralism.* Chicago: University of Chicago Press, 2005.

Mattar, Philip. "The PLO and the Gulf Crisis." *Middle East Journal* 48, no. 1 (1994): 31–46.

Mattes, Michaela. "Reputation, Symmetry, and Alliance Design." *International Organization* 66, no. 4 (October 2012): 679–707.

Mattes, Michaela, and Mariana Rodríguez. "Autocracies and International Cooperation." *International Studies Quarterly* 58, no. 3 (September 2014): 527–538.

Matthiessen, Toby. "Saudi Arabia and the Cold War." In *Salman's Legacy: The Dilemmas of a New Era in Saudi Arabia*, edited by Madawi al-Rasheed, 217–235. New York: Oxford University Press, 2018.

McAdam, Douglas, Sidney Tarrow, and Charles Tilly. *Dynamics of Contention.* New York: Cambridge University Press, 2001.

McDougall, Walter. *Promised Land, Crusader State: The American Encounter with the World since 1776.* Boston, MA: Mariner Books, 1998.

Mead, Walter Russell. "God's Country?" In *Rethinking Religion and World Affairs*, edited by Timothy Samuel Shah, Alfred Stepan, and Monica Duffy Toft, 247–262. New York: Oxford University Press, 2012.

Mearsheimer, John. *The Tragedy of Great Power Politics.* New York: W. W. Norton, 2001.

# BIBLIOGRAPHY 193

Miller, Judith. "War in the Gulf: Muslims; Saudis Decree Holy War on Hussein." *New York Times*, 20 January 1991.

Mitchell, Chris. "Egyptian President Meeting with US Evangelicals 'Prophetic' and 'Historic.'" *Christian Broadcasting Network*, 3 November 2017.

Mitzen, Jennifer. "Illusion or Intention: Talking Grand Strategy into Existence." *Security Studies* 24 (2015): 61–94.

——. "Ontological Security in World Politics: State Identity and the Security Dilemma." *European Journal of International Relations* 12, no. 3 (2006): 341–370.

Moore, Gregory J. *Niebuhrian International Relations: The Ethics of Foreign Policy-making*. New York: Oxford University Press, 2020.

"Moscow-Led Ukrainian Orthodox Church Breaks Ties with Russia." *Reuters*, 28 May 2022.

Motadel, David. "Uneasy Engagement." *World Today* 67, no. 1 (January 2011): 27–29.

Mufson, Steven. "Bush Saw Putin's 'Soul': Obama Wants to Appeal to His Brain." *Washington Post*, 1 December 2015.

Murray, Michelle. *The Struggle for Recognition in International Relations: Status, Revisionism and Rising Powers*. New York: Oxford University Press, 2019.

Narizny, Kevin. "On Systemic Paradigms and Domestic Politics: A Critique of the Newest Realism." *International Security* 42, no. 2 (Fall 2017): 155–190.

Nasr, Vali. *The Shia Revival: How Conflicts within Islam Will Shape the Future*. New York: W. W. Norton, 2006.

"National Security Strategy." The White House, Washington, DC, May 2010.

"The National Security Strategy." The White House, Washington, DC, 2006.

"The National Security Strategy of the United States of America." The White House, Washington, DC, September 2002.

Nexon, Daniel H. "Religion and International Relations: No Leap of Faith Required." In *Religion and International Relations Theory*, edited by Jack Snyder, 141–168. New York: Columbia University Press, 2011.

——. *The Struggle for Power in Early Modern Europe: Religious Conflict, Dynastic Empires and International Change*. Princeton, NJ: Princeton University Press, 2009.

Nexon, Daniel H., and Thomas Wright. "What's at Stake in the American Empire Debate?" *American Political Science Review* 101, no. 2 (May 2007): 253–271.

Ngoun, Kimly. "Thai–Cambodian Conflict Rooted in History." East Asia Forum, 27 January 2012.

Niebuhr, Reinhold. *The Irony of American History*. Chicago: University of Chicago Press, 1952.

Nielsen, Richard A. *Deadly Clerics: Blocked Ambition and the Paths to Jihad*. New York: Cambridge University Press, 2018.

Norris, Pippa, and Ronald Inglehart. *Sacred and Secular: Religion and Politics Worldwide*. New York: Cambridge University Press, 2004.

Nye, Joseph S., Jr. "How Sharp Power Threatens Soft Power: The Right and Wrong Ways to Respond to Authoritarian Influence." *Foreign Affairs*, 24 January 2018.

——. *The Paradox of American Power*. New York: Oxford University Press, 2002.

——. "Public Diplomacy and Soft Power." *ANNALS of the American Academy of Political and Social Science* 616 (March 2008): 94–109.

——. "Soft Power." *Foreign Policy* 80 (1990): 153–171.

# BIBLIOGRAPHY

———. "Soft Power and American Foreign Policy." *Political Science Quarterly* 119, no. 2 (2004): 255–270.

"Obama's Egypt Speech: What He Said to the Muslim World." Brookings Institute, Washington, DC, 4 June 2009.

"Obama 'Talks to the Enemy.'" *Sahara Reporter*, 26 February 2009.

Ochsenwald, William. "Saudi Arabia and the Islamic Revival." *International Journal of Middle East Studies* 13, no. 3 (August 1981): 271–286.

O'Neill, Mark. "Europe Closes Confucius Institutes." *EJ Insight*, 16 July 2021.

Oren, Michael B. *Six Days of War: June 1967 and the Making of the Modern Middle East.* Novato, CA: Presidio Press, 2003.

Owen, John M., IV. *The Clash of Ideas in World Politics: Transnational Networks, States, and Regime Change, 1510–2010.* Princeton, NJ: Princeton University Press, 2010.

———. "Springs and Their Offspring: The International Consequences of Domestic Uprisings." *European Journal of International Security* 1, no. 1 (2016): 49–72.

Owens, John E., and John W. Dumbrell, eds. *America's War on Terrorism: New Dimensions in US Government and National Security.* Lanham, MD: Lexington, 2008.

Ozturk, Ahmet Erdi. *Religion, Identity and Power: Turkey and the Balkans in the Twenty-First Century.* Edinburgh, UK: Edinburgh University Press, 2021.

Pandith, Farah. *How We Win: How Cutting-Edge Entrepreneurs, Political Visionaries, Enlightened Business Leaders, and Social Media Mavens Can Defeat the Extremist Threat.* New York: HarperCollins, 2019.

Pankin, Alexei. "A Boost for the Kremlin's Soft Power." *Moscow Times*, 23 December 2013.

"Parliament Demands Significantly Tighter EU Sanctions against Russia." Press release, News European Parliament, 21 January 2021.

Patrick, Stewart. "How U.S. Allies Are Adapting to 'America First.'" *Foreign Affairs*, 23 January 2018.

Payne, Daniel P. "Spiritual Security, the Russian Orthodox Church, and the Russian Foreign Ministry: Collaboration or Cooptation?" *Journal of Church and State* 52, no. 4 (2010): 712–717.

Permoser, Julia Mourao, and Kristina Stoeckl. "Reframing Human Rights: The Global Network of Moral Conservative Homeschooling Activists." *Global Networks* 21, no. 4 (2020): 681–702.

Petro, Nicholas N. "Russia's Orthodox Soft Power: U.S. Global Engagement Initiative." Washington, DC, Carnegie Council for Ethics in International Affairs, 23 March 2015.

Phillips, Andrew. *War, Religion and Empire: The Transformation of International Orders.* New York: Cambridge University Press, 2011.

Philpott, Daniel. "The Challenge of September 11 to Secularism in International Relations." *World Politics* 55, no. 2 (October 2002): 66–95.

———. "Explaining the Political Ambivalence of Religion." *American Political Science Review* 101, no. 3 (August 2007): 505–525.

———. "Has the Study of Global Politics Found Religion?" *Annual Review of Political Science* 12 (2009): 183–202.

———. "The Religious Roots of Modern International Relations." *World Politics* 52, no. 2 (January 2000): 206–245.

Pikayev, Alexander A. "Rise and Fall of Start II: The Russian Perspective." Carnegie Endowment for International Peace, Washington, DC, 1999.

"Pope Francis Holds Largest Rally against US-Led Military Action on Syria, 100,000 Attend Peace Vigial in Rome, Others around the World." *International Business Times*, 9 September 2013.

"Pope Francis Leads Global Fasting, Prayer Day for Syria Peace." *Al-Arabiya*, 7 September 2013.

Popkhadze, Miro. *Standing Up to Russia's Sharp Power*. Philadelphia, PA: Foreign Policy Research Institute, 2018.

Pospielovsky, Dimitry V. "The Russian Orthodox Church in the Postcommunist CIS." In *The Politics of Religion in Russia and the New States of Eurasia*, edited by Michael Bourdeaux, 41–78. Armonk, NY: M. E. Sharpe, 1997.

Pouliot, Vincent. *International Security in Practice: The Politics of NATO–Russia Diplomacy*. New York: Cambridge University Press, 2010.

Powell, Emilia Justyna. *Islamic Law and International Law*. New York: Oxford University Press, 2020.

Pravda, Alex. "The Public Politics of Foreign Policy." In *Internal Factors in Russian Foreign Policy*, edited by Neil Malcolm, Alex Pravda, Roy Allison, and Margot Light, 169–230. London: Oxford University Press, 1996.

"Preah Vihear Temple: Disputed Land Cambodian, Court Rules." *BBC News*, 11 November 2013.

Preston, Andrew. *Sword of the Spirit, Shield of Faith: Religion in American War and Diplomacy*. New York: Alfred A. Knopf, 2012.

Prodromou, Elizabeth H. "U.S. Foreign Policy and Global Religious Pluralism." In *Religious Pluralism, Globalization, and World Politics*, edited by Thomas Banchoff, 297–325. New York: Oxford University Press, 2008.

"Public Opinion Runs against Syrian Airstrikes." Pew Research Center, Washington, DC, 3 September 2013.

Pullella, Philip. "Analysis: Ukraine Invasion Splits Orthodox Church, Isolates Russian Patriarch." *Reuters*, 14 March 2022.

Quandt, William. *Peace Process: American Diplomacy and the Arab–Israeli Conflict since 1967*. Washington, DC: Brookings Institution, 1993.

Rabasa, Angel. *Eurojihad: Patterns of Islamist Radicalization and Terrorism in Europe*. New York: Cambridge University Press, 2015.

——. "Where Are We in the 'War of Ideas?'" In *The Long Shadow of 9/11: America's Response to Terrorism*, edited by Brian Michael Jenkins and John Paul Godges, 61–70. Washington, DC: RAND, 2011.

Rascoff, Samuel J. "Establishing Official Islam? The Law and Strategy of Counter-radicalization." *Stanford Law Review* 64 (January 2012). 125–190.

Reed, Stanley. "Jordan and the Gulf Crisis." *Foreign Affairs*, Winter 1990/1991.

Reiter, Daniel. "Learning, Realism and Alliances: The Weight of the Shadow of the Past." *World Politics* 46, no. 4 (July 1994): 490–526.

Renshon, Jonathan. *Fighting for Status: Hierarchy and Conflict in World Politics*. Princeton, NJ: Princeton University Press, 2017.

Resnick, Evan N. "Strange Bedfellows: U.S Bargaining Behavior with Allies of Convenience." *International Security* 35, no. 3 (Winter 2010/2011): 144–184.

## 196 BIBLIOGRAPHY

Rieber, Alfred J. "How Persistent Are Persistent Factors?" In *Russian Foreign Policy in the Twenty-First Century and the Shadow of the Past*, edited by Robert Levgold, 205–279. New York: Columbia University Press, 2007.

Roberts, Kari. "Understanding Putin: The Politics of Identity and Geopolitics in Russian Foreign Policy Discourse." *International Journal* 72, no. 1 (2017): 28–55.

Rock, Stephen R. *Faith and Foreign Policy*. New York: Continuum, 2011.

Roy, Olivier. *The Failure of Political Islam*. Translated by Carol Volk. Cambridge, MA: Harvard University Press, 1994.

Rubin, Lawrence. *Islam in the Balance: Ideational Threats in Arab Politics*. Stanford, CA: Stanford University Press, 2014.

Rudolph, Susanna Hoeber. "Introduction: Religion, States and Transnational Civil Society." In *Transnational Religions and Fading States*, edited by Susanna Hoeber Rudolph and James Piscatori, 1–26. Boulder, CO: Westview Press, 1997.

Ryan, Curtis. *Inter-Arab Alliances: Regime Security and Jordanian Foreign Policy*. Gainesville: University Press of Florida, 2009.

"Saddam Hussein Is No Saladin." *New York Times*, 26 January 1991.

Sahlins, Marshall. "Confucius Institutes: Academic Malware." *Asia-Pacific Journal* 12, no. 46 (November 2014): online.

Sandal, Nukhet A. "Religious Actors as Epistemic Communities in Conflict Transformation: The Cases of South Africa and Northern Ireland." *Review of International Studies* 37, no. 3 (July 2011): 929–949.

——. *Religious Leaders and Conflict Transformation: Northern Ireland and Beyond*. New York: Cambridge University Press, 2017.

Sandal, Nukhet A., and Jonathan Fox. *Religion in International Relations Theory: Interactions and Possibilities*. New York: Routledge, 2013.

Sarkissian, Ani. *The Varieties of Religious Repression: Why Governments Restrict Religion*. New York: Oxford University Press, 2015.

"Saudi Arabia Arrests More Women's Rights Activists." *Reuters*, 20 June 2018.

Schwarz, Tanya B. *Faith-Based Organizations in Transnational Peacebuilding*. Lanham, MD: Rowman and Littlefield, 2018.

Schweller, Randall L. "Unanswered Threats: A Neoclassical Realist Theory of Underbalancing." *International Security* 29, no. 2 (Fall 2004): 159–201.

Seawright, John, and John Gerring. "Case Selection Techniques in Case Study Research: A Menu of Qualitative and Quantitative Options." *Political Research Quarterly* 61, no. 2 (2008): 294–308.

Seiple, Robert, and Dennis R. Hoover, eds. *Religion and Security: The New Nexus in International Relations*. Lanham, MD: Rowman and Littlefield, 2004.

Semedov, Semed A., and Anastasiya G. Kurbatova. "Russian Public Diplomacy and Nation Branding." In *Russia's Public Diplomacy: Evolution and Practice*, edited by Anna A. Velikaya and Greg Simons, 45–61. Cham, Switzerland: Palgrave Macmillan, 2020.

Shaffer, Brenda. "Introduction: The Limits of Culture." In *The Limits of Culture: Islam and Foreign Policy*, edited by Brenda Shaffer, 1–26. Cambridge, MA: MIT Press, 2006.

——, ed. *The Limits of Culture: Islam and Foreign Policy*. Cambridge, MA: MIT Press, 2006.

## BIBLIOGRAPHY

Shah, Timothy Samuel, Alfred Stepan, and Monica Duffy Toft, eds. *Rethinking Religion and World Affairs*. New York: Oxford University Press, 2012.

Shah, Timothy, Alfred Stepan, and Monica Toft, eds. *Rethinking Religion and World Affairs*. New York: Oxford University Press, 2012.

Shakhanova, Gaziza, and Petr Kratochvil. "The Patriotic Turn in Russia: Political Convergence of the Russian Orthodox Church and the State?" *Politics and Religion* 15 (2022): 114–141.

Shellnutt, Kate. "Still No Churches in Saudi Arabia, but Small Steps toward Religious Freedom." *Religion News Service*, 5 October 2018.

Simons, Greg. "Aspects of Putin's Appeal to International Publics." *Global Affairs* 1, no. 2 (2015): 205–208.

Sinai, Ruth. "Saddam's Goal to Be Like Saladin, Nasser." *Associated Press*, 17 February 1991.

Sindi, Abdullah M. "King Faisal and Pan-Islamism." In *King Faisal and the Modernisation of Saudi Arabia*, edited by Willard A. Beling, 184–202. London: Croom Helm, 1980.

Singer, J. David. "Reconstructing the Correlates of War Dataset on Material Capabilities of States, 1816–1985." *International Interactions* 14 (1987): 115–132.

Sivertsev, Mikhail. "Civil Society and Religion in Traditional Political Culture: The Case of Russia." In *The Politics of Religion in Russia and the New States of Eurasia*, edited by Michael Bourdeaux, 95–112. Armonk, NY: M. E. Sharpe, 1997.

Smucker, Philip. "Iraq Builds 'Mother of All Battles' Mosque in Praise of Saddam." *Guardian*, 29 July 2001.

Snyder, Jack, ed. *Religion and International Relations Theory*. New York: Columbia University Press, 2011.

Soroka, George. "Putin's Patriarch: Does the Kremlin Control the Church." *Foreign Affairs*, 11 February 2016.

Sothirak, Pou. "Cambodia's Border Conflict with Thailand." *Southeast Asian Affairs* 2013 (2013): 87–100.

Soysa, Indra de, and Ragnhild Nordas. "Islam's Bloody Innards? Religion and Political Terror, 1980–2000." *International Studies Quarterly* 51 (2007): 927–943.

Stamatov, Peter. *The Origins of Global Humanitarianism: Religion, Empires and Advocacy*. New York: Cambridge University Press, 2013.

Stepan, Alfred C. "Religion, Democracy, and the 'Twin Tolerations.'" *Journal of Democracy* 11, no. 4 (October 2000): 37–57.

Stetsko, Elena. "The Role of Civil Society in Russian Public Diplomacy." In *Russia's Public Diplomacy: Evolution and Practice*, edited by Anna A. Velikaya and Greg Simons, 147–157. Cham, Switzerland: Palgrave Macmillan, 2020.

Stewart, Dona J. "The Greater Middle East and Reform in the Bush Administration's Ideological Imagination." *Geographical Review* 95, no. 3 (July 2005): 400–424.

Stoeckl, Kristina. "Double Bind at the UN: Western Actors, Russia and the Traditionalist Agenda." *Global Constitutionalism* 7, no. 3 (2018): 383–421.

——. "European Integration and Russian Orthodoxy: Two Multiple Modernities Perspectives." *European Journal of Social Theory* 14, no. 2 (2011): 217–233.

——. "The Rise of the Russian Christian Right: The Case of the World Congress of Families." *Religion, State and Society* 48, no. 4 (2020): 223–238.

# 198    BIBLIOGRAPHY

——. *The Russian Orthodox Church and Human Rights*. New York: Routledge, 2014.

Stoeckl, Kristina, and Kseniya Medvedeva. "Double Bind at the UN: Western Actors, Russia, and the Traditionalist Agenda." *Global Constitutionalism* 7, no. 3 (2018): 383–421.

Stone, Jon. "Nigel Farage Says Ukraine Invasion Is Result of EU and NATO Provoking Putin." *Independent*, 24 February 2022.

Svensson, Isak. "Fighting with Faith: Religion and Conflict Resolution in Civil Wars." *Journal of Conflict Resolution* 51, no. 6 (2007): 930–949.

Tabaar, Mohammed Ayatollahi. *Religious Statecraft: The Politics of Islam in Iran*. New York: Columbia University Press, 2019.

Te Brake, Wayne T. *Religious War and Religious Peace in Early Modern Europe*. New York: Cambridge University Press, 2017.

Tharoor, Ishan. "Why Putin Says Crimea Is Russia's 'Temple Mount.'" *Washington Post*, 4 December 2014.

Thies, Cameron. "A Pragmatic Guide to Qualitative Historical Analysis in the Study of International Relations." *International Studies Perspectives* 3 (2002): 351–372.

Thomas, Scott. *The Global Resurgence of Religion and the Transformation of International Relations: The Struggle for the Soul of the Twenty-First Century*. New York: Palgrave Macmillan, 2005.

Toft, Monica Duffy. "Getting Religion? The Puzzling Case of Islam and Civil War." *International Security* 31, no. 4 (Spring 2007): 97–131.

Toft, Monica Duffy, Daniel Philpott, and Timothy Samuel Shah. *God's Century: Resurgent Religion and Global Politics*. New York: W. W. Norton, 2011.

Torbati, Yeganeh. "How Mike Pence's Office Meddled in Foreign Aid to Reroute Money to Favored Christian Groups." *Propublica*, 6 November 2019.

Torres, Diego. "China's Soft Power Offensive." *Politico*, 26 December 2017.

Torriero, E. A. "Hussein Dots Iraq Landscape with Mosques." *Chicago Tribune*, 10 October 2002.

Troy, Jodok. "The Pope's Own Hand Outstretched: Holy See Diplomacy as a Hybrid Mode of Diplomatic Agency." *British Journal of Politics and International Relations* 20, no. 3 (2018): 521–539.

Tsygankov, Andrei P. *Russia's Foreign Policy: Change and Continuity in National Identity*. Lanham, MD: Rowman and Littlefield, 2016.

Turek, Lauren Frances. *To Bring the Good News to All Nations: Evangelical Influence on Human Rights and U.S. Foreign Relations*. Ithaca, NY: Cornell University Press, 2020.

"Ukraine War: The Role of Russia's Patriarch Kirill." *Deutsche Welle*, 16 May 2022.

Uzlaner, Dmitry, and Kristina Stoeckl. "From Pussy Riot's 'Punk Prayer' to *Matilda*: Orthodox Believers, Critique and Religious Freedom in Russia." *Journal of Contemporary Religion* 34, no. 3 (2019): 427–445.

——. "The Legacy of Pitirim Sorokin in the Transnational Alliances of Moral Conservatives." *Journal of Classical Sociology* 18, no. 2 (2018): 133–153.

Van Evera, Stephen. *Guide to Methods for Students of Political Science*. Ithaca, NY: Cornell University Press, 1997.

Van Herpen, Marcel H. *Putin's Wars: The Rise of Russia's New Imperialism*. Lanham, MD: Rowman and Littlefield, 2015.

Van Rythoven, Eric. "The Securitization Dilemma." *Journal of Global Security Studies* 5, no. 3 (July 2020): 478–493.

——. "Walter Lippmann, Emotion, and the History of International Theory." *International Theory* 14, no. 3 (2022): 526–550.

Vassiliev, Alexei. *King Faisal of Saudi Arabia: Personality, Faith and Times*. London: Saqi Books, 2012.

Velikaya, Anna A., and Greg Simons. "Introduction." In *Russia's Public Diplomacy: Evolution and Practice*, edited by Anna A. Velikaya and Greg Simons, 1–27. Cham, Switzerland: Palgrave Macmillan, 2020.

"Waging Peace: Asean and the Thai–Cambodian Border Conflict." International Crisis Group, 6 December 2011.

Wainscott, Ann Marie. *Bureaucratizing Islam: Morocco and the War on Terror*. New York: Cambridge University Press, 2017.

Wald, Kenneth D., and Clyde Wilcox. "Getting Religion: Has Political Science Rediscovered the 'Faith Factor.'" *American Political Science Review* 100, no. 4 (November 2006): 523–529.

Walker, Christopher, and Jessica Ludwig. "The Meaning of Sharp Power: How Authoritarian States Project Influence." *Foreign Affairs*, 16 November 2017.

Walker, Shaun. "Europe's Far-Right Divided Over Russia as Salvini Stages Pre-Election Rally in Milan." *Guardian*, 17 May 2019.

Walt, Stephen M. *The Origins of Alliances*. Ithaca, NY: Cornell University Press, 1987.

——. *Taming American Power: The Global Response to US Primacy*. New York: W. W. Norton, 2004.

Waltz, Kenneth. *Theory of International Politics*. Reading, MA: Addison-Wesley, 1979.

Wang, Hao, Yonghui Han, Jan Fidrmuc, and Dongming Weie. "Confucius Institute, Belt and Road Initiative, and Internationalization." *International Review of Economics and Finance* 71 (2021): 237–256.

Way, Lucan A. "The Rebirth of the Liberal World Order?" *Journal of Democracy* 33, no. 2 (April 2022): 5–17.

Westall, Sylvia, and John Irish. "Four Years On, Some in Europe Support Talking to Assad." *Reuters*, 18 February 2015.

Wilson, Erin K. "Beyond Dualism: Expanded Understandings of Religion and Global Justice." *International Studies Quarterly* 54, no. 3 (September 2010): 733–754.

Wittes, Tamara Cofman. *The New U.S. Proposal for a Greater Middle East Initiative: An Evaluation*. Washington, DC: Brookings Institute, 2004.

Wright, Lawrence. *The Terror Years: From Al-Qaeda to the Islamic State*. New York: Alfred A. Knopf, 2016.

Yin, Kai, and Allison Haga. "Rising to the Occasion: The Role of American Missionaries and Korean Pastors in Resisting Communism Throughout the Korea War." In *Religion and the Cold War: A Global Perspective*, edited by Philip E. Muehlenbeck, 88–113. Nashville, TN: Vanderbilt University Press, 2012.

Zarakol, Ayse. *After Defeat: How the East Learned to Live with the West*. New York: Cambridge University Press, 2011.

Zellman, Ariel, and Davis Brown. "Uneasy Lies the Crown: External Threats to Religious Legitimacy and Interstate Dispute Militarization." *Security Studies* 31, no. 1 (2022): 152–182.

# INDEX

Abdullah Al Saud (crown prince and later king of Saudi Arabia), 39
Abdullah II (king of Jordan), 3, 76, 93
abortion, 92, 96, 108
Abrahamic religions, 118, 123, 137. *See also* Christianity; Islam
Aburish, Said, 48
Afghanistan: and Iran, 54; Soviet invasion of, 64, 75; and the war on terrorism, 64, 68, 72
Africa, 69; East, 67
Albright, Madeleine, 3
Alexander, Gerard, 137
al-Qaeda, 63, 83; background on, 64–65, 67; criticism of Saudi Arabia by, 117; Bush administration and religious appeals against, 68–71, 76–78; and Europe, 112, 123; "moderate" Islam harnessed to defeat, 3, 11, 61, 85, 140; Muslim opposition to, 142; Obama administration and religious appeals against, 67, 71–74
alt-right. *See* far-right groups
Ansary, Hushang, 54
Arab League, 54
Arab nationalism, 45, 46, 53, 58, 59: Hussein and, 115, 116; Nasser and, 39, 113, 142; and opposition to Saudi Arabia and the Islamic Pact, 46, 48, 49, 56, 58, 124. *See also* pan-Arabism
Arab Spring, 4, 82, 119, 120, 130
Aram, Abbas, 50, 54
Asad, Hafez, 49
Assad, Bashar al-, 96, 97, 103, 119
Association of Southeast Asian Nations (ASEAN), 117
atheism: of China, 4; Cold War framed as battle between faith and, 142; considered threat in Middle East, 44, 54; of the Soviet Union, 12, 57
Australia, 122
Austria, 95, 97, 98, 104

authoritarianism: liberal international order versus, 67; in Muslim states, 62, 75–76, 129, 142; Putin's, 90, 92; in states that twist "moderation" to their own ends, 84, 126, 142; Trump's embrace of, 143; in US-supported states during the Cold War, 75
Azzam, Abdullah, 64

Bahrain, 12, 112, 113, 120, 123, 125. *See also* "Free Bahrainis"
Bakker, Jim, 103
Balkans, 114
Bannon, Steve, 99, 103
Belarus, 93, 94, 96
Belt and Road Initiative, 12, 115, 123, 126
Berkley Center for Religion, Peace, and World Affairs (Georgetown University), 9–10
Bettiza, Gregorio, 71, 72, 133
Biden administration, 131, 141, 171n192
bin Laden, Osama, 64
bin Salman, Mohammed, 129–30
Bourguiba, Habib, 44
BRI. *See* Belt and Road Initiative
Brown, Brian, 103
Brownback, Sam, 129
Brunei, 79
Buchanan, Pat, 99
Buddhism, 111, 117–18, 126
Bulgaria, 95
Bundy, McGeorge, 52
Busby, Joshua W., 16, 26
Bush, George W., 75; faith of, and evangelical support for, 65, 66, 71; and Putin, 107
Bush administration, 94; and IRF, 129; religious appeals by, 3, 64, 67, 68–71, 72, 73, 74, 76–78, 79, 83; and tensions with Russia, 104

201

## 202   INDEX

Cambodia, 12, 111, 115, 117–18, 122–23, 126

Cambridge Institute for Religion and Global Affairs, 9

Cameron, David, 101

Carlson, Tucker, 131

Catholic Church: and early modern struggles with Protestants, 24; and the legacy of Pope John Paul II, 21; and the Syrian civil war, 118–19; and Truman, in the struggle against the Soviets, 66; in Vietnam, 66. *See also* Vatican

Center for American Progress, 9, 10

Central Intelligence Agency (CIA), 46, 48, 50, 54

Chechnya, 90; Chechen wars, 94

Chicago Council on Global Affairs, 9

China: aggression of, 122; atheism of, 4; and future use of religious appeals, 140; religious appeals used by, as part of BRI (as an example of low credibility and material incentives), 4, 12, 111, 115, 121–23, 126; repression of religious communities in, 21, 122; Russia's relationship with, 94

Christianity, 17, 82, 90–91, 118, 136; Bush's, 65, 66, 71; in China, 122; in Cuba, 21; in Europe, 97, 113, 114; evangelical, 4, 65, 66, 99, 100, 102–104, 107, 129, 142; and persecution, 114, 122, 141; Russia appealing to, particularly conservative, 4, 87–88, 90–93, 99–100, 101, 106–108; in the united States, 65–67, 68. *See also* Catholic Church; Middle East: Christians in

CIA. *See* Central Intelligence Agency

classical realism, 135–36

Clegg, Nick, 101

Clinton, Bill, 90, 104

Clinton administration, 67

Cold War, 3–4, 62; end of, and impact on Russia, 88, 89–90; end of, and impact on United States, 64, 67, 116; as an ideological struggle, 66, 67; influence of religion in US foreign policy during, 63; Niebuhr's warnings during, 139; Saudi Arabia and, 38; US religious appeals during, 68, 70, 142; US support for authoritarian regimes during, 75

communism, 4, 49, 113; in China, 21, 121; and the former Soviet Union, 87, 90, 93; ideology of, and the Cold War, 66, 70; Saudi Arabia opposed to and using Isam as a defense against, 40–42, 43, 44, 51, 55; and the "Twin Pillars" policy, 38

Conchita (Austrian drag artist), 97

Confucianism, 111, 121

Confucius Institutes, 4, 115, 121–23, 126, 140

constructivism, 15, 16, 133, 134–35, 136, 138

Council on Foreign Relations, 9

countering violent extremism (CVE), 12, 71–74, 78–83

counterterrorism, 4, 9, 63, 64, 124; policies, in Europe, 111–14, 123; US appealing to Muslim states to work together on, 31, 61, 67, 68–86, 126; US coordinating with Russia on, 90. *See also* countering violent extremism (CVE)

credibility (of religious appeals), 7, 11, 12, 14, 16, 17, 18, 25, 26, 27, 30, 33, 34, 110–11, 123, 126, 127, 128, 139, 140–43. *See also under specific countries*

Crimea, 87, 90, 101–103, 107. *See also* Ukraine

Crimean war of 1853, 90–91

Cuba, 21

CVE. *See* countering violent extremism

Denmark, 95, 104

"Eastern" religions, 123, 137. *See also* Buddhism; Confucianism; Hinduism

Egypt, 97, 113, 126, 130; authoritarianism and repression in, including under the guise of combating extremism, 78, 129; evangelicals visit, 129; faith in, 142–43; Russia's close relationship with, 93; Saudi Arabia's rivalry with, and attempts to form an Islamic Pact, 11, 35–60, 112, 124, 138; as a US ally, 75

Eilts, Hermann, 42

Eisenhower, Dwight, 3–4, 38, 66

Eisenhower administration, 47, 66

Elshtain, Jean Bethke, 10

England. *See* United Kingdom

Eqbal, Manouchehr, 112–13

Estonia, 105

Europe, Western, 12, 92; far right in, 98, 99–100, 104, 106, 107, 108, 109, 124; and the invasion of Ukraine, 131; lower moral authority of religion in, 111, 112, 113–14, 123; Muslim minorities in, 113–14; Putin's criticism of, 97, 98; US relationship with, 100–101. *See also* European Union; *specific countries*

European Parliament, 101–102, 105

European Union, 90, 101

evangelicalism. *See* Christianity: evangelical

extremism: connection of, with religion, 74, 76, 77, 81, 132; roots of, and recruitment, 72, 73, 83, 113, 130, 132; solutions for, 67,

69, 71, 74, 77, 78, 80, 100, 114. *See also* countering violent extremism (CVE); counterterrorism; far-right groups; terrorism; *and specific extremist groups*

Faisal bin Abdulaziz Al Saud, or Faisal II (king of Saudi Arabia), 51, 54, 112, 113, 130; credibility of, 56–57, 59; efforts of, to form an Islamic Pact, 35, 40–48, 50–52, 55, 133, 142–43; piousness of, 57
Falun Gong, 122
Falwell, Jerry, Jr., 103
far-right groups: in Europe, 95, 98, 99–100, 102, 104, 106, 107, 108, 109, 124; Russia's appeals/outreach to, 88, 95, 98–102, 104, 106, 107, 108, 124; in the United States, 98–99, 106, 108, 109, 124. *See also* authoritarianism; extremism
Farage, Nigel, 100, 131
Farr, Thomas, 10
Fox, Jonathan, 15
France, 52, 65, 98, 117; and China, 121; as a colonial power, 117; election interference in, by Russia, 101; and the National Front, 95, 100, 102, 106; and the Syrian "red line," 119
Francis (pope), 111, 118–19

G8 nations, 90
Georgia (nation), 90, 107
Gerges, Fawaz, 64
Germany, 90, 94, 104–105, 122; West Germany, 4
Gerring, John, 31
Gerson, Michael, 67, 69, 71
Goddard, Stacie E.: on power politics framework, 2, 15, 137; and public rhetoric, 16, 28, 29; and states' legitimation of their policies, 6, 14–15, 16; and typology of integrating and fragmenting goals, 119, 133–34
Gorbachev, Mikhail, 91
Graham, Billy, 4
Graham, Franklin, 99, 102, 103
Great Britain. *See* United Kingdom
Greece, 95
Grzymala-Busse, Anna, 17, 22–23
Guinea, 41

Hamas, 120
Hamid, Shadi, 11, 141
Hassan II (king of Morocco), 51
Hassner, Ron, 10, 17
Haykal, Mohammed, 47

Hinduism, 117
Hizballah, 120
homosexuality, 92. *See also* LGBTQ equality/protections
Hughes, Karen, 69
Hughes, Seamus, 73, 79, 80, 82
humanitarianism, 5, 9, 17, 95, 132
human rights, 22, 79; China's abuses of, 122; Middle Eastern countries' abuses of, 80, 118; Putin/Russia on, 96, 98, 106; in UN discussions, 93; US's lack of credibility on, 75
Hungary, 95, 100, 114
Huseynov, Vasif, 104
Hussein (king of Jordan), 53, 54, 55
Hussein, Saddam, 4, 12, 39, 111, 115–17, 120, 126

ideologically charged international crises, 7, 14, 18, 22, 27, 33, 34, 110. *See also under specific countries*
India, 121
Indonesia, 79
Institute for Global Engagement, 9
instrumentalism/instrumentalists, 28, 29, 33, 127; and religious appeals by Saudi Arabia, 57–58; and religious appeals by the United States, 71, 84
International Center for Religion and Diplomacy, 9
International Court of Justice (IC), 117
international religious freedom, 4, 67, 103–104, 129
International Religious Freedom Act, 129
International Religious Freedom (IRF) office, 114, 141, 143
Iran, 17, 22, 36, 119, 130; and the Iran-Iraq War, 115, 120; and King Faisal's Islamic Pact, 41, 48, 49, 50, 53, 54–55, 56–57; 1979 revolution in, 21, 22, 36, 120; postrevolutionary, and use of religious appeals (as an example of high credibility and material incentives), 12, 21, 111, 115, 118, 120–21, 123, 126; Saudi Arabia's tensions over Bahrain with, 12, 112, 113, 115, 120, 123, 125, 140; and the "Twin Pillars" policy, 38
Iran-Iraq War, 115, 120
Iraq, 4, 36, 39, 50, 53, 54, 66, 111; Christians in, 103; critical of the Islamic Pact, 48, 49; and the Iran-Iraq War, 115, 120; ISIS in, 103; and Operation Desert Storm, 115–17, 123; US invasion of, 64, 68, 72, 75, 94, 120

204    **INDEX**

IRF. *See* international religious freedom
ISIS, 61, 68, 78, 85, 112, 119, 140; Christians
living under, 103, 105; Obama's strategy
to defeat, 67, 71–72; origins of, 65; and
recruitment, 79, 80; Russian appeals
against, 97; success of coalition building
to defeat, 76, 83
Islam, 3, 11–12, 100, 118, 136; debates over
connection to extremism, 74, 76–83,
132; displacing onto, blame for other
problems, 78, 81, 82–83; in Europe,
113–14; holy sites of, 116; and *hudud*
punishments, 79; and Hussein's appeals
to counter the US in Operation Desert
Storm, 115–17, 123, 126; Iran's credibility
on, 120; "moderate," 3, 8, 12, 61, 67–71,
77, 78, 80, 83, 85, 140; moral authority
of, in Saudi Arabia, 38–39; political, as a
competing ideological frame to liberalism, 24, 138; in Saudi foreign policy,
36–37, 112–13, 123, 130 (*see also* Islamic
Pact); theological debates about, 20;
UAE's appeals to, 4; US fear of addressing, 81–82; Wahhabi, 45. *See also* Islamists;
Shia Muslims; Sunni Muslims; Uighur
Muslims
Islamic Pact, 11, 34, 35, 37, 38, 40–42, 140,
142; impact of religious appeals aimed at
building, 45–60, 124, 126, 138
Islamic Republic of Iran. *See* Iran
Islamic State of Iraq and Syria. *See* ISIS
Islamists, 70, 120; al-Qaeda distinct from
other, 64; and the Arab Spring, 130;
Egyptian, 57; engaging with, 82, 114;
ideology of as focus of counterterrorism,
113; in opposition to the US war on
terrorism, 24; pursuit and repression
of, 78, 116; Putin on, 97; relocation of,
to Saudi Arabia; Saudi oil wealth supports, 58
Israel, 48, 93; and the Arab-Israeli conflict,
54; opposition of other Middle Eastern
countries to, 4, 116, 120; and the Six-Day
War, 39, 44
Italy, 93, 94, 100, 102

Jackson, Patrick Thaddeus, 134–35
Jacobs, Larry, 99
Japan, 121
Jeffress, Robert, 103
Jehovah's Witnesses, 142
John Paul II (pope), 21
Johnson, Lyndon Baines, 47, 51–52

Johnson administration, 37
Jordan, 3, 48, 49, 59, 93; and Egypt, 46; and
Operation Desert Storm, 116; and Saudi
Arabia (and the Islamic Pact), 41, 50, 52–54,
55, 57, 130; and the United States, 76
Justice and Development Party (AKP;
Turkey), 21

Kazakhstan, 96
Kenya, 64
Kerry, John, 4, 74
Khalid (crown prince of Saudi Arabia), 52
Khammash, Amer, 53
Khomeini, Ayatollah Ruholla, 120
Komer, Robert, 40, 51, 52
Korean War, 66
Krebs, Ronald R.: and public rhetoric, 28, 29
Kuwait, 41, 51, 55, 115, 116, 126

LaRossa, Connie, 70, 72, 77, 82
Latimer, Matthew, 69
Latvia, 92, 105
Lavrov, Sergei, 98
Le Pen, Marine, 98, 102
Lebanon, 120
Lepgold, Joseph, 139
LGBTQ equality/protections, 93, 96, 98, 108
liberalism, 22, 89; criticized by far-right
Europeans, 99, 100; criticized in Russia,
91, 94, 96, 98, 100, 131; ISIS as a threat to,
67, 68, 83; Islam as a competing
framework to, 24, 82; US emphasis on
spreading, 62, 67
Lieber, Kier A., 137
Lieberman, Joseph, 3

MacDonald, Paul K., 137
Mali, 41
Malofeev, Konstantin, 99
Mandaville, Peter, 11, 72, 74, 141
material incentives and disincentives, 7, 14,
17, 18, 25–28, 30, 33, 34, 110, 126, 127,
128; for China's efforts to mobilize support for the BRI, 12, 111, 115, 122, 123;
for future US appeals, 140–42; for Iran's
postrevolutionary Middle East mobilization, 12, 111, 115, 120, 123; during Operation Desert Storm, 12, 111, 115, 123; for
Middle East states when considering
whether to join the Islamic Pact, 11, 46,
56, 58; for Muslim states in working with
the United States after 9/11, 12, 61, 62,
75, 83, 84, 86; for Thailand and Cambodia's

## INDEX

border dispute, 12, 111, 115, 118, 123; for the Vatican intervening in the Syrian civil war, 12, 111, 119, 123; for Western states in opposing Russian influence, 12, 98, 100, 101, 108
McKinley, William, 66
Medvedev, Dmitry, 93
Mellon Foundation, 9
Merkel, Angela, 107
Metropolitan Kirill. *See* Patriarch Kirill
Middle East: Bush administration approach to, 68–71, 126; Christians in, 92, 96–97, 103, 105, 129; in the Cold War, 38; communism in, 51; and human rights, 80, 118; Obama administration approach to, 71–74, 83; and Operation Desert Storm, 115–17; Russia's approach to, 93, 95, 97–98, 103–104, 105. *See also specific countries*
Moldova, 92, 100
Montenegro, 100
moral authority (of religion), 7, 14, 17, 18, 19, 22–23, 24, 27, 33, 34, 112, 114, 123, 125, 127, 137. *See also under specific countries*
Morocco, 41, 50, 51, 59, 73, 76, 130
Mrouh, Kamel, 50, 56
Muslim Brotherhood, 47, 52, 97
Muslims. *See* Islam

Nasser Hussein, Gamal Abdel: pan-Arabism of, 35, 39, 40, 58; Saudi relations with, and the Islamic Pact as a reaction to influence of, 35, 38–48, 50, 52, 54, 55, 56, 57, 58, 59, 66, 113, 138, 140, 142; ; and the Six-Day War, 138; Soviet support for, 38, 40, 44, 50, 66
National Counterterrorism Center, 73, 79
National Front (France), 95, 100, 102, 106
National Security Strategy, 68, 72
NATO, 90, 94, 100, 101, 102, 106
"near abroad," 86, 88, 89, 90, 93, 94, 124
Nexon, Daniel H.: on classical realism, 135; on power politics framework, 2, 15, 137; on social forces as the products' of actors' behavior, 134–35; and typology of integrating and fragmenting goals, 119, 133–34
NGOs. *See* nongovernmental organizations
Niebuhr, Reinhold, 136, 139, 143–44
Nigeria, 78, 92
Nincic, Miroslav, 139

9/11 terrorist attacks: centrality of religion to foreign policy recognized as a result of, 9, 22, 60, 70; European response to, 125; war on terrorism as a response to, 3, 11–12, 31, 61, 67, 68, 71, 77, 85, 140, 142
Non-Aligned Movement, 38
nongovernmental organizations (NGOs), 95
North Atlantic Treaty Organization. *See* NATO
Northern League (Italy), 100, 102
Nye, Joseph S., Jr., 10, 141

Obama, Barack, 104; on al-Qaeda, 67; on Bush's foreign policy, 71; on Putin, 97, 103, 104, 107; on Syria, 119
Obama administration: and IRF, 129; and religion in foreign policy, 4, 67; religious appeals by, 67, 68, 71–74, 78–83
oil: influence of, on foreign policy, 36, 58, 108; in Kuwait, as a factor in Operation Desert Storm, 115; and the "oil for security" deal, 38; prices, rise of in the 1970s, 35; Saudis as stewards of, 45; Saudis attempt to diversify away from, 130. *See also* Russia: and energy markets
Oman, 82
Operation Desert Storm (as an example of low credibility and lacking material incentives), 12, 111, 115–17, 123, 126
Orbán, Viktor, 95, 104, 114
Otaiba, Yousef al-, 4

Pakistan, 45, 54, 75, 82
Palestinian Liberation Organization (PLO), 49, 116
Palestinians/Palestine, 39, 47, 48, 49, 54, 93, 116, 120
pan-Arabism, 35, 39, 40, 58, 59, 138. *See also* Arab nationalism
Pandith, Farah, 67, 69, 70, 71, 77
Patriarch Kirill, 91, 92, 93
Patton, James, 70, 72, 77, 80, 81–82
Pence, Mike, 4, 129
Pew Research Center, 9, 10
Pharaon, Rashad, 112
Poland, 98, 104
Pouliot, Vincent, 16
Preah Vihear Temple dispute (as an example of low credibility and lacking material incentives), 111, 115, 117–18, 122–23, 126
process tracing, 32
Prodromou, Elizabeth H., 71
Protestantism, 24, 65. *See also* Christianity

## 206 INDEX

Putin, Vladimir, 133, 142, 165n11; appeals of, to conservative Christian values, and Western evangelicals' support for, 4, 87–90, 92–101, 103–109, 131, 142; and the invasion of Ukraine, 131; and Middle East Christians, 103; and Trump, 97, 103–104, 106, 108

Qatar, 4, 130

radicalization. *See* extremism
realpolitik, 22, 36, 42, 43, 66
religion skeptics/skepticism, 8, 28–29, 33, 34, 36, 127; and religious appeals by Russia, 88, 89, 105, 107; and religious appeals by Saudi Arabia, 57, 59; and religious appeals by the United States, 62, 63, 84, 86
religion triumphalists/triumphalism, 8, 29, 33, 34, 36, 127; and religious appeals by Russia, 88, 89, 105, 107; and religious appeals by Saudi Arabia, 58; and religious appeals by the United States, 62, 63, 85
Religious Freedom Initiative, 9
Republican Party (US), 97, 99, 103, 104. *See also* far-right groups
Riesebrodt, Martin, 2
ROC. *See* Russian Orthodox Church
Roosevelt, Franklin D., 38
Rosand, Eric, 69, 73, 74, 78, 79–80, 81
Rostow, Walt, 41, 51, 52
Roy, Olivier, 120
Rusk, Dean, 52
Russia, 165n11; aggression of, 12, 88, 90, 93, 98, 99, 101, 104, 105, 109, 124, 131, 140; and appeals to traditional/conservative values, 4, 8, 12, 87–109, 131, 142; Biden administration policies on, 171n92; conditions in, predicting use of religious appeals, 90–95, 125; and control over former Soviet states, 12, 31, 90, 93; corruption and inequality in, 89; credibility of, on religion, 88, 98–99, 101; Crimea invasion by, 87, 90, 101–103, 107; cyberwarfare, hacking, and election interference by, 8, 88, 90, 103, 104; and energy markets, 88, 100, 108; and exceptionalism, 94; and future use of religious appeals, 140; ideologically charged international crisis confronts, 12, 89, 94, 95; impact of religious appeals by, and analysis, 98–109, 124, 126, 128, 141–42; inferiority and dissatisfaction of, 89, 93; and the Middle East, 93, 95, 97–98, 103–104, 105, 119;

moral authority of religion in, 12, 89, 90, 95, 106, 110; nationalism in, 91; nuclear arsenal of, 88; religious freedom in, 103, 142; resurgence of Russian Orthodox faith in, 12, 87, 89–95; sanctions against, 90, 100, 102, 103, 104, 106, 131; and "soft power," 94–95; and Ukraine invasion (2022), 108, 129
Russian Orthodox Church: and invasion of Ukraine, 131; prominence of, 108; resurgence of, 12, 87, 89–95
*Russky Mir* (Russian World), 12, 87, 90, 93, 95, 98

Sadat, Anwar, 47
Salal, Abdullah al-, 43
Salvini, Matteo, 98, 100, 102, 104
Sandal, Nukhet, 15
Sandler, Shumuel, 15
Sannousi, Mohammed el-, 114
Saqqaf, Omar, 43, 45
Saud bin Abdulaziz Al Saud (king of Saudi Arabia), 38, 39, 45, 66
Saudi Arabia, 82; al-Qaeda attacks in, 67; authoritarianism of, 129; and the Cold War, 38; conditions in, predicting use of religious appeals, 38–39, 125; credibility of, on religion, 11, 45–46, 55, 56–57, 59, 61; counterrevolutionary mobilization of, under Mohammed bin Salman, 129–30; ideologically charged international crisis confronts, 11, 38–40, 112–13; impact of religious appeals by, and analysis, 45–60, 124, 128, 138, 140, 141–42; Iran's tensions over Bahrain with, 12, 112–13, 115, 125; moral authority of religion in, 11, 38–39, 40, 55, 59, 110, 112; in the 1960s, and religious appeals that were less ideologically charged, 110–11, 112–13, 123, 126, 140, 142; and religious appeals as a foreign policy tool, 45; and religious appeals re: the Islamic Pact, 40–42; Shia populations in, 120; and Yemen, 37, 39, 40, 42–45, 46, 49, 50, 51–52, 53, 60, 130
Seawright, Jason, 31
security studies, 1, 5, 9, 10, 128, 133–34, 137, 138
Shariah law, 79
Shia Muslims/Shiites, 21, 50, 116, 120–21
Siam. *See* Thailand
Six-Day War, 35, 39, 44, 59, 126, 138, 140
soft power, 10–11, 88, 94–95, 105, 122, 133, 140, 141
South Korea, 66

## INDEX 207

South Vietnam. *See* Vietnam
Soviet Union: Afghanistan invasion of,
  64, 75; atheism of, 12, 57; and the Cold
  War, 62, 66, 67, 88, 89–90; control of the
  church by, 91; fall of, 88, 89, 93; former
  states of, 12, 31, 90, 92, 93, 121; influence
  of in relationship to the Middle East, 38,
  42, 44, 47, 50, 51, 57, 120. *See also* Russia
Sudan, 41, 51, 66
Suez crisis, 46
Sultan bin Abdulaziz (Saudi defense
  minister), 40, 42, 44, 51, 52
Sunni Muslims, 120
Syria: critical of Saudi Arabia and the
  Islamic Pact, 48–49, 50, 51; and Iran,
  120; ISIS in, 65, 79, 103; minorities in,
  97, 120; Russia's support for, 92, 96–97,
  105; Vatican's international mobilization
  against military action in, 111, 115, 118–19,
  123, 126. *See also* Syrian civil war
Syrian civil war, 12, 118–19, 120, 123, 130

Taiwan, 122
Tanzania, 64
Tell, Wasfi, 53
terrorism: European states and, 113–14;
  research on, 5, 132; US-led global war on,
  3, 11, 24, 61–86, 110, 112, 122, 124, 126,
  141. *See also* countering violent extrem-
  ism (CVE); counterterrorism; 9 / 11
  terrorist attacks; *and specific terrorist
  groups*
Thailand, 12, 111, 115, 117–18, 122–23, 126
Trans-Pacific Partnership, 79, 121
Truman, Harry, 66
Trump administration, 4, 101, 103–104, 129,
  143
Trump, Donald: and evangelical support,
  103–104, 108; and IRF, 129, 143; and
  Putin, 97, 103–104, 106, 108
Tunisia, 41, 44, 82
Turkey, 17, 21, 41, 54, 65, 79, 130

UAE. *See* United Arab Emirates
Uighur Muslims, 122
UKIP. *See* United Kingdom Independence
  Party
Ukraine, 99, 101, 104; pro-European tilt of,
  106; the ROC in, 92; Russian appeals to,
  and fear of losing, 93, 94, 96, 98; Russian
  invasion and annexation of Crimea in, 87,
  90, 101–103, 105, 131; Russian invasion
  and war of 2022 in, 108, 129. *See also*
  Crimea

UNESCO, 117, 118
United Arab Emirates, 4, 8, 76
United Arab Republic, 40
United Kingdom: election interference
  in, by Russia, 101; far right in, 98, 104,
  114; and the Middle East, 46, 47, 48, 50,
  52; poisoning of Russian agent in, 104;
  settlers from, in the United States, 65;
  views of Russia in, 95, 100, 101–102
United Kingdom Independence Party
  (UKIP), 95, 100, 101–102, 106
United Nations, 9; and the importance of
  religious engagement, 22; Human Rights
  Council, 93; Security Council, 40, 116,
  117. *See also* UNESCO
United States, 11–12, 31, 61–62, 88, 142;
  Bush administration, and religious appeals, 68–71, 76–78; and China, 121; and
  the Cold War, 3–4, 38, 62, 63, 64, 66, 67,
  68, 70, 75, 116, 139, 142; conditions in,
  predicting use of religious appeals, 65–67,
  125; counterterrorism in, 31, 61, 67,
  68–86, 90, 113, 114, 126; credibility of, on
  religion, 12, 72, 75–76, 83, 84, 86; election interference by Russia in, 90, 97, 103,
  104; Europe's relationship with, 100–101;
  evangelicals in, 4, 65, 99, 100, 102–104,
  107, 129; far right in, 98–99, 106, 109, 124;
  focus on, in study, 138; and future use of
  religious appeals, 139–43; ideologically
  charged international crisis confronts, 11,
  61, 67, 83, 85–86; impact of religious
  appeals by, and analysis, 75–86, 124, 128,
  141–42; and Iran, 120–21; moral authority of religion in, 11, 61, 62, 65, 67, 68,
  83, 85, 86, 110; Obama administration,
  and religious appeals, 71–74, 78–83; and
  Operation Desert Storm, 12, 111, 115–17,
  123, 126; Putin's criticism of, 97–98, 99,
  100; and the role of religion in foreign
  policy, 1, 62–63, 83–86; Saudi Arabia as
  ally of, 36, 37, 38, 42; and the Syrian "red
  line," 119; and the war on terrorism, 3,
  11, 24, 61–86, 110, 112, 122, 124, 126, 141
United States Agency for International
  Development (USAID), 143
Universal Declaration of Human Rights, 98
USCIRF. *See* US Commission on Interna-
  tional Religious Freedom
US Commission on International Religious
  Freedom (USCIRF), 129
US Department of Homeland Security, 64
US National Security Council, 40
USSR. *See* Soviet Union

## INDEX

US State Department: Office of Religion and Global Affairs, 4, 72, 74, 78–79, 80, 129, 143; and religious factors in foreign policy, 10, 74, 77, 81, 129; and religious training, 143; and the Six-Day War, 44
Uzbekistan, 83

Vanas, Tomas, 100
Vassiliev, Alexei, 44
Vatican, 25, 66, 92, 94; religious appeals by (as an example of high credibility and material incentives), 12, 115, 118–19, 123, 126. *See also* Catholic Church
Vietnam, 42, 44, 66
Vistisen, Anders, 104

Walt, Stephen M., 16
Waltz, Kenneth, 22
war on terror/terrorism. *See* terrorism: US-led global war on
Wilders, Geert, 98
World War II, 90, 105

Xi Jinping, 121

Yamani, Ahmad, 112
Yeltsin, Boris, 90, 92
Yemen, 40, 50, 82; Saudi and Egypt proxy war in, 37, 39, 42–46, 49, 51–52, 53, 60, 130

Zionism, 41, 49

Milton Keynes UK
Ingram Content Group UK Ltd.
UKHW011813150923
428767UK00007B/254